The Macmillan Book Of
BOATING
By William N. Wallace

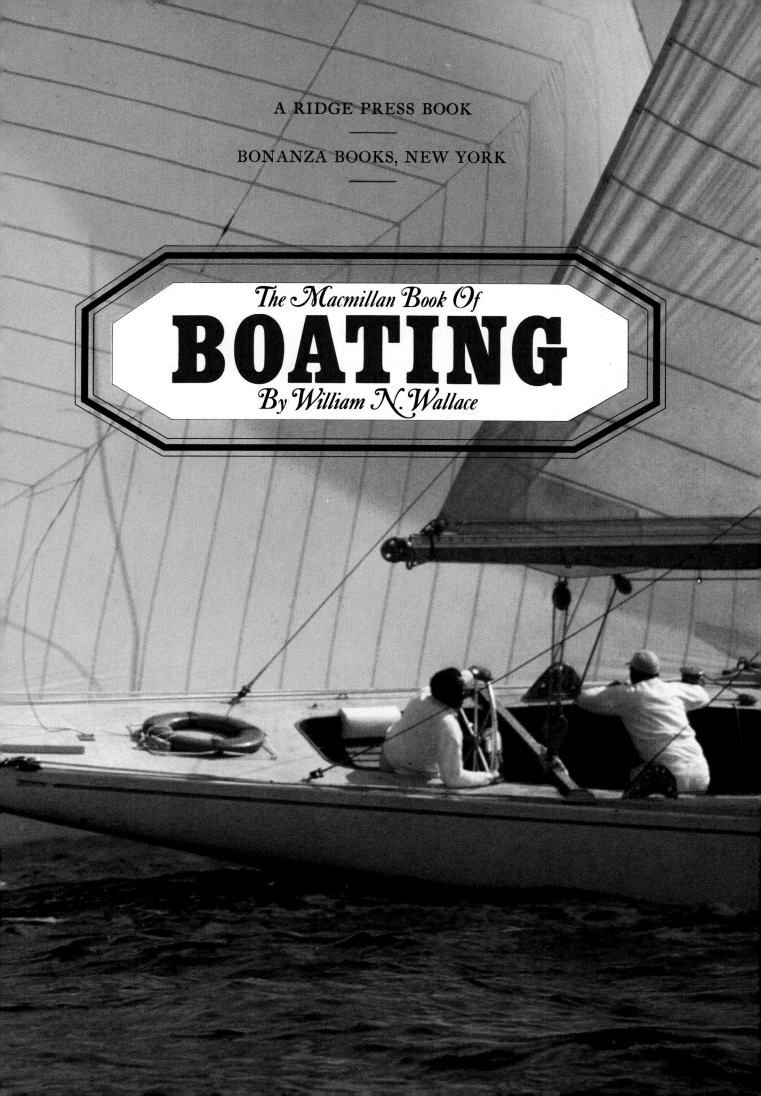

A RIDGE PRESS BOOK

BONANZA BOOKS, NEW YORK

The Macmillan Book Of
BOATING
By William N. Wallace

CONTENTS

Editor-in-Chief: JERRY MASON

Editor: ADOLPH SUEHSDORF

Art Director: ALBERT SQUILLACE

Associate Editor: EVELYN HANNON

Picture Editor: PETER LACEY

Art Associate: DAVID NAMIAS

Art Production: DORIS MULLANE

INTRODUCTION

*T*he concept of America most widely held is that of a nation first extending and conquering its western frontier and then growing rich and strong through industrial growth. Less well known and appreciated is our seafaring tradition. But it still is true that ours is a nation of sailors and always has been.

Geography has made the United States a boating country. The great land mass is superbly architected for the passage of work boats and pleasure craft. It is bounded east and west by serrated coasts where lie the sailing grounds of generations of yachtsmen. The rivers and lakes reach deep into the interior of the land, and in this century there have been developed vast, man-made waterways, by-products of the effort to dam and discipline water.

Today the owners of boats in these fifty states number at least 2,000,000. Of course, no one knows for certain exactly how many boatowners there are, but the grand total probably exceeds any count of all the men who pulled an oar for Phoenicia, sailed a galleon for Spain, or fired broadsides from Britain's seventy-four-gun men-o'-war.

The original American boats were working craft used for trade and fishing along the eastern coast. Yachting, which we take to mean the use of all kinds of boats for pleasure, came later and came slowly. In the early days of the republic, citizens for the most part had neither the time nor the wealth for nautical frivolity. Still, it must have been that many of the early American boatowners had a pleasurable hour or two aboard their shallops and scows. We would like to think that on a day when the burdensome tasks of making a livelihood could be for a moment put by, a few of these serious folk took their boats out for the sheer enjoyment of being on the water.

The goal of this book is to show how Americans have used their boats for pleasure. It is essentially a story of the evolution of naval architecture, which means the interplay between men capable of designing fine boats and men capable of paying for them. Usually and appropriately, the design innovations preceded the demand. But the creation of a boat being what it is, no designer has ever gone very far without a score or two of loyal yachtsmen who have won races in his craft and urged him onward. The interplay has made for some quite wonderful and exciting and amusing history. Clean cut, too. There is very little inconclusive milling around in the story of yachting. Some designer and his boats generally are supreme until the sad and triumphant day when a better design appears. In the pages which follow, there is a parade of bold, inventive, curious, strong-minded people whose urge to win a race or build or possess the best have helped to bring about change and progress.

For quite a while, boating was a pastime of the wealthy. The nation's first leisure class was established following the Civil War and among the "swells" there was no better expression of one's financial stature than possession of a yacht, preferably a big one.

The seafaring population of the United States diminished and the merchant marine contracted in the last half of the nineteenth century, but public interest in nautical affairs remained. The America's Cup proved this to be so. *Repeated defenses of this prize against foreign invaders made cup racing a glamorous and widely publicized sporting event. The series prompted William Picard Stephens, the nineteenth century's most noted yachting historian, to write in 1904: "The story of American yachting is a rope of many strands, each made of innumerable yarns. The 'core' is the America's Cup. About it twine many other subjects, the New York Yacht Club, the growth of a national club system, the racing of small yachts, the improvement in model and construction."*

Some sixty years have passed since Mr. Stephens wrote his rhapsody. Today, of course, it is the not-so-wealthy yachtsman who makes up the majority of Americans upon the water. For the western frontier was, indeed, extended and conquered. And the fabulous productivity of an industrial economy grown rich and strong has put sail and power within the reach of thousands upon thousands of people. Significantly enough, market-research studies have shown that the typical purchaser of a boat these days is a skilled factory worker out of the vast American labor force.

The availability of boats is not a reason in itself for buying them, but no one who has ever been a part of a raft of powerboats in a cove or a company of sailboats spreading their wings in the fresh breeze on any day in summer can doubt the deep and heartfelt affection for boats in a nation of sailors. George Emlen Roosevelt, a commodore of the New York Yacht Club, said it very well in a piece he wrote for the club's centennial yearbook in 1944:

"The love of the sea is bred in a large part of the human race and, therefore, knowledge of the sea is eagerly sought."

The author's search for knowledge of the American boating heritage took him primarily to the Marine Historical Association at Mystic, Connecticut, and the New York Yacht Club, on West Forty-Fourth Street, in New York City. The help cheerfully provided by Edouard A. Stackpole, curator of the association at Mystic, is gratefully acknowledged. This book tapped the resources of the Mystic Seaport, a remarkable, living museum that ably represents and preserves nautical history. The New York Yacht Club's library is unsurpassed in its subject, American yachting. Thanks go to the librarian, Sohei Hohri, for his guidance in using the collection, and also to Robert H. Wessmann and the late Drake Sparkman, members who have shown a continuing interest in the library.

Stanley Crane, librarian of The Pequot Library, Southport, Connecticut, was a helpful consultant. Other sources were the Sterling Memorial Library, Yale University, New Haven; the New York Public Library; the New-York Historical Society, and the Great Lakes Historical Society, Cleveland, Ohio. Roger Olmsted of San Francisco was an invaluable contributor of material regarding the beginnings of yachting on the Pacific Coast. Stanley Rosenfeld, the talented marine photographer, provided interesting facts regarding the use and expenses of giant yachts. Critchell Rimington, editor of "Yachting" magazine, added sage advice and clues leading to the discovery of material. Edwin Gaynor, a neighbor and an accomplished yachtsman, permitted long-term borrowing from his fine library.

To all of them, many thanks.

WILLIAM N. WALLACE, *Southport, Connecticut*

AMERICA'S
FIRST
YACHT

AMERICA'S FIRST YACHT

From stern and rock-bound New England comes a costly, luxurious sailing vessel dedicated to pure pleasure—"Cleopatra's Barge."

Preceding pages: Yachting and merchant-shipping relics of the nineteenth century from Mystic Seaport museum.

In the town of Salem, Massachusetts, in the fall of 1816, the subject of constant and excited conversation was that ship of Captain Crowninshield's being built at Becket's shipyard—by name, *Cleopatra's Barge*. And what kind of a name was that for a ship?

As a matter of fact, it was a very good name. For if it implied lavish appointments and a display of gilt, this was entirely justified. The *Barge* was going to be as sumptuous as anything anyone had seen around Salem for a long time. And if, furthermore, anyone had visions of an aimless voyage through limpid waters, he could be forgiven. The *Barge* had no purpose but pleasure.

Self-indulgence was not exactly an accepted way of life in Salem, a town where nineteen inhabitants had been hanged for alleged witchcraft only 118 years before, but George Crowninshield could get by with his project. He belonged to one of Salem's wealthiest families and he was a respected, popular man who tipped his hat to almost everyone as he rode around town in his two-wheeled yellow buggy. If he wanted a plaything and chose to give it a preposterous name, no one would oppose him.

So, in November, 1816, *Cleopatra's Barge*—America's first yacht—was launched. The designation is somewhat arbitrary. It is possible that lesser American ships may have fit the definition of "yacht" prior to the launching of the *Barge,* but certainly no prior ship was built so obviously for pure pleasure or on so grand a scale. And this, after all, is the criterion: Yacht—a relatively small vessel, characteristically with a sharp prow and graceful lines, and ordinarily privately owned and used for pleasure.

Crowninshield himself had an earlier craft, a sloop called *Jefferson,* which was built in 1801 and most likely never did an honest day's work. But *Jefferson* later went into grubby service as a privateer in the

War of 1812, a circumstance that detracts from her qualifications as a yacht. *Cleopatra's Barge* also served briefly as a packet in later years, hauling customers for hire, but she ended her days with a flourish, driven on to a Pacific reef by an Hawaiian king. On balance, she *deserves* to be the first yacht and is so regarded by most yachting historians.

Other boats found at Salem and nearby Beverly harbor in the early years of the nineteenth century were strictly utilitarian. There were no "pleasure" craft. Life was too hard in the new republic and extracting a living from the New England coastal economy left no time for recreation. The smallest craft, from 15 to 20 feet in length, were the heavy longboats developed from the kind carried in davits by navy ships. These were powered by oars or one or two sails. There were sloops, like the *Jefferson,* of various sizes up to 50 or 60 feet, and then the brigs and brigantines. *Cleopatra's Barge* was a hermaphrodite brig, meaning that she was square-rigged on her foremast; fore-and-aft rigged on her mainmast, the sails being set on the long axis of the hull from bow to stern. (Brigs were square-rigged, brigantines had a fore-and-aft mainsail below the square topsails of the mainmast.) The work boats were built for hauling cargo and passengers or for fishing. They were constructed with little or no thought to comfort or aesthetics, and many were roughly finished. But there were no splinters on *Cleopatra's Barge*.

It would seem that Crowninshield had been inspired by Plutarch's description of the original Cleopatra's barge, with which the Queen of Egypt first traveled to meet Antony at Cilicia. That was a yacht if ever there was one:

"She [Cleopatra] came up the river Cydnus in a vessel," Plutarch says, "the

CLEOPATRA'S BARGE *was an 83-foot
schooner built for a "voyage of pleasure" by
George Crowninshield (right),
a wealthy, imaginative shipping captain.*

stern whereof was gold, the sails of purple
silk, the oars of silver which gently kept
time to the music. She placed herself under
a rich canopy of cloth-of-gold, habiting like
Venus rising out of the sea with beautiful
boys about her, like cupids, fanning her; and
her women leaned negligently on the sides
of the vessel while troops of virgins, richly
drest, marched on the banks of the river,
burning incense and rich perfumes, which
were covered with an infinite number of
people gazing in wonder and admiration.

"The Queen's success with Antony was
answerable to her expectations."

And the *Barge* was answerable to Crowninshield's.

She was a whim. She was outrageously
expensive—a cool $50,000 in 1816 dollars.
But George Crowninshield did not care. He
had in abundance the requisites for being
a yachtsman: time and money.

In 1816 he was fifty years old, unmarried,
and rich. He was a short fellow, a mere
five foot, six inches, but an extrovert and a
dandy. He wore a shaggy beaver hat, with
a skin like that of a terrier dog, and under
it a seaman's pigtail. His father had died
and the family shipping business had dissolved with no objections from George and
his brothers. They didn't need it. A prime
asset of the business had been an extremely
fast, 114-foot brigantine called *America*
that, it was said, had never been outsailed.

During the war of 1812, the *America* had
been equipped for duty as a privateer by
the Crowninshield clan and had captured
British vessels and cargo which sold in
Boston for $1,100,000, a fabulous sum in
those times. A portion of this money went
into the *Barge*.

Crowninshield also used the *America* as
a model for his yacht. He wanted the vessel,
he said, for a voyage of "amusement and
travel" across the Atlantic Ocean to Europe
and the Mediterranean. Captain Crowninshield intended to make the yacht his permanent home.

Cleopatra's Barge was built by Retire
Becket, a descendent of John Becket, who
first came to Salem in 1655, and established
a shipyard which occupied the same site for
145 years. Retire was sixty-three years old
and had a nickname, Tyrey. He was skilled
at his trade, and around Salem it was agreed
that Crowninshield's yacht was probably the

best-built boat in the world. She was 83 feet long on the water line, about 100 on deck, with a beam of 22 feet, 11½ inches and a draft of 11 feet, 5½ inches. Her tonnage came to 191½. She was equipped with every species of light sail known at the time (mainsail, square sails, staysails, and jibs), which would serve her well in the Mediterranean's light airs. The gear was first class—for example, "the best patent horizontal windlass; a rudder fixed to move with great ease and safety upon a new patent device."

Those were the basics of the ship. The embellishments were unbelievable. According to William Bentley, pastor of the East Church, the *Barge* had "elegant settees with velvet cushions, chairs with paintings upon them, mirrors, buffets loaded with plate of every name, the best glass and porcelain...."

Also furniture of mahogany and bird's-eye maple covered in red velvet and gold lace with gilt bronze ornaments. In the main saloon, which measured 19 by 20 feet, there was a chandelier, a magnificent sideboard, and mirrors adorned with gilt eagles. The vessel's ropes, in different colors, were served with velvet and belaying pins at the mast were of brass.

"The expence [sic]," wrote Dr. Bentley, "must have been very great. Nothing has been suffered to enter not in the highest style of excellence." The owner himself admitted,

Crowninshield's Wharf at Salem was headquarters for the merchant fleet that was the source of the family fortune.

"Her accommodations are very stilish [sic] indeed."

Mary Crowninshield, George's sister-in-law, tried to explain what was going on in a letter to her husband Benjamin, who was in Washington serving as President Madison's Secretary of the Navy:

"He [George] is so taken up with his vessel. He is getting furniture. Thinks of having chairs made like those two of ours you bought at Norrises. Is going to have his cabin as large as our parlour. Is getting his spoons and tumblers made. I tell you these particulars as you seem to doubt it all."

Doubting Benjamin didn't know the half of it. Before George was through he had spent $8,000 on furniture alone.

The *Barge's* name had posed a problem for the Captain, despite the obvious parallel with Cleopatra's Nile runabout. At first he proposed *Car of Concordia,* clearly the most unsuitable name to be suggested for a boat since 1588, when England's Queen Elizabeth called her yacht the *Rat of Wight.* He was persuaded to try again.

Cleopatra's Barge was launched on November 21, 1816, before a huge crowd. She was easy to identify. Horizontal stripes

Benjamin Crowninshield, George's brother, was Secretary of the Navy under Madison. Below: A page from the BARGE's log in midwinter. Right: Reproduction of the BARGE's dining saloon in the Peabody Museum at Salem contains original furniture.

Journal

Of an intended Voyage of pleasure in the Brig Cleopatra's Barge of Salem, (Benj.ⁿ Crowninshi Commander) of the burthen of one hundred & ninety one tons

God Speed the Cleopatra's Barge.

Salem Harbour, Thursday January 23 18

1817 Thursday January 23	Commences with fresh breezes from the N. & extremely cold — — — — — — — — — Middle part rather more moderate, the Harb froze over nearly down to the Aqua Vitea. up the Fore Top. St. Yard & listed the Vice

in various colors ran along her starboard side, a zigzag pattern on her port side. Gifts were numerous. (Crowninshield's cousin, a Mrs. Smith, presented the ship with a barrel of mincemeat for which she later charged him $160. He was furious.)

It was a hard winter in Salem. The harbor froze over and the *Barge* stood idle, a captive of the ice. Crowninshield spent the time entertaining aboard the vessel. For the *Barge* was extremely popular, and paid the traditional penalty of popularity by playing cordial host to visitors. One day in December, some 1,900 women and 700 men came for a look at the yacht.

As soon as the thaw came, there was a forty-mile trial voyage to Cape Ann and back, a merry one according to Mary Crowninshield, who wrote to Benjamin: "Captain Beach was one so badly off they had to put him to bed." Mrs. Crowninshield also detected her brother-in-law's pleasure with his new toy. "He appears so happy and satisfied," she wrote, "much as our boys with their new sled."

Cleopatra's Barge set sail for the Mediterranean on March 30, 1817, with fourteen persons aboard. Those who wished to go on the voyage of amusement were subject to discussion by the people of Salem, and Mary Crowninshield wrote: "Much is said about his [George's] choice of companions—and I am sorry—but they may appear better abroad than at home."

The new yacht sailed beautifully, eight knots in a moderate breeze, ten to eleven in a stiff breeze. The owner was delighted. "I'm not going to push her," he wrote home. The Azores were reached on April 18, after a very fast passage. Along the way a member of the ship's company, Samuel Curren Ward, went on record as one of the very first yachtsmen who enjoyed being at sea just for fun. Ward wrote of this experience:

"The night was dark and rainy, the sea ran wonderfully high, and the wind being ahead it continually dashed over the bows of our vessel.

"She appeared to be moving on waves of fire. Upon looking over the stern a bright stream of light seemed to dart from her rudder and extend itself to a great distance behind.

"On each of the quarters, other streams proceeded parallel with that from the rudder. They gave light enough to read the name on our stern.

"The appearance of this light resembles the Milky Way more than anything I can compare it to. It is a large broad belt of faint and indistinct light, interrupted with brilliant stars of every magnitude. Upon going forward and looking over the bows, there appeared nothing but rows of brilliant fire, sparkling and foaming under the bows, and moving off in right angles on both sides of the ship, and fading into the darkness of the surrounding sea. As I stood forward two large grampuses came up under the bow and sported there for two or three hours.

"As I stood wondering at this singular scene, a sea came over our bows and drenched me from head to foot. Upon looking down on our deck, I found it covered with brilliant stars, and my shoes were ornamented with several studs that shone elegantly. In a few moments they all disappeared, and soon after I retired for the night."

From the Azores, the ship went on to Gibraltar, Tangier, and Majorca, creating curiosity and enthusiasm everywhere. Captain Crowninshield had armed himself with 300 letters of introduction (including one from Secretary of State James Monroe to John Quincy Adams, then minister to England) and used them liberally. He also had $5,000 in cash for expenses.

The voyage continued around the Medi-

Italian artist painted BARGE'S *picture
(below) in harbor of Genoa.
The yacht went to work following her
sale, advertised at right, in 1818.*

terranean coast. At Barcelona, where they seemed never to have heard of America, 8,000 people visited *Cleopatra's Barge* in one day.

The stream of visitors in every port tested the crew and annoyed the owner's nephew, another Benjamin Crowninshield—"Philosopher Ben," as he was called. He wrote of the visitors:

"They must see the salon, examine the buffet, hear a dissertation on bird's-eye maple, know the price of each article in America; take some wine; then sit down until another crowd pushes into the room eager to enjoy the same privilege. And what with seasickness among the ladies; the strong and offensive odors of the friars, beggars and garlic, the company below is subjected to undergo a regular inquisition.

"When the vessel rolls, it is no uncommon sight to see fifteen or twenty ladies in a most miserable plight, reclining over the rail or stretched out on deck. Some gentlemen, full of love or pity for the ladies, will caress them. Others stare at them when their lovely faces are not wearing their most beautiful smiles. Alas for poor human nature. What a miserable feeling is seasickness but what a fine appetite it gives us on shore."

At Marseilles, the owner felt it was time to sharpen up the ship. On board came four upholsterers to make cushions, four gilders to paint gold leaf, three girls to sew curtains with tassel cords, a sailmaker to produce an awning, two tailors, a shoemaker, and "dozens" of mechanics, according to Philosopher Ben. In his journal he wrote that the *Barge* had been completely painted

twice in forty days and that many parts of the upper works never dried between paintings. The ship's company was forever brushing into wet paint and ruining clothes.

(Philosopher Ben may have been a wet blanket. He became gloomy and disgruntled, calling his uncle "My Lord," and was put ashore at Gibraltar, at his own request, on the return voyage.)

It was at Marseilles that Captain George brought aboard two paintings for the saloon. He was under the impression they had been done by Rubens; it was probably just as well that they had not. At Genoa, 4,000 visitors added a complication. They brought aboard fleas. At Leghorn, the Mediterranean bounced so much that a chest of pickles emptied into the tea and rice went into the pork.

On deck as decoration was a full-sized, carved American Indian, gloriously war-painted and the object of great curiosity. A nearsighted Frenchman saluted it. The bored crew told Genoese visitors it was an American saint and the Italians kissed its feet. In Spain, the crew told the peasants it was alive and introduced them to it.

Crowninshield, an impressionable, small-town American, doted on big shots. He greatly enjoyed entertaining admirals and princes and consuls aboard his vessel. Everyone told him the *Barge* far exceeded in beauty and appointments any English yacht ever seen in the Mediterranean. The climax of the trip for Crowninshield came when he took a side trip to Rome, where he was entertained by the Bonaparte family and by Princess Pauline of Naples.

Cleopatra's Barge then sailed for home, reaching Salem on October 3, 1817. The success of his first cruise encouraged him to plan a second one. He decided that the next year he would sail to northern Europe and cruise the Baltic on his wonderful yacht. But it was not to be. He succumbed to heart

disease and died on board the *Barge* on November 26.

The *Barge* was converted to a merchant vessel, and the next year sold at auction to a brother of the late captain for $15,400. There was no demand for a yacht and there were no other George Crowninshields about. The pursuit of pleasure, in this land of Cotton Mather, was still looked upon as wicked.

Cleopatra's Barge was sold again and became a packet ship on a run from Boston to Charleston, South Carolina. Then, in 1820, she set sail for the Sandwich Islands, as Hawaii then was called. King Kamehameha II took a great fancy to her and bought her on November 16, 1820, for a price payable in sandalwood over the next year. The king put her back to her original use as a yacht, but soon after through carelessness she ran aground on a reef and was wrecked. The hulk was towed to Honolulu, where it lay on the beach for years.

"AMERICA"
WINS
A
CUP

2

"AMERICA"
WINS
A
CUP

Commodore Stevens
and his
friends beat the
British in
their home waters
and return
with a silver mug
worth a hundred
guineas.

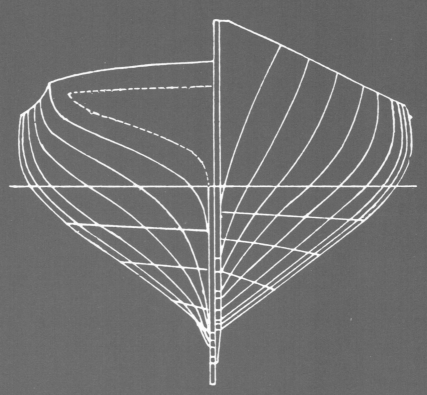

Preceding pages: The AMERICA was
similar to the swift New York pilot boats of her time.
Her schooner rig had no topsails.

Louis Augustus Depau was a distinguished New Yorker. He concerned himself with his family's shipping firm, which had originated regular passenger service by sailing packet between New York and Le Havre, and for a wife he had taken Sylvie, daughter of a hero of the American Revolution, the Admiral Count François Joseph Paul de Grasse of France.

Late one summer's afternoon, Depau left his offices in lower Manhattan and walked a few blocks down to that graphic point of land at the end of the island, the Battery. There he fell in with two friends, John C. Jay and George L. Schuyler, of equally prominent New York families. A few hundred yards offshore, a yacht with the gleam of newness about her lay at anchor. This was *Gimcrack,* a blunt-bow, short-ended schooner measuring 51 feet from stem to stern, 49 feet along her water line. *Gimcrack* was one month out of William Capes' shipyard in Hoboken, New Jersey, and her design model had been carved from a block of wood by a young modeler named George Steers. The vessel's owner was John Cox Stevens and he had sailed her down from the mud flats of Hoboken to the Battery that day for the purpose of holding a meeting.

Depau and Schuyler and Jay were rowed out to *Gimcrack,* assembling on the hard cushions of the yacht's saloon at 5:30 p.m. There were six others present: Stevens, Captain James Rogers, James M. Waterbury, George B. Rollins, Hamilton Wilkes, and William Edgar. All owned yachts and were there for the purpose of organizing a yacht club. The date was July 30, 1844.

The idea of a yacht club was not original to New York. England's Royal Yacht Squadron had been founded in 1815, and it was well-known to cosmopolitan Americans like those seated in *Gimcrack's* cabin. Even in this country there was then in existence the first Boston Yacht Club (which later disbanded) and the Detroit Boat Club. The New Yorkers, however, were not abashed. Jay was recording secretary, and if we are to take his minutes literally, few club meetings have proceeded with greater purpose and speed than the one that created the New York Yacht Club. The gentlemen present agreed on the name, agreed to designate themselves the original members. Stevens, the host, was chosen commodore. A five-man committee was appointed to draft club rules and regulations. Lastly and boldly, the members decided to have a club cruise to Newport, Rhode Island, under command of the commodore. It was to begin three days hence at nine o'clock in the morning. And it did, with all the club's yachts but one in the fleet.

The founding of the New York Yacht Club, fittingly enough aboard his own yacht, was one of many triumphs for John Cox Stevens. The mainstream of yachting in this country traces back to him, and those who bestow titles have called him "the father of American yachting." He came from a remarkable family. His father, Colonel John Stevens, was one of the foremost engineers of the new nation and deserves a share of the credit for the early development—if not the invention—of the steamboat. A Stevens vessel, the *Phoenix,* made the first run by steam from New York to Philadelphia, in 1809, two years after the maiden voyage of Robert Fulton's *Clermont.*

Colonel Stevens had a family of twelve children. He raised them at Castle Point, an imposing home he had bought in 1784 in Hoboken, on the west side of the North River. With water at their doorstep, the Stevenses inevitably were a nautical clan. At early ages the boys were rowing passengers across the river to Manhattan. Like many restless minds of the nineteenth century,

those of the Stevens boys turned to a variety of endeavors: yachts and yacht designing, steam engines and steamboats, railroads, cricket, and race horses.

The second son, Robert Livingston Stevens, was an inventor. He made numerous improvements in steamboats and introduced spring piling for use in ferry slips. He imported the famous steam locomotive, *John Bull,* from England, and invented the T-shaped railroad rail.

Robert's brother, Edwin Augustus Stevens, was the inventor of the Stevens farm plow, a pioneer builder of ironclad warships, and the founder of the Stevens Institute of Technology, which was erected in 1870 on the family homesite.

John Cox Stevens, the eldest son, shared all the interests of his father and brothers. He was also very much the sportsman, and as a yacht owner he established the precedent of dissatisfaction that has kept boat-builders and designers in business ever since. He owned boat after boat, beginning in 1809, when he was twenty-four, with a 20-footer called the *Diver*. It was used to carry Stevens, his friends, and family on frequent trips across the Hudson to New York.

In 1816, Stevens cast aside the *Diver* and stepped up to *Trouble,* a considerably larger vessel, 56 feet in over-all length. In 1820, he experimented with a twin-hulled catamaran, although, like others who came after

him, he could not get the design to sail properly. In 1832, he had a big schooner, *Wave,* 65 feet on the water line. And in 1839, he had the even larger *Onkahaye* built. It was 91 feet on the water line, weighed 250 tons, and had an iron keel. Then, in 1844, came *Gimcrack*.

In the genealogy of American yachts, *Onkahaye* and *Gimcrack* are descendents of *Cleopatra's Barge,* although not direct ones. During the intervening decades of the 1820's and 1830's, there were isolated boats which qualified as yachts by the manner in which they were used. A few were found around Boston, a few in New York. But *Cleopatra's Barge* had started no fad. English society had a leisure class and, therefore, a flourishing yachting movement, but there was no comparable community in America. Stevens and his guests aboard *Gimcrack* provided the first significant impetus for one.

On that first New York Yacht Club cruise, August 2 to 12, *Gimcrack* was similar to the seven companion vessels. They were sturdy types, 17 to 45 tons, and from models in the present clubhouse one can see that they had full, bluff bows, broad sterns, little overhang, stumpy bowsprits, and short masts. All save one was schooner rigged.

The next year the club introduced racing, and competition brought some unhappiness to Commodore Stevens because *Gimcrack* did not do as well as he would have liked.

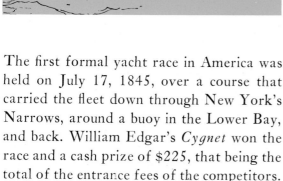

The first formal yacht race in America was held on July 17, 1845, over a course that carried the fleet down through New York's Narrows, around a buoy in the Lower Bay, and back. William Edgar's *Cygnet* won the race and a cash prize of $225, that being the total of the entrance fees of the competitors. *Gimcrack* was third.

Stevens took action after that setback. He and his brother Edwin had an imposing sloop built and named it *Maria,* after John's wife. The new vessel was inspired by the *Eliza Ann,* swiftest of the commercial North River sloops which worked the Hudson River towns. *Maria* was big—110 feet on deck, 92 at the water line—and she had a tremendous beam (26½ feet), but a shallow draft of only 5 feet, 2 inches. That was with the centerboard up. It was quite a board: seven tons of iron, counterbalanced by huge springs.

Maria had an enormous rig, and when sailing off the wind, with the centerboard raised, steering could be downright treacherous. So a small, second centerboard was run through the deadwood aft to add stability. It was a less than perfect rig. *Maria* often broke down. She was more efficient later on when transformed from a sloop to a schooner.

Maria's hull form was extreme for her time, and she was unique in other ways. The Stevens genius hit upon hollow masts and

John C. Stevens (far left) was a founder of the New York Yacht Club and its first commodore. The club came into being on July 30, 1844, at a meeting aboard the Stevens yacht GIMCRACK *(next left). Winner of America's first formal yacht race, held by the N.Y.Y.C. in 1845, was William Edgar's* CYGNET *(above, left). The prize was $225. For years the Stevens brothers'* MARIA *(above) was the fastest yacht in New York harbor.*

booms to lighten rigging; no one had thought of it before. The panels of sailcloth were cut parallel to the boom, rather than vertically as was the custom. The seams, therefore, offered less resistance to the wind flowing over the surface of the sails.

Old records state that she could do seventeen knots. This may have been a generous estimate, but there is no doubt that she was swift. Her career as a yacht was short and impressive.

John Stevens, who never kept a boat for long, finally sold his share of her to brother Edwin, who altered her rig to that of a two-masted schooner and sold her into commercial work. The former flagship of the New York Yacht Club thus ended her days sailing the Atlantic Coast in the fruit trade. In 1870, she went down off Cape Hatteras in a storm.

In her first race, on October 6, 1846, *Maria* won easily, defeating *Siren* by over one hour on elapsed time. Four days later,

The New York Yacht Club's first clubhouse
was erected on the Elysian Fields at Weehawken,
N. J., and John Stevens paid for it.
The building now is a part of Mystic Seaport.

Commodore Stevens had her out again, taking on *Coquette* in a match race for a $1,000 side bet. The course was twenty-five miles to windward in the ocean and back again. *Coquette*, carrying full sail, beat the reefed *Maria*. The *Maria's* crew had not carried all of her vast canvas in the ocean for fear of tearing the rig right out of the boat.

Match races like these usually were sailed on a boat-for-boat basis. However, in club events between several yachts of different sizes and speeds, some effort at reaching an equitable handicap had to be made. So yachts were handicapped on the basis of their tonnage as determined by the U. S. Customs House formula, each ton costing forty-five seconds per mile of course. This was the first handicap formula for yachting and it was far from satisfactory—like all those that have come after it.

Although the waters around New York were extensive and varied, a yachting delight, they were shallow in many places. Such conditions dictated local yacht design throughout the nineteenth century, and were evidenced in a wealth of wide, beamy centerboarders of shallow draft, as opposed to the narrow-keel craft which sailed the deeper waters of New England and Great Britain.

New York waters influenced *Maria's* design and so did the favored club racing courses of the time. They began off Hoboken, carrying down the river through the Narrows into the Lower Bay, rounding the Southwest Spit buoy, or the Sandy Hook lightship, and then returning. Distances worked out to about thirty-five miles, which could be sailed in four hours or might take all day, depending upon the wind. Under the prevailing southwest breezes of summertime the course evolved into two long reaches, down to the turning mark and back. Those were perfect points of sailing for *Maria's* long water line, her shoal underbody, and her big sloop rig of mainsail and jib. Commodore Stevens had something.

He also had the New York Yacht Club virtually in his front yard. The first club-house, "a handsome Gothic cottage in a pleasant grove," was located at the Elysian Fields, a popular picnic ground of the era at Weehawken, New Jersey, just north of the Stevens home at Castle Point. John Stevens paid for the clubhouse. He had his club, he had his yacht, and he had the sporting spirit to bet and lose $1,000 on a yacht race. Here was a man ready for bigger game. George Schuyler provided the challenge.

Schuyler had a letter from England which suggested that inasmuch as New York was famous for its pilot boats, a sample craft should be sent abroad in connection with the first world's fair, England's Crystal Palace exhibition of 1851. And why not? Schuyler, John Stevens, and Stevens' brother Edwin formed a syndicate with three other N.Y.Y.C. members: Colonel James A. Hamilton, J. Beekman Finley, and Hamilton Wilkes, one of the club's founding fathers. All agreed that a New York pilot boat would be the perfect instrument for American representation in England.

The New York pilot boats—two-masted schooners 80 to 100 feet long—had a world-wide reputation for speed. And speed was necessary in their line of work which sent them offshore to place pilots on incoming merchantmen. Since the first pilot aboard got the job, competition was fierce and there was pressure on designers to build more and more speed into the boats. George Steers designed the fastest ones, the same George Steers who produced *Gimcrack*. He was an advocate of the longer bow, of filling out the middle sections of the yacht, and of running long, clean lines aft.

America is and always has been famous for her schooners. The concept of the two-masted rig originated here and the name "schooner" was fixed to it one day in 1713 when Andrew Robinson launched such a vessel from his yard at Gloucester, Massachusetts. As the boat slid off the ways into the bay, a bystander is reputed to have called out, "Oh, how she schoons!"—meaning, how she skims the water. Robinson replied, "A schooner let her be."

The Stevens syndicate commissioned Steers to design and build a yacht following the lines of the pilot boats. A letter from London encouraged them greatly. The Earl of Wilton, commodore of the Royal Yacht Squadron, wrote to Stevens, whom he had never met, on February 28, 1851:

"Sir: Understanding from Sir H. Bulwer that a few of the members of the New York Yacht Club are building a schooner which it is their intention to bring over to England this summer, I have taken the liberty of writing to you, in your capacity as commodore, to request you to convey to them and to any friends that may accompany them on board the yacht, an invitation on the part of myself and the members of the Royal

Yacht Squadron to become visitors at the clubhouse at Cowes during their stay in England.

"For myself I may be permitted to say that I shall have great pleasure in extending to your countrymen any civility that lies in my power, and shall be very glad to avail myself of any improvements in shipbuilding that the industry and skill of your nation have enabled you to elaborate. I remain sir, your obedient servant, Wilton (Commodore, Royal Yacht Squadron)."

That was the most gracious kind of invitation for the commodore of a six-year old yacht club in "uncivilized" America to receive. Stevens fell all over himself in expressing his gratitude to Lord Wilton and at the same time revealed a little more of what he planned for the impending yacht and voyage.

He wrote: "Should she [the yacht] answer the sanguine expectations of her builder, we propose to avail ourselves of your friendly bidding, and take with a good grace the sound thrashing we are likely to get by venturing our longshore craft on your

Lines of the AMERICA. *But George Steers (right) drew no lines when he designed her. As was the custom of the day, he whittled a model from a block of wood. He helped build her and was a crew member. Boat was produced at William H. Brown's shipyard (far right) in New York City.*

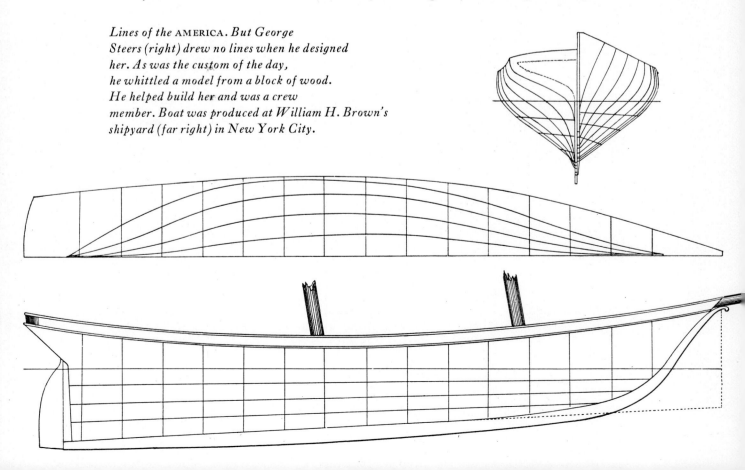

rough waters. I fear the energy and experience of your persevering yachtsmen will prove an overmatch for the industry and skill of their aspiring competitors."

What Stevens and Schuyler and the others had in mind was the use of their yacht as a betting instrument, in addition to a world's fair exhibit, and they were preparing fertile ground for their wagers.

The yacht was launched and named *America*. The syndicate took delivery on June 18, 1851, and George Steers was paid $20,000. *Maria* beat *America* in a trial run, but no one was dismayed because *Maria* was an inshore racing machine, incapable of crossing the ocean as *America* was about to do.

With the exception of *Cleopatra's Barge* in the dim past, no yacht had ever crossed the Atlantic Ocean. But there was little trepidation about that because the New York pilot boats went 'way offshore and had proved their seaworthiness. The *America* would do likewise.

In all of his early work Steers adhered to the conventional hull form, the "cod's head and mackerel tail" shape. But in 1849, when

he received an order for a pilot boat for Captain Richard (Dick) Brown, a noted New York pilot, he had cut loose from his usual style and worked out a radically different form. The result was the *Mary Taylor*, named after an actress who was a great favorite in New York. The new pilot-boat design was an instantaneous success and Steers used the hull form again for the *America*.

He built into the forward sections of the hull the sharp, concave lines that were a departure from the contemporary blunt-bow "cod's head" boats. Also the widest part of the ship—the maximum beam—did not fall at the middle of the hull as had previously been the practice, but aft of amidships. The result for the *Mary Taylor* and the *America* was less drag, better balance, more speed.

America was a true sister ship of the pilot schooners—with a few concessions to yachting such as white-and-gold decorations and velvet-covered sofas below. Steers built from a half-model he had carved in solid wood, following the custom of the time. No lines were drawn on paper.

The *America's* over-all length measured 101 feet, 9 inches. On the water line she was 90 feet, 3 inches, and she had a maximum beam of 23 feet. She drew 11 feet (to *Maria's* 5 feet, 2 inches) and possessed no centerboard. Her rig carried 5,263 square feet of sail, and it was a simple one: mainsail, foresail, and jib. Below decks, she had one large main saloon extending from the mainmast aft, along the sides of the saloon were six berths. Foreward were four large

staterooms, then the galley and the pantry. The large forecastle in the bow contained accommodations for some fifteen men.

Her sails were probably her best racing feature. They were of cotton-duck cloth, cut with well-formed curves aloft, if the portraits of her that survive are accurate. To the London *Times,* however, they were "flat boards" compared to English sails, which were made of baggy flax and hung loose at the foot instead of being secured to the booms.

America made a fast passage, from New York to Le Havre in twenty days, sailed by a crew of thirteen which included George Steers, his fifteen-year-old nephew, Henry Steers, and the Sandy Hook pilot, Captain Dick Brown, who was in charge. Commodore Stevens came aboard in France. The yacht completed her fitting out at Le Havre before setting sail across the English Channel on July 31, for Cowes, on the Isle of Wight. Because of heavy fog, *America* anchor-ed that night five miles from her destination.

The next morning the English cutter *Lavrock* came out from Cowes with the intention of testing the invader. As Stevens later found out, this was one of the newest and fastest cutters. At a dinner given him and his associates on their return to the United States, October 1, 1851, Stevens said:

"The news spread like lightning that the Yankee clipper had arrived and that the *Lavrock* had gone down to show her the way

Sail plan of one of AMERICA'S *British contemporaries (below) called for topsails and multiple headsails. The British were astounded at* AMERICA'S *raked masts (bottom).*

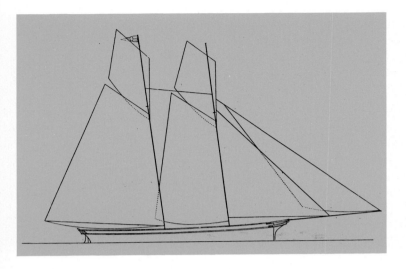

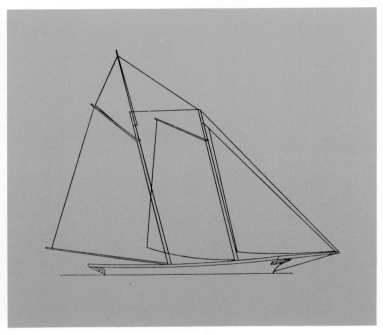

India voyage and were some four or five inches too deep in the water. We got up our sails with heavy heart—the wind had increased to a five or six knot breeze—and after waiting until we were ashamed to wait longer, we let her go about two hundred yards ahead, and then started in her wake."

During the first five minutes Stevens said, there was not a sound aboard the *America,* "save the beating of our anxious hearts," as she strove to overcome the Englishman. Captain Brown crouched in his cockpit, his hand on the tiller, his eyes on *Lavrock.* The others were spread flat and motionless on the deck, reducing the windage of their bodies. They too were watching the other boat. By Stevens' account, *America's* position was not a particularly favorable one. She was to leeward and behind *Lavrock.* Under such circumstances, it usually takes the trailing yacht a goodly time, if not forever, to go ahead of an antagonist blocking the source of the wind. That morning the *America's* crew soon realized that they had a going vessel under them. The invading schooner sailed right up to windward of the Englishman and the brush was over. Stevens said: "We worked quickly and surely to windward of her wake; the crisis was past and some dozen of deep drawn sighs proved that our agony was over."

Afterwards, when the yacht returned to Cowes, the *Lavrock* crew talked. Within a few days a legend had grown concerning the *America's* speed. She lay in the roadstead at Cowes, her crew enjoying Lord Wilton's promised hospitality and Englishmen by the dozen coming around to have a look. Most of them were confounded by the pilot-boat appearance which was quite different from the typical British cutter.

Differences were obvious to the eye. The English cutter type had a rounded blunt bow, a high-sided hull, a rig not as tall as *Amer-*

up. The yachts and vessels in the harbor, the wharves, and the windows of all the houses bordering on them, were filled with thousands of spectators, watching with eager eyes the eventful trial they say we could not escape; for the *Lavrock* stuck to us, sometimes lying to, and sometimes tacking around us, evidently showing she had no intention of quitting us.

"We were loaded with extra sails, with beef and pork and bread enough for an East

ica's, and less relative sail area. The English yachtmen criticized the *America's* long, sharp bow, the low black hull, and the stiff-looking raked masts. But they wanted no part of a race with her.

Stevens had accepted the implied challenge of *Lavrock* and he is to be commended for that. But under the circumstances, his discretion might be questioned. No doubt it never occurred to this sportsman to hold back and hide some of *America's* speed so as to lure the yachtsmen of Cowes into making a money challenge. Later he may have wished he had.

Stevens was feted at Cowes, a popular visitor with impeccable manners. But he could not entice any yacht owner into a race, and he soon had to drop his ideas about friendly match races for large stakes. In a final attempt to arouse some interest, however, he did post a challenge in the club-house, "To sail the *America* against any British vessel whatever, for any sum from one to 10,000 guineas, merely stipulating that there should be not less than a six-knot breeze." George Schuyler, a good man with words, set down the terms. Still there were no takers.

The summer plans of the Royal Yacht Squadron, however, called for a race around the Isle of Wight on August 22 "for yachts of all nations," and the prize was to be the Royal Yacht Squadron Cup, which had cost one hundred guineas. Continuing their hospitality to the visitors, the squadron's officers invited Stevens to sail his yacht in the race. After three weeks of inactivity, the commodore accepted gladly.

The conditions of the race were simple. It was to be a free-for-all, sailed without time allowance, and the first yacht to finish would take the cup. From a prestige standpoint it was to be all the British yachts against the American. The course of some

fifty miles was highly complex, going clockwise around the island, from Cowes on the north side, thence south to St. Catherine's Point, finishing in the Solent, the western approach to Cowes. The London *Times,* which had chided local yachtsmen for refusing to race the *America,* said of the route:

"The course around the Isle of Wight is notoriously one of the most unfair to strangers that can be selected, and, indeed, does not appear a good race ground to anyone, inasmuch as the current and tides render local knowledge of more value than swift sailing and nautical skill."

A swarm of rivals and a tricky course that would reward local knowledge were less than ideal prospects for a first race, but the New York sailors were cocky. Stevens and Schuyler scoured the water front trying to get a bet down on themselves, but were unsuccessful. Only one wager was made. George Steers, the builder, wanted a little more sail area for the boat and so he added a flying jib set on a boom. Michael Ratsey, of the Isle of Wight Ratseys, a family that has made sails and spars and boats for hundreds of years, produced both spar and sail, and Steers bet him their cost against the outcome of the race. Ratsey was allowed to choose one English boat against *America* and he took *Beatrice.* There were no other bets.

It was the custom in those days to start races at anchor, with the yachts lined up in rows. On the morning of August 22, 1851, there were two rows of yachts intending to race: seventeen British schooners and cutters, ranging in size from 47 tons to 393, plus the 170-ton *America* which was the fifth largest boat in the fleet. It was not a propitious racing day. The wind was light and came from the west, which meant that the yachts would be sailing down wind at the outset.

The preparatory gun, five minutes before the start, was fired at 9:55 a.m., and after that the crews were allowed to hoist sails. The *America* ran into trouble right here. With sails up, the boat wanted to take off, but the anchor could not be pulled until the second gun had gone off. The schooner overran her anchor again and again, turning and twisting on the rode. To get the anchor up, the sails had to be dropped. Meanwhile, the starting signal had sounded and all of the fleet was under way. The *America* was last.

But the crew worked quickly. The anchor was pulled and the schooner set out in pursuit of the others. With the breeze aft, the *America* charged through the water and began to pick up and pass one boat after another. Many years later, in 1877, a description of the race was given at a Sewanhaka Yacht Club dinner by Henry Steers, who had been the fifteen-year-old cabin boy. Steers said: "By the time we got to the Nab [twelve miles away], we had walked through the whole fleet except for four, *Beatrice, Aurora, Volante,* and *Arrow.* We were running wing and wing and these boats would steer close together, so that when we tried to get through them we could not without fouling and we had to keep cutting and sheering about, very often being near jibing."

It was the opinion of this eyewitness that the four British yachts were sailed in collusion, which was against the spirit of a free-for-all race. Their object seemed to be to block off the foreigner, to stop him from getting through. If in the melee *America* should jibe all standing, well, that would be her crew's misfortune.

But the British yachts could not block the way forever and finally *America* broke through. From the Nab down to St. Catherine's Point at the south end of the island, the wind, having shifted to south-southwest, was ahead of the beam, and this was the *America's* best point of sailing. "We left them so fast," Steers recalled, "that when we got down to the point there was not a yacht in sight."

America had gone from last to first. Behind her in the fleet other events were favoring her, as well. Three of the fastest British yachts were out of the race. The cutters *Arrow* and *Volante* had had a collision and dropped out. *Arrow* ran aground and *Alarm* turned back to stand by her.

After passing St. Catherine's Point, the *America* raced to the Needles on a favorable port tack under a good breeze. Steers said the boat's speed was "thirteen or fourteen knots." Off St. Catherine's that flying jib boom, which had been acquired by speculation, broke in two and the new sail could not be carried. That delighted Dick Brown, the pilot-boat skipper, who said he was "damned" glad the jib boom was gone because he didn't believe in carrying a flying jib to windward.

The *America* reached the Needles at 5:30 p.m., and it was estimated that she had a lead of eight miles over the second boat, the little *Aurora.* The rest of the squadron was far out of sight astern. But the wind fell light again, the tide ran against the boats, and in the run up the Solent to the finish *Aurora* slowly but decisively closed on *America.*

The *America's* lead was substantial enough to last, however, and when she finished the race, at 8:37 p.m., *Aurora* was about two miles behind. The latter, at 47 tons the smallest boat in the race, finished at 8:55. Then came *Bacchante* at 9:30, *Eclipse* at 9:45, and the big *Brilliant* at 1:20 a.m. the following day. The times of the other boats were not taken.

Would *America* have beaten *Aurora* if the boat had been able to use her customary handicap in the race? Yes, she would have won by about two minutes, according to the handicapping formula then favored by the

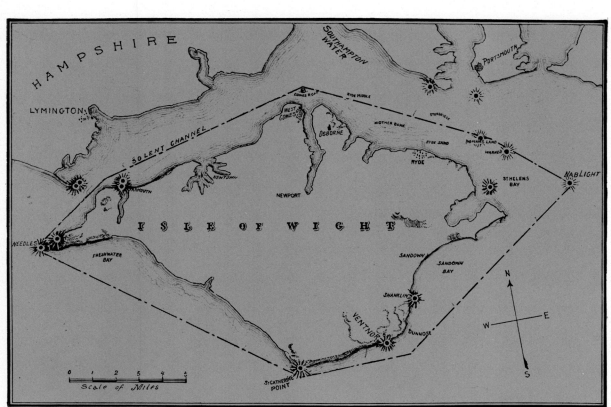

Royal Yacht Squadron. This was "Acker's time-allowance scale," which dated back to 1730. Nonetheless, *Aurora's* respectable margin behind *America* at the finish makes one wonder whether the anecdote about that notable yachting enthusiast, Queen Victoria, is not apocryphal. The Queen saw parts of the race aboard the royal yacht, and is said to have inquired which yacht was second, behind the *America*. By way of answer, the story goes, she was told: "There is no second, Your Majesty." For the sake of the thousands who have come to believe this story, it may be suggested that the innocent question and the bleak answer were made sometime in the afternoon, before the *America* began to buck the tide in the Solent and *Aurora* gained six miles on her.

Queen Victoria was certainly interested in *America*. She and Prince Albert came aboard for a visit a few days after the race. By this time, said Steers, "there was an awful crying and moaning about Cowes." Ratsey and other builders said they could build a boat to take the *America*. They claimed she was a "mere shell—a Yankee trick." It was pointed out that the race had been less than perfect by any standards, the wind light, variable, and, therefore, fickle with regard to the competitors. Besides, three of the fastest British yachts were among the eight which never did finish the race.

Ratsey and some others firmed their talk into a proposition and John Stevens was willing to listen. The English wanted ninety days to build a boat. Then they would race for a $2,500 wager. Stevens did not think the prize was in proportion to the required three-month wait and, speaking like a twentieth-century Texan, proposed that the stakes be $125,000. Ratsey and his contemporaries backed off.

America did sail once more that summer. The week after winning the Squadron Race she took on the schooner *Titania* for a side bet of $500 and won easily.

There were no further racing possibilities for the vessel, but there was a buyer. Stevens sold the *America* to an Englishman, Sir John de Blaquiere, for $25,000. At that price the syndicate members got back their original investment and their expenses, too.

Commodore Stevens had had a fine summer. He had created a stir in England with a rakish and newfangled yacht and brought home a cup worth one hundred guineas, plus considerable fame and prestige. Only in

terms of gambling earnings was the voyage a bust.

Thereafter, the *America* had a long, varied, and generally unsuccessful career. Her new owner immediately altered her rig, cutting the masts by five feet because, it was reported, they were rotten at the base. She had only moderate racing success and was sold again the next year. Then she was hauled up in the mud at Cowes and remained inactive until another sale and a complete rebuilding in 1859. At this time the large gilt eagle on the *America's* stern was removed and placed over the door of an inn on the Isle of Wight. It stayed there until given to the New York Yacht Club many years later.

Steers, the man responsible for the model and the construction of the *America,* was dead by then. He had owned a country place at Great Neck, Long Island, in addition to the family home at 91 Cannon Street in New York City. On September 25, 1856, he set

AMERICA *in August, 1891, after hull and sail plan were altered by designer Edward Burgess for her owner, General Ben Butler.*

out with a road wagon and a team of horses to drive to Great Neck. The horses took fright and Steers was thrown or jumped from the wagon. In any event, he struck his head and lay in the road, unconscious, until found by some friends. He died the next day at his home in the city.

George Steers was only thirty-six years old at his death. In the perspective of time he has come to be recognized as a truly great shipbuilder. The *America,* the "yacht built to represent a nation," as Stevens had put it, outlasted her creator by eighty-nine years.

Her name was *Camilla* when the Civil War broke out and a Savannah man bought her in England. With guns mounted on her decks and *Memphis* on her bows, she had a fling as a Confederate dispatch boat and blockade runner. That career quickly ended when the Union gunboat *Ottawa* chased her up the St. John's River in Florida in 1861 and her crew scuttled her. Lieutenant Thomas H. Stevens, of the *Ottawa,* went up the river in a small boat and seventy miles above Jacksonville, in Dunn's Creek, he found the *America* sunk in three fathoms of water, only her port rail showing above the surface. She was without masts and five two-inch auger holes had been bored through her bottom. She was raised, repaired, renamed *America,* and assigned to the blockade fleet off Charleston, South Carolina. In 1863 she went north to Annapolis, becoming a training ship for the midshipmen at the Naval Academy.

The United States Navy spent $10,343 (which did not include new sails) repairing and refitting *America* in 1870. She was a great favorite of the naval officers and proudly entered the New York Yacht Club's international race of that summer, being one of twenty-three yachts defending the Royal Yacht Squadron Cup that she had won nineteen years before. In the contest, which came to be known as the "first" America's Cup

Race, the original cup winner finished in fourth place.

General Ben Butler of Boston bought the *America* in 1873 at a Navy Department auction for $5,000 and sailed her as a yacht for another nineteen years.

During a long lifetime, the yacht was poked, prodded, planked, and painted many times. General Butler scarcely let a year go by without making some changes in her. He underwrote two major rebuilding efforts. The first, in 1875, was done under the direction of Donald McKay, the designer and

AMERICA *memorabilia at Mystic. Left: Her rudder. Above: Nails from garboard strake, part of a deck cover, dolphin used by Steers, a block, and oil painting of yacht itself.*

builder of many of America's fastest clipper ships. Edward Burgess, the leading yacht designer of the 1880's, "modernized" the *America* a second time in 1886.

Butler died in 1893, and his ship went out of commission as a yacht following the season of 1901. A group of yachtsmen purchased her in 1921 and returned her to the Naval Academy as a gift to the nation. She was berthed alongside a pier at Dewey Basin in Annapolis and attracted thousands of visitors until 1945, when, rotten beyond restoration, she was broken up.

Because the America's Cup competition grew to such tremendous proportions, the *America* gained stature as the years went by —stature beyond the results of her racing efforts. Many a yacht has posted a better racing record than *America's*. She had fifty-one races and won twelve of them. But the first race was the one that counted.

LENGTH ON DECK	99 FEET.
WATER LINE	90
BREADTH OF BEAM	23
DEPTH OF HOLD	9 6 IN.
DRAUGHT OF WATER	11
REGISTER	205 TONS

THE YACHT "HE

MODELLED BY Mr Wm TOOKER, N.Y. BUIL

Owned by Mr James

WINNER of the GREAT OCEAN YACHT RACE, With the "FLEETWING" and "VESTA" from New Yo

THE
GREAT
OCEAN
RACE

—

3

ETTA" 205 TONS.

STEERS, GREENPOINT, L. I.

Gordon Bennett Jr

Cowes, Engd for $ 90,000, Dec. 25th 1866. Making the run in 13 days 22¼ hours, mean time.

LENGTH OF MAIN MAST		79 FEET.	
" FORE MAST		77	
" MAIN BOOM		57	
" MAIN GAFF		27	6 IN
" FORE D°		26	
" BOWSPRIT (OUTBOARD)		26	
" FLYING JIB BOOM		19	

LITH. CURRIER & IVES. N.Y.

THE
GREAT
OCEAN
RACE

---

*A daredevil
bet for
high stakes sends
three schooners
across the
Atlantic in the
dead
of winter.*

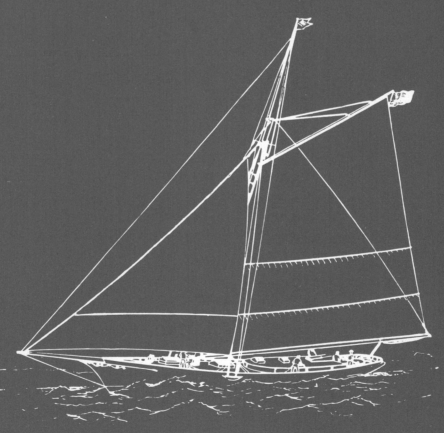

Preceding pages: James Gordon Bennett's
HENRIETTA. *She was faster than her predecessor,
the sloop* REBECCA *(above).*

The impact of the *America's* victory in 1851 was immense. Much of the race had been a drifting match, the outcome was decided largely by chance, but the event received wide publicity at home, and the story in time became a part of our national folklore. After all, there was nothing quite like beating our British cousins, in men-o'-war or yachts. A favorite chant among small boys of the 1850's ran:

> *"Where did she come from?*
> *New York town.*
> *Who was her skipper?*
> *Old Dick Brown."*

The *America* brought an international quality to yachting and measurably increased its popularity. With the exception of *Cleopatra's Barge* thirty-four years before, the *America* also was the first yacht to cross the Atlantic Ocean and call at foreign ports. Her visit inspired a feeling of good will for American yachtsmen among the English and began a transoceanic parade of yachts that was curbed only slightly by Britain's Crimean War of 1854-55 and the American Civil War of 1861-65.

These peregrinations reached a climax in 1866 with the first transatlantic race, an event that came to be called the "Great Ocean Race." It was a bizarre affair, born in brandy, foolhardy in concept, courageous in execution. The race took six lives and served to introduce James Gordon Bennett, Jr., to the world of international sport, a world that was never the same thereafter.

Bennett belonged to the new breed of yachtsmen that grew in numbers after the Civil War. They all were immensely rich and regarded their large, expensive yachts as toys. They lacked the scientific background and investigative interest of the Stevens family, and most of them left the design and equipment of their vessels to sailing masters.

None of these "new" yachtsmen was quite as flamboyant as Bennett. His father ran the New York *Herald;* he would inherit it later on. The pair of them, said the late Elmer Davis, "invented almost everything, good and bad, in modern journalism." James, Junior, was a spoiled brat raised without direction by estranged parents in Paris and New York. In 1857, at age sixteen, he became a member of the New York Yacht Club, the youngest ever accepted. His father gave him a yacht, the sloop *Rebecca,* and with her went a skipper, Captain Samuel "Bully" Samuels, whose unenviable assignment was to keep boat and owner out of trouble. "Bully" never quite succeeded.

In June, 1858, the New York Yacht Club staged a race around Long Island, the first of its kind. It began off the clubhouse at Elysian Fields, followed a course down the Narrows, around Montauk Point, to a finish at Throgs Neck. *Rebecca* won the race, but was disqualified. She had entered Long Island Sound by way of Plum Gut, rather than The Race, which had been forbidden in the instructions as too dangerous. Although his fellow yachtsmen admired Bennett's daring and offered no rebuke at the disqualification, the senior Bennett was outraged—not for the first time—at his son's conduct. The boy was shipped off to France.

But Jimmy was back the next summer, racing *Rebecca* against the larger schooner *Restless* from Brenton's Reef, off Newport, to Throgs Neck for a $500 stake. When he lost not only this race, but one the following season that cost him an additional $250, Bennett promptly got a new yacht for 1861. This was *Henrietta.* She was a big schooner, 107 feet long, built by William Tooker at Greenpoint, New York, and designed by Henry Steers, who proved to be as talented a designer as his ill-fated Uncle George. Captain Samuels went along with *Henrietta.*

The Civil War began as the vessel was

launched. Bennett, Senior, sought a place for junior in the conflict and, not surprisingly, went right to the top, wielding the influence of the *Herald* all the way.

The following letter is from Abraham Lincoln to Salmon P. Chase, his Secretary of the Treasury: "The Secretary of State [William H. Seward] introduces to me James Gordon Bennett, Jr., who tenders to the United States the service of a fine yacht of 160 tons burthen. If you allow him an interview, which I ask for him, he will talk with you about putting other vessels of the same class into the service. We send this subject to you because we believe these vessels may be made most available in the Revenue Service."

Yacht and owner were commissioned in the government's service, young Bennett as a

James Gordon Bennett as a lieutenant in the Union navy. He and HENRIETTA *served briefly during the Civil War, were both decommissioned in 1862. Bennett lived high, raced hard, welcomed the risk of "Great Ocean Race." Below: The start.* FLEETWING (*left*), VESTA, HENRIETTA.

third lieutenant. *Henrietta,* armed with two six-pound guns and a twelve-pound cannon, cruised Long Island Sound under twenty-year-old Bennett's command that summer of 1861, possibly as a deterrent to Confederate raiders who might become lost in those waters.

The yacht, now with cutter rig, was next assigned to the blockade of Charleston, South Carolina, but the United States Navy soon had enough of its millionaire third lieutenant and *Henrietta* was ordered decommissioned in April, 1862. Bennett resigned his commission on May 11 and went back to New York.

For the next few years Bennett was a spirited, uninhibited rake around the town. In yachting matters he belonged to a group of owners that laid high stakes and sailed hard races. Yachting experienced a great boom following the Civil War and the tonnage of the New York Yacht Club's fleet soon exceeded anything seen in the home of the sport, the English Channel. A large shoal-draft schooner about 100 feet in length was the favorite American type. It was natu-

ral that Bennett and his cronies soon found the patch of Atlantic Ocean between Cape May and Montauk to be too small for their ambitions.

One October evening of 1866, there was a dinner at the Union Club, a favorite hangout of rich young males. The brothers Osgood—George and Franklin—were engaged in debate with Pierre Lorillard, Jr., regarding the merits of their respective yachts, the schooners *Fleetwing* and *Vesta*. It was a debate heated by alcohol and resolved by a race. The conversation went this way:

"Let it be outside."

"Agreed."

"What do you say, Sandy Hook to Cowes?"

"Done."

"In December."

"Yes."

The last provision was pure bravado. The idea was to assure plenty of wind for the yachts, and the Osgoods and Lorillard did not at the moment consider the inherent risks of midwinter ocean racing. On reflection, they

personally withdrew from the afterguard of their schooners and arranged for their dispute to be settled by professional crews.

There were stakes, big ones. The words of the wager were these: "George and Franklin Osgood bet Pierre Lorillard, Jr., and others $30,000 that the *Fleetwing* can beat *Vesta* to the Needles on the coast of England. Yachts to start from Sandy Hook on the second Tuesday in December, 1866; to sail according to rules of the New York Yacht Club, waiving the allowance of time. Sails to be carried are mainsail, foresail, jib, flying jib, jib topsail, fore and main gaff topsails, storm staysail, and trysail."

When he heard about this daring challenge, Bennett, of course, wanted in. He was accepted by the other principals through payment of his $30,000 subscription, "20 per cent of the money to be deposited with Mr. Leonard W. Jerome [Sir Winston Churchill's grandfather] by November 3rd, the balance on the first Tuesday of December—play or pay."

The three schooners were quite similar. *Henrietta* and *Fleetwing* were keel types, *Vesta* had a centerboard. *Fleetwing* had been designed for the Osgoods by J. P. Van Dusen and launched in 1865. *Vesta* came out the next year, designed and built by David Carll. *Henrietta* was then five years old. The dimensions of the three schooners:

	LENGTH OVER-ALL	BEAM	DRAFT	TONNAGE
Henrietta	107	22-0	11-6	205.4
Fleetwing	106	23-8	11-8	206
Vesta	105	25-0	7-6	201

In preparing *Henrietta,* owner Bennett was industrious and thorough, which came as

At the annual New York Yacht Club regatta, yachts started the race from moorings in the Narrows, off Staten Island.

a surprise to his father, because James, Junior, had displayed none of those qualities during an apprenticeship at the *Herald*.

One of the problems for all three parties was crew. The idea of sailing these big boats to England during the winter with full racing sail did not appeal to many sailors. The requirements, which all met eventually, were four officers and twenty-two in crew, excluding passengers, for each. To fill out her complement *Fleetwing* signed on nine whaler captains at great expense.

Bennett went long on intellect. He had in his afterguard of amateurs Charles Longfellow, the poet's son and an excellent sailor, and Stephen Fiske, a playwright and drama critic. On the day of departure—December 11—Bennett took *Henrietta* out of the harbor at seven in the morning because he had

heard that worried friends of his crew had arranged for court trials the sailors knew nothing about. The service of subpoenas at dockside would have withdrawn them from the foolhardy venture.

A fleet of steamers followed the contestants from Staten Island to Sandy Hook. It was a cool, clear winter's morning with a fresh westerly blowing. The crowd aboard an excursion steamer had a cheer for *Henrietta* and "for the man who crosses in the boat he owns." This, of course, was Bennett, the one owner aboard his yacht for the race. He was relishing the prospect of every tumultuous moment ahead.

The start was at one in the afternoon and by eight that night the three were scattered, never to see one another thereafter during the race. The logs of the three ships later showed that *Vesta* was the early leader, then *Henrietta* through the fourth day, then *Vesta* again until a landfall was reached.

Trouble came on December 19 in the shape of a gale. *Fleetwing's* log entries tell the tale in part:

"Wednesday, December 19, 1866. This day commences with a light breeze from S.S.W. 2 p.m. Took in all light sails; gale increasing with heavy seas. 7 p.m. Blowing a gale; running under double-reefed foresail and forestay sail. 9 p.m. Shipped a sea which washed six of the crew out of the cockpit; hove to for 5 hours under double-reefed foresail. 2 a.m. Kept off; later part moderate; wind hauling to westward."

The sea that boarded *Fleetwing* washed the watch of eight men out of the cockpit, but two of them managed to hang on to some-

thing and were saved. It was later said, without confirmation, that *Fleetwing's* cockpit was open while the other two boats had covered theirs over. With the watch gone *Fleetwing* broached, losing her jib boom, and lay hove to for five hours. That put her out of the race, although *Henrietta* also gave in to the storm for a few hours. Her logbook told with what gloom the sailors had hauled out the storm trysails: "A pause in a race like this seemed a burial of all our hopes."

Vesta was the first to sight land—and to be sighted. The Scilly light picked her up the evening of December 24. *Henrietta* appeared a mere fifty minutes later. After 3,000 miles of racing, only ten miles separated the two, and they had sailed the course without a tack.

Bennett's boat passed the Lizard at three o'clock Christmas morning, picking up a Cowes pilot at noon. This fellow told the Americans, " '*Enrietta's* a good 'un and first hin." The schooner reached the Needles at 3:45 p.m., the two judges aboard her marking the time, and *Henrietta* dropped anchor in Cowes Roads that evening.

Vesta's pilot became lost in the fog on Christmas Eve, nearly putting the vessel aground, and she did not finish until 1:40 a.m., the day after Christmas. *Fleetwing* had come in forty minutes earlier.

Henrietta took thirteen days, twenty-one hours, and fifty-five minutes to sail 3,106 miles. Her average speed was nine and a quarter knots and on her best day she covered 280 miles. *Fleetwing* took 14:06:10 for 3,135 miles with 270 miles on her best day. *Vesta* required 14:06:50 for 3,144 miles and had a top twenty-four-hour total of 270 miles. Those were excellent speeds for the time, comparable to the west-east records of the much larger commercial sailers: H.M.S. *Newcastle,* New York-Falmouth, eleven days; clipper ship *Dreadnought,* New York-Liverpool, thirteen days, eight hours, and clipper *Independence,* New York-Liverpool, thirteen days, fifteen hours.

Bennett had won $60,000, and he and his friends spent a great deal of that in the ensuing weeks. In recognition of the hospitality accorded him, Bennett offered to give *Henrietta* to a noted British yachtsman, Prince Alfred, but the gift was declined. The prince said, "We must find a rival to her and do our best in common with all Englishmen."

The news of *Henrietta's* victory was a big story at home, in father's *Herald* among other papers, and the elder Bennett for the first time took pride in his son.

When James, Junior, did come home, he was a changed man. He settled down and took hold of the *Herald* with such convincing purpose that his father turned it over to him. Fiske later said that the "Great Ocean Race" was the turning point of young Bennett's career. For the first time he had accomplished something on his own and made that powerful, competitive father of his take a back seat. Junior became a successful businessman and used to advantage his connections among the N. Y. Y. C. membership.

Bennett was an active yachtsman for the rest of his astounding and controversial life. Following *Henrietta* came *Dauntless*, a larger schooner. Her owner had another transatlantic race in her, against *Cambria*, the first America's Cup challenger. That was in 1870, from Gaunt Head, Ireland, to Sandy Hook, *Cambria* winning a $1,250 cup by one hour, seventeen minutes. Two sailors aboard *Dauntless* were swept overboard and lost.

A later Bennett vessel was *Polynia*, but she was too slow for her owner's tastes and he replaced her in 1884 with *Namouna*, a huge iron-hulled three-masted schooner built at Newburgh, New York. *Namouna* was 226 feet long, weighed 845 tons, and had four-cylinder compound steam engines driving her screw propeller. She was a yacht of Oriental magnificence and unparalleled luxury, the first to be called "a floating palace."

Bennett, who for a while lived in France, often commuted to New York in *Namouna*. And the *Herald* staff, loathing these disruptive visits, called the yacht *Pneumonia*.

(It was also in 1884 that Bennett played a hand in America's Cup affairs. He was in his second term as commodore of the New York Yacht Club, and he and his old friend, Vice-Commodore William P. Douglas, built the *Priscilla* to defend the cup. But she was beaten in trials by *Puritan*, from Boston, and Bennett went back to France after that, having no further role in club affairs.)

Namouna was exceeded, in every way, by her successor, *Lysistrata*. She was named, Bennett said, "for a Greek lady reputed to be very beautiful and very fast." *Lysistrata*, a steam yacht, cost him $625,000, and there

*James Gordon Bennett
enjoyed life on land and sea.
At far left, he lounges
on afterdeck of his steam
yacht* LYSISTRATA, *with
a dog on his lap and friends at
his elbow. They are on a
Mediterranean cruise. His*
NAMOUNA *(right) was 226 feet
long, had screw propeller
driven by compound
steam engines. She was first to
be called "floating palace."*

was an owner's suite on each of her three decks. Those suites were said to be for Bennett's convenience in dealing with the ladies who accompanied him on his cruises.

There is little left of Bennett in the New York Yacht Club's way of life. Even the cups that he donated when he first became commodore in 1871—the Brenton's Reef Cup, the Cape May Challenge Cup, the New York Yacht Club Racing Course Cup—are no longer in competition.

In some ways, however, Bennett can be said to have encouraged the development of a better type of yacht. During his lifetime there were steady and spectacular advances in the technology of boats, and Bennett accepted progress. He ordered the latest and the best, thereby setting an example for fellow yachtsmen, who were in awe of him. He also set a standard of personal courage that unfortunately was not followed by many. In the "Great Ocean Race," he took the position that an owner belonged aboard his yacht and that the delegation of responsibility to a professional crew was not an act of valor. Bennett accepted all challenges, from contestants and the sea alike.

HARPOON.

1891

A
NEW
TACK

Naval architects
ponder the
merits of the
beamy centerboarders
against the
narrow, deep-keeled
British cutter.
The "Mohawk"
disaster
hastens a decision.

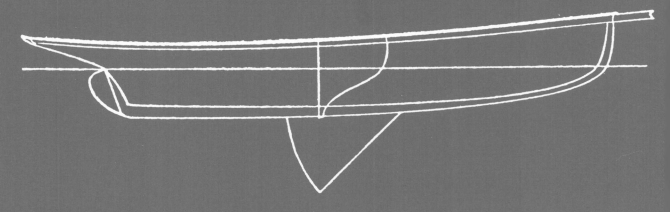

Preceding pages: Half models show
the change in hull shapes from centerboarder
(top) to keel and deep-keel types.

The band—stressing brass, of course—created a great din and added to the excitement of this special occasion. Boston's Fanueil Hall was full, and the crowd had overflowed into the square in front of the building. The noise touched the rafters of the old hall. The moment was a proud one for Boston. Two of her sons, General Charles J. Paine and Edward Burgess, were being honored. Paine had been a syndicate organizer and an underwriter of three centerboard sloops, *Puritan, Mayflower,* and *Volunteer,* which defended the America's Cup, and Burgess had designed them.

The last defense, *Volunteer* over *Thistle,* had just ended and Mayor O'Brien of Boston decided to hold a public reception for General Paine and Burgess at 6 p.m. on October 7, 1887. The mayor had hit the right chord and the oratory touched heights of patriotic fervor seldom attained before, even in Boston. It was one of those rare evenings when everyone present seemed delighted to be there, and the speeches were full of praise. From Adams Academy in Quincy, where he was headmaster, came Dr. William Everett, believed by some to be an orator equal to his father, Edward Everett, who had spoken for two hours at Gettysburg preceding Abraham Lincoln.

"The Mersey builds her keels of steel," Dr. Everett declaimed, with a gracious nod in the direction of Britain's shipbuilding center.

> *"The Clyde her keels of flame.*
> *Our Burgess builds no keels at all*
> *But he gets there just the same."*

There was an archly humorous letter from Oliver Wendell Holmes, in which the autocrat of the breakfast table said: "Proud as I am of their achievement, I own that the General is the only commander I ever heard of who made himself illustrious by running away from all his competitors."

Paine was then fifty-four years old. He came from an old Massachusetts Bay family and had been educated as a lawyer. He was graduated from Harvard in 1853, but never practiced law. During the Civil War he served the Union as a brevet major general of volunteers. Paine inherited a fortune which was increased by a successful marriage and successful investments in western railroads. He also figured in a group of Eastern Yacht Club members who decided to have a go at the America's Cup themselves. He became managing director of the syndicate which put up the money for one cup defender, *Puritan,* in 1885, and was sole owner of the next two, *Mayflower* and *Volunteer.*

Edward Burgess was first exposed to boats and the sea in his youth at his father's large summer home at Sandwich, on Cape Cod. Burgess was one of six brothers, all of whom owned and sailed small sloops and catboats. But Edward's chief interest was in natural history, especially entomology, and his friends called him a "bugologist." Following his graduation from Harvard in 1871, he was a teacher of entomology for twelve years. His life changed in 1883 owing to the business failure of his father, Benjamin Franklin Burgess, who had been a prominent merchant with sugar plantations of his own in Cuba and vessels to carry the sugar from the island to the United States.

With the loss of the family fortune, Edward and his brother Sidney opened an office as yacht brokers in Boston. Sidney soon became discouraged and went to England, leaving the business to Edward. Bugs and boats apparently were not too far apart because Edward soon built a reputation as an excellent draftsman and designer. He was thirty-seven years old in 1885 when Paine and his associates decided to build a cup defender entirely new in concept and entrusted its design to him.

Two-and-a-half years later, in Fanueil Hall, Burgess and Paine deserved all the plaudits that came their way. They had beaten the stuffing out of the New Yorkers, who had dominated the sport of yachting up to that time. They had put Boston on the yachting map and earned respect for her yachtsmen. They had defended the America's Cup three times for the New York Yacht Club. Most important of all, they had changed the course of yachting by introducing to it a scientist's curiosity and a draftsman's exactitude in the planning and building of boats.

Once an unknown local designer with a dingy back office up three flights of stairs, Burgess now took rank among the foremost naval architects of the country. He had thrown tradition to the wind and taken what he thought was best in yacht design, no matter where it came from. That was not easy to do. Most of the country was convinced of the superior merits of the purely American type of shallow hull with its ballast of lead or iron bricks laid inside. Burgess preferred a narrower, deeper hull, outside lead ballast set in the keel, an overhanging stern, a modified cutter rig, and a centerboard dropping through a cut in the keel. These characteristics, taken as a whole, were more British then American.

For twenty-five years the boats that were built to defend the cup established the design of large yachts in America. It was not until the 1890's that the influence of the cup defenders dimmed with the coming of the giant, specialized racing machines that had no other utility.

Cup racing burst into prominence in 1870. The cup itself had gone from the drawing room of John Stevens' home in New York City's Washington Square to the New York Yacht Club in 1857. Stevens and the four remaining members of the original syndicate gave the trophy to the club in trust, to be held as a permanent challenge cup in match-race competition open to any organized yacht club of any foreign country.

There was no immediate interest abroad, and by the end of the Civil War in 1865, memory of the prize had dimmed. The first challenge began a new era. Between 1870

*General Paine (far left) and designer
Edward Burgess, three-time defenders of the
America's Cup. Below: Yacht racing was
a man's sport. The ladies watched.*

and 1903 there were twelve challenges for the America's Cup—ten from Great Britain and two from Canada.

On the East Coast, at least, a cup challenge became the leading sports event for three reasons. Because water transport was still so important, the sailing arts were understood and appreciated by a large part of the population. Second, the young country was provincial in thought, and national pride grew around defense of "The Cup," especially against British challengers. Lastly, there was something of a vacuum in popular sports. Professional baseball's National League would not be organized until 1876. College football had begun in 1869 but would not become a notable attraction for another fifteen years. Boxing's first famous figure, John L. Sullivan, would not emerge until the 1880's. Horse racing was sporadic and somewhat disreputable; a Jockey Club would not be formed to give it leadership and class until 1894. So yacht racing, one of the very oldest of sports, ranked as a major one in people's minds.

The first challenger, James Lloyd Ashbury, helped to make it so. Ashbury was the son of an English wheelwright who invented a car-

riage support for railway wheels and laid the foundation of a fortune. Ashbury came from Manchester but moved to London and, with his considerable money, attempted to enter the social swim in the city. His standing was not high, as is often the case with possessors of new wealth, and he used the sport of yachting to gain distinction for himself. In this, however, he was not successful and when he died, in London in 1895, his passing was neither noticed nor mourned. His aggressiveness and his gall faulted his ambitions.

Ashbury knew all about the cup that the *America* had won from the Royal Yacht Squadron in 1851 and the fact that it was now a prize of the New York Yacht Club, open to challenge.

In the summer of 1868, Ashbury's yacht *Cambria* (188 tons) won a race sailed around the Isle of Wight, defeating two English cutters and *Sappho,* a large New York Yacht Club schooner of 310 tons. *Sappho* had been brought to England with the hope of emulating the *America*—success in a race or races and then a sale at a profit to a local yachtsman. In these matters she was a failure, but her defeat by *Cambria* inspired Ashbury to think bigger. That fall he began a lengthy correspondence with the New York Yacht Club to discuss a challenge for the America's Cup. The details of his first proposal were colossal. He wanted a designated schooner of *Cambria's* size to come to England for the summer yachting season, then to race the Ashbury yacht back across the Atlantic for a side bet of $1,250. That was the first half of the proposition. Next, the two yachts were to race around Long Island,

View from the deck of the steamer
RIVER QUEEN (left) as the New York Yacht Club
fleet passes in review in the
Upper Bay, June 19, 1866. Bottom: CAMBRIA
crosses SAPPHO to windward in winning
1868 race around Isle of Wight.
Victory over American yacht inspired CAMBRIA's
owner, James Ashbury (below)
to challenge for the America's Cup.

two races out of three. To the winner would go the cup.

The New York Yacht Club replied that the only possible race it could consider would have to meet the conditions of Commodore Stevens' deed of gift for the cup: a challenge to a match race from an organized foreign yacht club rather than from an individual. Ashbury never did grasp this point and the correspondence rambled on through 1869. In the fall of that year, he informed the New York Yacht Club that he intended to sail *Cambria* to America the following season, in any event, and continuing to ignore the club's stipulations, he challenged again for the America's Cup.

Cambria did come over in the summer of 1870 and loudly, too. She raced James Gordon Bennett, Jr.'s, schooner *Dauntless* from Ireland to Sandy Hook and beat her by one hour, seventeen minutes. *Dauntless,* a topnotch $70,000 schooner, had led most of the way until a wind shift spoiled her chances 250 miles from the finish. This point was overlooked in the widely publicized *Cambria* victory, and Bennett blamed defeat on a superabundance of experts—including himself—aboard *Dauntless*. Besides the owner, there were Bennett's old mentor, "Bully" Samuels, and Dick Brown, who had been *America's* captain.

Not long after his arrival, Ashbury and the New York Yacht Club officers tried to work out agreeable conditions for a match race. Finally, the Englishman was invited to enter the club regatta and race against the club fleet over the club course in New York Bay. Apparently the New York officers were interested in coming as close as possible to duplicating the conditions under which the *America* had won the cup at Cowes nineteen years before. Here, as there, the conditions were unfair to the challenger, asking him to race over a course where tides, currents, and "local knowledge" were paramount considerations. Furthermore, a single competitor is at a disadvantage in attempting to gain free air and brook no interference from a dozen rivals determined to defeat him. Ashbury did protest the unfairness of the proposed race to the club officers, but at the same time he accepted their invitation.

On August 8, 1870, *Cambria* took on twenty-three N. Y. Y. C. yachts. The America's Cup was at stake, even though its use as a prize was contrary to a strict interpretation of Commodore Stevens' deed of gift. The yachts began the competition from anchor off Staten Island, the course carrying the fleet through the Narrows, around the Southwest Spit buoy in the Lower Bay, out to the Sandy Hook lightship, and back—a distance of thirty-eight nautical miles.

The little schooner *Magic* won the race. *Cambria* was never a factor and finished tenth. The old *America,* refitted by the United States Navy at a cost of $30,000, placed fourth. *Dauntless* was fifth and *Fleetwing,* veteran of the "Great Ocean Race," was twelfth.

Ashbury accepted his defeat in good spirit, and *Cambria* went off on the New York Yacht Club cruise, losing consistently. Her owner took her back to England and sold her into commercial work. *Cambria* ended her days in the West African coasting trade.

Ashbury ordered a new schooner, *Livonia,* with an eye to another challenge in 1871, and he started writing letters again. He wanted a match race for the cup, and a number of people agreed with his proposal, including George L. Schuyler, the last survivor of the Stevens' syndicate.

"It seems to me," Schuyler said, "that the present ruling of the club renders the America's trophy useless as a 'Challenge Cup,' and that for all sporting purposes it might as well be laid aside as family plate. I cannot con-

Currier & Ives print, "Rounding the Lightship," shows flag-decked Sandy Hook Lightship, traditional turning mark of N.Y.Y.C. racecourse, during first cup defense in 1870. Winner was schooner MAGIC, whose main cabin (below) had no shortage of velvet pillows and tufted cushions.

LIVONIA (*far left*) *was Ashbury's second America's Cup challenger. She came to New York in 1871, but was unsuccessful and Ashbury went home angry.* LIVONIA'S *opponent in the first three races of the series was* COLUMBIA (*left; foreground*). COLUMBIA *won the first two races, one of which is shown below. The American schooner breaks out a topsail as she leads the challenger.* LIVONIA *is reducing sail, her crew appearing to be taking in a lowering staysail.*

ceive of any yachtsman giving six months' notice that he will cross the ocean for the sole purpose of entering into an almost hopeless contest for the Cup. . . ."

The club moved a little bit, but not all the way. It was decided to accept Ashbury as a contender and to sail a best-of-seven match-race series. But the New York side would have four yachts from which to choose on the morning of the race: two centerboard schooners for light weather, two keel schooners for heavy. This was patently unfair, but it would not be the last time that retention of the cup would mean more to the New York Yacht Club than sportsmanship.

Ashbury accepted the conditions and the series bordered on the ludicrous. The wind for the first race, October 16, was light; the club named as defender *Columbia,* a center-

Life aboard the schooners was plush.
Below: Main saloon and cabin accommodations of
William B. Astor's AMBASSADRESS *(right).*

board schooner which drew only 5 feet of water compared to *Livonia's* 12½. *Columbia,* called "a skimming dish" by the *Livonia* crew, pranced around the familiar course and beat the challenger by twenty-seven minutes.

Columbia also won the second race but in the third race *Columbia* had two breakdowns and *Livonia* won.

Fearing additional breakdowns by *Columbia,* the home side shifted to *Sappho,* which had been rebuilt and improved over her 1868 form. *Sappho* belonged to N.Y.Y.C. vice-commodore, William P. Douglas. The American schooner trounced *Livonia* in the next two races and that seemed to end the affair, four victories to one for the defenders. But Ashbury did not see it that way. He claimed that the protested second race belonged to *Livonia,* that the score was three to two, and that his yacht would show up the next day for race number six. The New York Yacht Club did not bother to reply and *Livonia* appeared for the sixth and seventh

"races" without an opponent. Ashbury claimed two more victories and demanded the cup.

It was not forthcoming and the Englishman went home in a huff, charging the New York Yacht Club—not unreasonably—with unfair and unsportsmanlike behavior. Ashbury entered into a heated correspondence with Commodore James Gordon Bennett, Jr., and the commodore, who had no superior in telling people off, sent back three cups which *Livonia's* owner had donated to the club. Bennett said the cups were no longer wanted. That silenced Ashbury. But his story of the events in America circulated among the British yacht clubs, and perhaps that was why thirteen years went by before another British yacht came out to challenge.

The two defenses of the America's Cup served to flatter the American schooner yacht, which was now nearing its zenith. There was a grandeur to these massive vessels, owned by rich men and worked by large crews of twenty to thirty sailors.

Their cabin appointments were the same as those in the parlor of a Fifth Avenue house: Oriental rugs, velvet-button cushions, silk drapes, gilt mirrors, and dripping lamps in the Victorian mode. Aboard Bennett's *Dauntless* the glasses were said to have had round bottoms so that a guest had to finish his drink before he put one down.

Commodore John M. Forbes of the Eastern Yacht Club at Marblehead bought the schooner *Rambler* from James H. Banker of the New York Yacht Club in 1872 for $35,000, She was a big schooner for her day, measuring 120 feet over-all, 103 feet on the water line, and with a 25-foot beam. She drew 10 feet and her tonnage was 240. Upon her foremast and mainmast, which stood 68 and 70 feet above the deck, could be rigged a mainsail, foresail, main topsail and fore topsail, flying jib, jib, and fore staysail—all at once or in any number of combinations. All the rigging was of rope, all the blocks of wood.

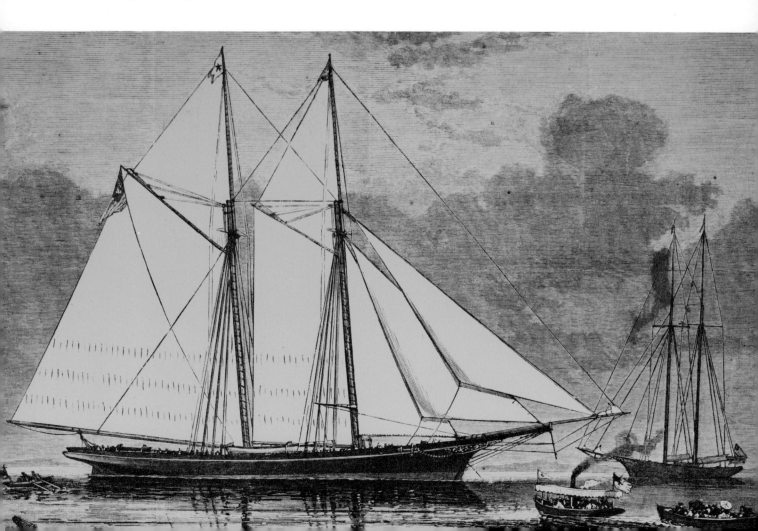

Rambler had a clipper bow and a long, thick bowsprit. The stem of the vessel terminated in a design of a lady returning from the fields, her right arm extended, the hand grasping a bouquet of flowers. The figure seemed to be emerging from a cornucopia. The design was neat, striking, and tasteful. High bulwarks went round the deck. A cockpit was located aft of the mainmast and a raised deckhouse was aft of the foremast.

Commodore Forbes had considerable confidence in *Rambler*. In the spring of 1872 he took her on a cruise to Fayal in the Azores, leaving Boston on April 28. By July 25, *Rambler* was back again and racing 280 miles

from Sandy Hook lightship to Brenton's Reef lightship, off Newport, and back for James Gordon Bennett's New York Yacht Club Challenge Cup. She won the cup, beating one other schooner, *Madeleine*. During the race, *Rambler* experienced some very heavy weather, but proved herself to be a thoroughly good sea boat. She combined the finest attributes of the American schooner.

Sappho, twice the conqueror of *Livonia,* was another of the large schooners, 134 feet in over-all length, 120 feet on the water line, with a beam of 24 feet, 9 inches, and a draft of 12 feet, 8 inches. She was a keel schooner, although the centerboard type was much pre-

ferred around New York. There were two reasons for the popularity of the centerboard design—moorings and speed. Anchorages were in shallow water off the flats of Hoboken, Communipaw, and Gowanus, and it was not uncommon for a centerboarder to lie in the mud at low tide where a keel boat would founder. The New York Yacht Club's racing courses were fixed ones in the protected waters of the Lower Bay, and the prevailing

*American schooners clustered at
Newport for a summer's sailing were finest
yachts afloat in the early 1870's.
Right:* SAPPHO *under sail.*

southwest breeze of the summer months made reaching and running the usual point of sailing. This suited the shoal-draft centerboarders perfectly. The keel boats could not stay with them when they hauled up their boards on these legs.

These factors led yacht design away from the healthy seagoing schooner, such as the *America,* and toward the harbor-sailing, centerboard skimming dishes like *Maria.* Those were the kind of boats that the wealthy New York yachtsmen wanted, and builders like Bob Fish obliged.

Sappho had been placed in the hands of Fish in 1869 and he had "hipped" her at a little dock on South Street in lower Manhattan. The operation known as hipping consisted of stripping the planks above the water line, padding the frames (in *Sappho's* case to the extent of 7 inches on each side), and then replacing the planking. With 14 inches more in breadth, with her tonnage reduced from 310 to 274, and with Captain Bob in command, *Sappho* became a racing threat.

William Picard Stephens, the nineteenth

century's most noted yachting historian, tells us that at the time, "Yacht owners had little interest in design and naval architecture. They left those matters to sailing masters and modelers and builders. The owner swore by his modeler who in turn worshiped some model or form section which had proved successful. Models of larger yachts were mere enlargements of sailboats with all their faults magnified."

The modeler was the designer. He was not a scientific person and he put nothing down on paper. Rather he shaped yacht models of a desired design from a block of wood and built his boats from these models. That is the way it had been done in shipyards for hundreds of years and the best measurement was the rule o' thumb. Fish was a clever modeler who could make many a yacht go faster by means of his native skills, although he knew nothing of scientific yacht design. It was a long passage from Fish to Harvard-educated Edward Burgess, but yachting accomplished this passage in the late 1870's and 1880's.

It occurred to some yachtsmen, particularly those who had visited the British yachting centers, that the fat, shoal American hull might not be the last word in boats. They came to believe that more could be expected of a boat. Did a yacht have to spread all the canvas of a schooner to attain ten knots? Could not a cutter sail considerably closer to the source of the wind than a broad-beamed sloop or schooner? Was it not possible that a smaller hull, manned by a smaller crew, would perform just as well, if not better, in a rough sea? What was wrong with applying the technology of naval architecture to yacht design?

A leader of the reformers who were asking such questions was Robert Center, son of a New York merchant, and a young fellow who worked very hard at club and sporting life. Center joined the N.Y.Y.C. in 1862, at the age of twenty-two, and the Seawanhaka Yacht Club at Oyster Bay, Long Island, some fourteen years later. Yachts were his primary, but not sole, sporting interest. He was a founder of the Queens County Hounds, an officer of the New York Rowing Club, a founder of the Orpheus Glee Club, a founder of one of the city's leading social institutions, the Knickerbocker Club, and an avid horseman.

Center had become interested in yacht design as a young man and had been aboard *Fleetwing* in the "Great Ocean Race" of 1866. He had seen and appreciated the good qualities of the narrow, deep British cutters, with their lead ballast placed outside in the keel. Center also had come across a book published in London, *Yachts and Yacht Building,* by Philip R. Marett. It described the process of making calculations, then drawing the lines of a hull on paper with no reference to a model. This was revolutionary stuff.

Center took the book to a friend, Archibald Cary Smith, and awakened his interest in it. This was in 1870. Archie Smith was

then thirty-three, the son of the Reverend Edward Dunlap Smith, pastor of St. Paul's Episcopal Church on the corner of Ninth Avenue and Twentieth Street in New York City. As a youth Smith played on the nearby shore of the Hudson River, then in a more natural state, and at eighteen he was apprenticed to Captain Bob Fish, whose shipyard stood across the river, at Panrambo, New Jersey (part of what is now Bayonne). He soon became an expert boat handler and later a marine painter. Although a quiet type afflicted with a stutter, Smith joined in the rough life on the Hudson water front during the era of turbulent racing in sandbagger sloops. The sailors, Smith included, were great fanciers of New Jersey's native wine, applejack, and one Sunday morning a friend accosted him on the Panrambo water front: "What are you doing here?" Smith replied, "My father is over in New York preaching Heaven and salvation and I've been over here raising hell and damnation."

Center and Smith decided to build a boat, with Smith the designer. The result was *Vindex*, the first yacht in America built from design lines prepared on a drafting board. She was built of iron, another revolutionary step, and many yachtsmen predicted she would not float. Her hull shape was away from the accepted New York centerboard schooner. In fact, *Vindex* had a cutter rig and a keel hull. Her dimensions are particularly interesting when compared to *Vision*, a centerboard contemporary.

	LENGTH WATER LINE	LENGTH OVER-ALL	BEAM	DRAFT
Vision	66	52-4	20-9	5-9
Vindex	63-3	55-3	17-3	8-10

As a racer, *Vindex* had only fair success on Long Island Sound, but she did well when venturing into the deeper waters and before the stronger breezes east of Newport. In

MADELEINE (*above*), *a 106-foot schooner, defeats the British challenger,* COUNTESS OF DUFFERIN, *in 1876 America's Cup series.* MADELEINE *was the last of the beamy, centerboard schooners to defend the cup. For 1881 challenge, A. Cary Smith designed a "compromise" sloop,* MISCHIEF (*bottom, left*), *which won handily against Britain's* ATALANTA (*top, left*). MISCHIEF, *shown leading at start of race, was only 67 feet long and had an iron hull whose lines were somewhere between schooner and cutter.*

1877, Center and Smith joined forces again and built *Volante*, a more successful cutter. One feature was a bowsprit that could be brought inboard into its housing. This, coupled with the use of two jibs on a double head rig (two headstays rather than one on which to set jibs), made for a more flexible, easier-handling rig. Sail could be reduced quickly and efficiently.

A. Cary Smith, as he styled himself, soon

became known as an important naval architect. His celebrated and active career would span thirty years, and the kind of yachts that he and Center envisioned would gradually come to be accepted.

Smith was a moderate. His position was somewhere between the shoal-schooner school and the "cutter cranks," whose taste for extremes led to absurdly narrow, soaking-wet, plank-on-edge yachts. Smith's "compromise" cutters and sloops were not quite so beamy and shoal and light as heretofore,

and not so narrow and deep and heavy as the British types.

One was *Mischief,* the 1881 America's Cup defender. She was a sloop rather than a schooner. They called her the "iron pot," because of her iron hull, and she was considerably smaller than *Madeleine,* her immediate predecessor in the cup series: LOA 67-5; LWL 61; B 19-10; D 5-4. *Madeleine* of 1876 was a 106-foot schooner.

That same summer of 1881, a boat from Scotland had a profound effect on American

yachting. This was *Madge*. In a way, she reversed the voyage of the *America* thirty years before. She was a little cutter, quite unlike anything in this country: LOA 46-1; LWL 38-6; B 7-9; D 7-10. *Madge* had 10 tons of lead in her keel, was superbly built of wood, and had no need of a cabin trunk to provide headroom below, as did the American centerboard yachts. Her spars, blocks, and fittings, some of bronze, were lighter, stronger, and quicker to work than their American counterparts. Furthermore, her

crew was smartly dressed in neat uniforms. In almost every way she differed from the practice here.

Madge had been built by a Scotsman named George L. Watson, for another Scot, named James Coats. At the time Watson was just beginning an illustrious career. He was the son of a Glasgow physician, but as a youth had shown little interest in following his father's footsteps. By the time he was sixteen, no man could get him away from the famous shipyard of Napier & Son, on the Clyde. He began designing at twenty, and before he was done he turned out five America's Cup challengers, any number of large steam yachts bought by wealthy Americans, plus *Britannia,* one of the series of royal yachts by that name.

Watson was thirty years old when he designed *Madge* for Coats, who, in turn, entrusted the little cutter to James Duncan for the trip to America. Duncan proved to be a sly skipper. He sailed *Madge* around New York harbor for a while without displaying the yacht's big club topsail. Unlike Commodore Stevens, Duncan held something back and he was successful in making matches. With her topsail flying, *Madge* won a $100 cup from *Wave* and a $250 cup from *Mistral.* She won six out of seven races in America.

Madge encouraged the "cutter cranks." Ordinarily, cutters had a number of bad points that made them hard boats to defend. Their extremely narrow hull was crowded and uncomfortable, and so tender that they always sailed at a sharp angle of heel, even in a light breeze. A real blow laid them flat on the water, although the heavy lead ballast in the keel always righted them once the wind eased. *Madge's* success was an effective answer to these complaints. It is difficult to argue with a winner.

The America's Cup trials to select a defender in 1885 opposed two design styles in

Priscilla and *Puritan*. *Priscilla* was a sloop designed by Cary Smith for James Gordon Bennett and his pal, William P. Douglas. She was another *Mischief,* only bigger, and Smith was never happy with the commission. After the New York Yacht Club's conservative cup committee had left the order with Smith, on February 26, 1885, the designer blurted to W. P. Stephens, "Well, my b-b-oy, I've g-g-got to build a damned steel s-s-scow."

Up in Boston, Edward Burgess was under no pressure from General Paine's syndicate. Even though the largest yacht that Burgess had designed up to that time was a 35-foot sloop, his backers had confidence in him. Bur-

gess produced a second potential defender, *Puritan,* for them. *Puritan* represented the Eastern Yacht Club of Marblehead and was the first vessel from Boston waters built for America's Cup purposes.

Like Robert Center, Burgess had become dissatisfied with contemporary American yachts and had gone to England to study the products of Cowes and Torquay. He was deeply influenced by the British designs, and *Puritan* showed British strains with regard to her outside ballast and her beam measurement, which was narrower than was customary in American yachts. Her dimensions were: LOA 94: LWL 81-6; B 22-7; D 8-8. She had a plumb stem, high freeboard and bulwarks, and an outside keel containing 48 tons of lead through which a centerboard was dropped. *Puritan* was built in Boston by George Lawley. She promptly beat *Priscilla* in trials to decide the defender, and she also beat the challenger, Sir Richard Sutton's *Genesta,* 2-0.

Genesta was the narrow-hulled, deep-keel British type with characteristics admired by the extreme "cutter cranks." The victory of *Puritan* further diminished the popularity of the shoal, beamy American type and helped Burgess advance the principle of compromise on the American yachting scene.

Early in 1886, General Paine ordered from Burgess a larger yacht, which was to be an improvement on *Puritan.* In May, *Mayflower* was launched. Her over-all length of 100 feet made her the largest sloop in the country. *Mayflower* was another "compromise" vessel, a finer entrance and longer forebody made her a much better boat in a head sea than *Puritan.* But *Mayflower* was not so deep nor so full of lead as her America's Cup opponent, *Galatea.*

Galatea was an extreme example of the English style, a narrow plank-on-edge cutter with only 15 feet of beam for a hull 102 feet, 7 inches long. And she was a lead mine of ballast with 81 tons in her keel. *Galatea* was owned by Lieutenant William Henn of the royal navy, and he cruised in her with his wife. They became a popular couple in America and were entertained here for a full year following the cup races of 1886.

Mayflower defeated three others, including *Puritan,* in trial races and went on to take *Galatea,* two races to none, in the sixth challenge for the America's Cup.

The seventh challenge came the next year, 1887, and the matter of defense was left to General Paine and Burgess. They came out with another new boat, *Volunteer,* which in

general followed the forms of *Puritan* and *Mayflower. Volunteer,* at 106 feet in over-all length, was larger and she spread more sail, her total being 9,271 square feet. The challenger was *Thistle,* from Scotland's Royal Clyde Yacht Club. *Volunteer* defeated her easily in two straight races.

Burgess' stock as a designer went sky high. He designed 137 vessels in seven years, until his death in 1891, an end some felt was brought on by overwork.

Season after season, from the summer of the *Madge* invasion, it became more and more evident that the old centerboard schooners and sloops, "the American heritage," were all wrong in proportion, construction, ballasting, and rig. However, no red-blooded American yachtsman was ready to accept or borrow anything British, particularly since the schooners had been so consistently successful in competition. Despite the innovations in her design, *Puritan*

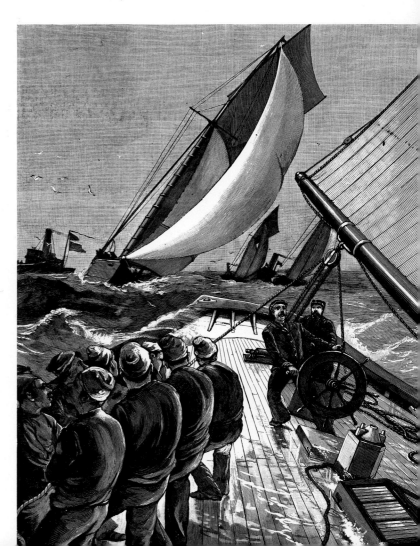

MAYFLOWER SALUTED BY THE FLEET.

CROSSING THE BOW OF GALATEA ON THE FOURTH TACK IN THE FIRST RACE FOR THE AMERICAS CUP
OVER THE INSIDE COURSE NEW YORK BAY SEPT. 7TH 1886.
[Won by Mayflower]

was hailed as "a Boston boat," as though her antecedents were in Massachusetts Bay, rather than the Solent.

Nonetheless, the day of the rule-o'-thumb modeler and the centerboarders was coming to a close. Bright progressives like Robert Center and scientifically oriented designers like Burgess and Smith insisted on pushing forward, on doing better, on trying new ideas.

It took more than men to change yachting concepts, however. It also took a tragedy. On July 20, 1876, a black line squall swept across the Jersey meadows and struck the New York Yacht Club anchorage off Stapleton, Staten Island. The squall was sudden and severe. Under its pounding the schooner *Mohawk* capsized and sank in a matter of minutes, drowning five persons aboard.

Mohawk, completed in 1875, had an overall length of 140 feet and was the largest yacht in the world at the time. She was commissioned by William T. Garner, a thirty-five-year-old New Yorker who could well afford her. Garner had inherited from his father the world's largest textile-manufacturing business. His personal fortune was believed to be $18,000,000 or $20,000,000, his annual income $2,000,000.

Garner had no particular yachting past. He joined the New York Yacht Club because that was the thing for wealthy young men of the city to do. Garner built and presented to the club its new $23,000 clubhouse at Stapleton, on Staten Island, and he had served a term as vice-commodore. In 1875, he headed a slate of officers which opposed

THE PURITAN AND GENESTA ON THE HOMESTRETCH.
IN THEIR SECOND AND FINAL INTERNATIONAL RACE FOR "THE AMERICA'S CUP" SEPT. 16TH 1885.
Won by the Puritan

those presented by the nominating committee and lost election to the post of commodore by a single vote, twenty-five to twenty-four. Pictures show him with a walrus mustache and a fleshy face.

Mohawk, the yacht he chose for himself, had measurements and a style typical of the direction taken in the building of expensive schooners between 1870 and 1875. She measured 120 feet on the water line, her beam was an immense 30 feet, 4 inches. Her draft with centerboard up was a mere 6 feet and the depth of her hull was only 9 feet, 4 inches. She followed the trend of *Tidal Wave,* another fat schooner said to look like "a snake with a frog in its belly."

All of *Mohawk's* ballast was inside in the form of loose lead blocks placed in her flat,

During the 1870's and 1880's, before today's spectator sports were well established, yacht racing was everyone's game. Currier & Ives prints like these and Frederic Cozzens paintings (see page 69) were part of the national enthusiasm for America's well-sailed, ever-victorious yachts.

shoal bilges. These pigs of lead weighed 150 pounds each. Atop her flat platform of a hull there was placed an enormous expanse of sail. The distance from the tip of the jib boom to the end of the main boom measured 235 feet, while the top of the main topsail yard stood 163 feet above water. Such dimensions created a vessel that was tricky to handle and left no margin for careless error or poor judgment. There was a lot of both on the afternoon of her disaster.

"The grossest stupidity caused her to capsize," wrote Roland Folger Coffin, a respected New York sea captain. "I have sailed in her, carrying three whole lower sails, with the water just bubbling along the lee-plank sheer, when all others were double reefed and staggering along with lee rails under."

There were four yachts moored close to *Mohawk* that day off Stapleton: *Magic, Dreadnought,* and *Idler,* all N. Y. Y. C. "regulars," plus the *Countess of Dufferin,* the Canadian challenger for the America's Cup.

To run the boat and its crew of twenty-three, Garner had Captain Oliver P. Rowland, who found himself in court after the capsizing, accused of negligence. Garner had left instructions with Captain Rowland that the ship was to be ready to sail on this Thursday afternoon, and at 4 p.m. the owner came aboard with a party of six. Besides Mrs. Garner, the thirty-one-year-old mother of three daughters, there were five guests: Miss Adele Hunter, thirty-one; Frost Thorne, twenty-five; Gardner Howland, thirty-six; J. Schuyler Crosby, thirty-four, and Miss Edith Sybil May, twenty-four. Miss May was the sister of Caroline May, the girl to whom James Gordon Bennett, Jr., was affianced.

It had been a squally day and as the sails were unfurled, someone from the *Countess of Dufferin* hailed Captain Rowland, calling his attention to the portents of more squalls. Rowland replied, "I guess we'll hold on," a remark which the subsequent coroner's jury interpreted as meaning that the *Mohawk's* preparation for sailing would continue. It did.

A sudden rain shower came, sending the guests below. The sky darkened, but Captain Rowland kept the crew busy getting the ship under way and all the canvas, save fore-gaff topsail, went up in a matter of minutes.

When the squall struck, *Mohawk* surged ahead until held by her anchor, which was stuck fast in the Stapleton mud. She headed downstream initially, but quickly swung upstream on her anchor and heeled over.

"Her masts were prone upon the water within three seconds," said a witness watching from the veranda of the clubhouse. "The whole scene was one that I cannot recall without shuddering. Not a single sheet was started."

Mohawk was in a vice, her vast expanse of sail locked inboard by sheets secured in their blocks, and the surging hull imprisoned by the anchor. "*Mohawk* had greater initial stability than any yacht ever built in this country," Captain Coffin maintained later, but the initial stability was gone when the gust of wind came down from the hills of Staten Island, out of west-southwest, and struck the vessel amidships.

The yacht seemed to want to right herself for a moment, but then she gave up, settled to leeward, and filled up. Her stern went down, her forefoot went up in the air, and she sank.

In the cabin below, the sofa, the piano, and the pigs of lead had come crashing down once the yacht had heeled over. Mrs. Garner was pinned under the sofa with Miss Hunter, the lead pigs piled to their waists. Mr. Garner attempted to free his wife and he shouted to Crosby, "Schuyler, for God's sake, try and help me pull her out."

The ladies screamed and Crosby fell over Miss Hunter. When he arose, the water had covered the lady, and the young man went to the aid of Mrs. Garner, grasping her hand. She did not come free. The cabin by this time filled with water and Crosby swam out through an opening cut by a boatswain in one of the skylights. "The last he heard was a gurgle," reported the New York *Tribune.*

Miss May was rescued by one of the seamen, as was Howland, through a skylight which had given way. The owner and his wife, Miss Hunter, Mr. Thorne, and Peter

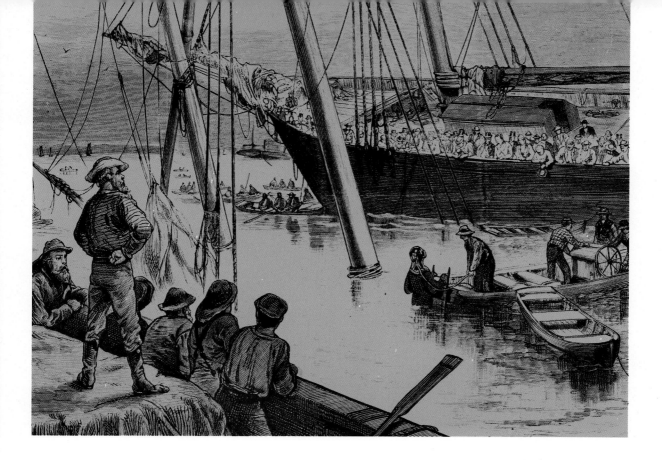

Sullivan, the cabin boy, all were drowned.

Mohawk went down in six fathoms within 500 yards of the Stapleton shore. Her center-board, the only stabilizing factor in her hull, was two thirds down, but even that was no help to the "snake with a frog in its belly." When the yacht was raised, the clock over the companionway had stopped at 4:23 p.m., and out of the muck and mud in the cabin came a painting of the "Great Ocean Race" of 1866. On Sunday, following the Thursday disaster, Thorne's body was found after a long search forward in the hull, and Crosby came across the ring which Mrs. Garner had torn from his hand during his vain attempt to free her.

The disaster caused a turmoil in the city and Captain Rowland, unpopular with his crew, was taken to jail upon a complaint registered by two of his quartermasters.

The captain later testified that he had tried to slack the mainsheet when the squall hit, but that the sheet jammed in the block. When the ship was raised the mainsheet was found belayed in the block, repudiating Rowland's testimony. The investigation also brought out that the chain had been raised part way, but not enough to free the anchor. Had the mainsheet and the anchor been free, *Mohawk* would not have gone over and Garner, who gave his life in an attempt to save the ladies, would likely have enjoyed a long and full existence.

The coroner's jury exonerated Rowland, nonetheless, and the *Mohawk* was sold into Federal service, becoming the coast survey vessel *Eagre*. The case was closed, but its repercussions continued to be felt in the yachting world. Although the *Mohawk* tragedy took place through the grossest carelessness and in consequence of unwarranted overconfidence in her stability, the affair made yachtsmen question the safety and practicality of their big, beamy schooners. "Her mishap caused a prejudice against centerboard vessels," wrote Captain Coffin, and very few of *Mohawk's* kind were built thereafter.

The capsizing helped to open the door for the new and better ideas of what a yacht should be, as advocated by Robert Center, A. Cary Smith, and, a few years later, by Charles Paine and Edward Burgess.

THE
AGE
OF
STEAM
—
5

THE AGE OF STEAM

"The yacht owner in America appears to understand only one thing —the speed attained by his vessel."
—W. P. Stephens

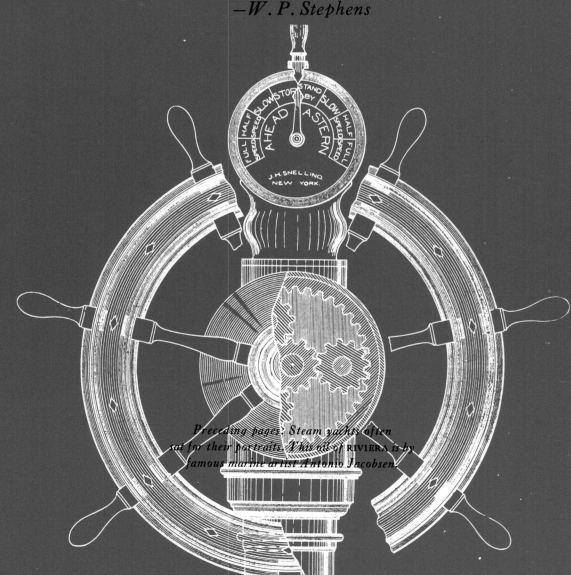

Preceding pages: Steam yachts often sat for their portraits. This oil of RIVIERA *is by famous marine artist Antonio Jacobsen.*

It was a lovely spring night over the Atlantic Ocean. The sky was swarming with stars. The twin paddle wheels of the yacht *North Star* churned away at the ocean and the ship made good twelve knots each hour on the way to England. This was in late May, 1853, and on the stern deck sat Cornelius Vanderbilt I, for the moment at least a man living in contentment.

Vanderbilt was fifty-nine years old and he had $11,000,000, which was more than anyone in America and more than any private citizen in the world. The vessel under him was his own, recently completed at a cost of $500,000. *North Star* came as close to being a floating palace as Vanderbilt and his builder, Jeremiah Simonson, of Greenpoint, New York, could make her. She was an enormous oaken ship, 270 feet in length with immense side wheels, 34 feet in diameter.

The Commodore, a title of no official significance but one which delighted him, was on a vacation of his own planning. He explained that he had a right to a rest after thirty years of business and no one could deny him that. In those three decades the farm boy from Staten Island had powered his way to control of water transportation in and around New York, and he had shipped thousands of gold seekers to California. This shrewd, grasping man had twenty-four years more to live, and by his death in 1877 he would be worth some $40,000,000.

Vanderbilt had no friends, or even cronies, but he did have a large family and to fill the many guest rooms on the *North Star,* the Commodore had brought along his wife, Sophia, and ten of his twelve children. Other guests were seven sons-in-law; one granddaughter; Mrs. Asa Eldridge, a friend of one of his daughters; a physician, Dr. Jared Linsly, and Mrs. Linsly, and a minister, Reverend John O. Choules, and Mrs. Choules.

The Reverend Choules kept an account of the voyage—it was a diary rather than a log —and in it he wrote: "There was discipline aboard that ship, sir. Each man attended to his own business. The Commodore did the swearing and I did the praying. So we never disagreed."

On this particular warm spring night, Vanderbilt was joined on the afterdeck by his eldest son, William Henry, to whom he would leave his empire. The son, by then thirty-eight years old, was puffing on a cigar. The Commodore, no doubt taken with the purity of the scene all around him, grumbled at the son. "My boy," he said, "I'll give you $10,000 to stop smoking."

The son replied, "Oh, father, you don't have to bribe me. Your wish is enough." And he threw the cigar over the side. The Commodore then proceeded to extract from his coat a large cigar of his own and to light up, blowing the smoke in his son's face, as the *North Star* steamed ever eastward.

The ill-natured tyrant and his brood had quite a voyage before they were done. The *North Star* had covered 15,024 miles when it passed Sandy Hook again four months later. The passage to Southampton took only ten days, and during one twenty-four-hour span the paddle steamer did 337 miles for an average speed of fourteen and five-tenths knots, consuming forty-two tons of coal. Those were fantastic speeds for the time, and the voyage heralded the start of yachting's age of steam, an era concerned with a search for speed and a display of opulence.

Although she went into commercial service as a passenger vessel upon her return from abroad, *North Star* was considered to be the first steam yacht, and she visited places where many others were to follow: Norway, the Baltic Sea, Denmark, France, Spain, and the Mediterranean. The vessel weighed 2,500 tons and she had four huge boilers, each twenty-four feet long. The walls of the saloon were decorated with ligneous marble. Silk lambrequins and lace curtains veiled the berths in the ten staterooms, and the furniture exactly matched the color of the hangings. Each stateroom also had a steam heater.

The purser, Mr. Keefe, came from the Racquet Club in New York and the ladies had their maids. The crew was made up in part of youths from some of the country's well-known families, the attraction being the Commodore's itinerary of faraway lands. (One of these lads, Robert Odgen Flint, was lost at sea, falling overboard in the Bay of Biscay.) The boys were not expected to do the dirty work of stoking the boilers, however. That task was up to the firemen, and Commodore Vanderbilt went through two sets of them.

The first set struck for higher wages in New York, one hour before the departure time. The Reverend Choules wrote of this: "True to his principles of action in all his business affairs, Mr. Vanderbilt refused to be coerced by the seeming necessity of the case. He would not listen for a moment to the demands so urged." Instead, Vanderbilt's captain signed on a group of green hands. One rural youth later in the voyage was ordered to strike two bells. After searching the vessel, he reported he could find only one bell.

North Star's departure date was set for May 19, and from 400 to 500 visitors were aboard her at the pier, intending to accompany the Vanderbilts as far as the Sandy Hook lightship where they would disembark. The pilot set the paddle wheels in motion and the *North Star* backed onto a reef just beyond the pier. There she remained, stuck fast, until the tide freed her hours later. Hurried telegrams were sent to the Secretaries of State and Navy, the latter giving permission for the government dry dock to be used to check damage to the *North Star*. No damage was found, and the trip began.

Later the Commodore gave the departing pilot a purse of gold to show there were no hard feelings. Within nine days of the incident, however, another pilot put the yacht aground again in a soft mudbank not far from the Needles on the channel approach to England. Again the *North Star* had to wait until the tide floated her off. This time the Commodore kept his gold.

The *North Star's* trip in general was a success and a considerable achievement. The Reverend Choules added this claim: "I hazard no contradiction from any of my messmates when I say that our table was equal to any hotel in America."

When Commodore Vanderbilt reached home, he was swept back into his rough-and-tumble business. He had left the Accessory Transit Company in the trust of two of his partners, Charles Morgan and C. K. Garrison, and they were bound to pay him twenty per cent of the gross receipts of the stage line in Nicaragua which carried California-bound travelers twelve miles across the isthmus to the Pacific Ocean. But the two had stopped the payments while the Commodore was out of sight and out of mind, faraway on the *North Star*. Soon Morgan and Garrison received a note. It said:

"Gentlemen: You have undertaken to cheat me. I won't sue you, for the law is too slow. I'll ruin you. (signed) C. V." And C. V. did.

The voyage of the *North Star* was the first of many yachting achievements made by members of the Vanderbilt clan. William Henry was no kind of a yachtsman, being principally interested in making money like his father. He managed to run the family fortune up to $90,000,000 before his death in 1885. But his son, William Kissam Vanderbilt, had a great love of the sea as did William Henry's two grandsons, William K. II and Harold—the latter a three-time

Commodore Vanderbilt's NORTH STAR, *the first steam yacht, was enormous: 270 feet long, with paddle wheels 34 feet in diameter.*

defender of the America's Cup (in 1930, 1934, and 1937).

If the *North Star* had been a sailing vessel alone, without her big paddles, how long can one suppose she would have taken to sail 15,024 miles. Not four months, certainly. A year perhaps? Yachtsmen in America became appreciative of steam's practicality, and following the Civil War, a new and growing crop of millionaires began to demand steam yachts for themselves.

The steam vessel had certain prejudices to overcome. Britain's Royal Yacht Squadron barred steam yachts from the fleet roster until 1856. The *Herald* of 1825 wrote of the commercial steamers: "Such clouds of smoke as completely obscured all distant objects. Murky vomitings of the furnaces covered the surface of Southampton water from side to side." In America, the Stevens brothers from Hoboken were early exponents of steam vessels, but not steam yachts. Applying steam to pleasurable uses on the water was the work of Vanderbilt, who did not pursue the project, and of a contemporary in New York, William H. Aspinwall, the president of the Pacific Mail Steamship Company.

In 1854, Aspinwall had built a small experimental steamer, the *Firefly*. She was of wood, 98 feet over-all, and in the center of her hull there was fitted a paddle wheel enclosed in a box, the invention of a Frenchman. The rig was a failure and Aspinwall replaced it with conventional twin paddles powered by a steam engine and a locomotive boiler. The *Firefly* was used for cruising and commuting between her owner's home on Staten Island and New York City. In later years the commuting steam launch was a conspicuous possession of the wealthy, running back and forth between large estates and large offices.

Aspinwall had a son, John, who built his first steamboat when thirteen years old, utilizing an engine driven by six alcohol lamps, and terrifying swans on the family pond. As he grew older, Aspinwall built one steam yacht after another and they grew larger. *Sentinel,* his thirteenth, was 160 feet long. And John knew how to run these boats. He served as a deck hand, cook, fireman, engineer, and captain. The Aspinwalls, father and son, set a good example with their yachts and a number of men, who knew far less

about steam, concluded that it was "safe" to have one of these vessels.

Commercial steamboats had been plying the oceans, coasts, and rivers for fifty years before the steam yacht became popular and considerable mechanical progress had been made. The force of expansion is the basis of all steam engines. A fired boiler heats water and the resulting steam is conveyed into a cylinder where its effort to expand moves a piston. (Steam requires about 1,600 times the amount of space as the water from which it is formed.)

A reciprocal action occurs when the expansive force drives the piston within the cylinder and then forces it back again. A crank and flywheel convert the back-and-forth action of the piston into rotational motion which, by means of a connecting rod, turns a shaft. And the shaft in turn powers a paddle wheel or a propeller.

On the water such a system was infinitely preferable to the sailing vessel's reliance upon the wind. Steamships and steam yachts had their limitations and problems. Coal to fire the boilers required considerable bunker space, which meant the hull had to be large. The initial cost of the engines plus the charges for fuel made for great expense. But the new affluent society of the late nineteenth century did not pause to count the cost.

The only things that money could not overcome were the smoke, the heat, the dirt generated by the engines, and the occasional danger of explosion from uncontrolled high pressures in cracked boilers. Yet explosions were rare and, as was frequently pointed out, the owners of steam yachts always "know when they will get back."

Captains of industry had to "get back" so they could make more money. Edwin S. Jaffray, a well-known writer on nautical matters, put it gently in an essay, "American Steam Yachting," in 1886: "There is a tide in the affairs of men which, taken at the flood, leads on to fortune. This tide is *steam!*"

One time Jaffray was steaming up the Hudson River near Irvington on a return trip from the city. He came across James Stillman's steamless yacht *Wanderer* setting off on a cruise. The next morning, on his trip back to the city from Irvington, Jaffray saw *Wanderer* again, off Yonkers. She had progressed down-river only seven miles since the previous encounter.

Speed on the water, which steam could deliver, went to yachtsmens' heads like the champagne so many of them guzzled. "The yacht owner in America appears to understand only one thing—the speed attained by his vessel." So wrote that sober commentator, W. P. Stephens. The interest in speed was perfectly understandable. The growing technology, spurred on by the industrial revolution, was reaching every aspect of American life. The pace of living was quickening and travel, previously so limited and full of discomfort, had new appeal.

Newport, Rhode Island's imposing resort with its beautiful cove for a harbor, came into its own as a social center following the Civil War, and a "milk run" developed between that port and New York for the

steam-yacht owners. They competed with one another for the fastest times, and those who had pride in the matter would not hesitate to scrap a comparatively new yacht, ordering another with the familiar command to the builder, "Make her a little faster."

On the Newport-New York "milk run," no one ever topped the mark set by *Now Then,* a yacht belonging to Norman L. Munro, a New York publisher. In 1887, this vessel ran the 170-mile distance in seven hours, four minutes, at a speed of twenty-four knots. There are few yachts today which can equal that speed, although few are around these days to try it. Nowadays, Newport's swells make the trip in private airplanes.

Besides speed, the steam-yacht owners of the 1880's and 1890's required space and luxury equivalent to what one might find in a substantial house ashore. To make the

Opposite: NOW THEN *averaged 24 knots in setting Newport-New York record. Britain's 300-foot royal yacht,* VICTORIA & ALBERT *(below), could do nearly 15 knots.*

ladies feel at home, the builders put in large rooms with high ceilings and rich appointments. Many of the yachts had a great dining hall in the center of the ship and a reception room. To assure adequate illumination, big windows, skylights, and high cabin trunks were demanded. In addition, the achievement of comfort required that elaborate and complicated plumbing systems be installed to pipe hot and cold water through the hull.

Inevitably, the creation of these vessels meant a conflict between speed and comfort —a conflict which never was resolved. The engines, boilers, and bunker space required for exceptional speed took up a great deal of precious room in the heart of the hull, where a sailing yacht of equivalent size might have any number of cabins. The wealthy men buying steam yachts, having little appreciation of the problems of naval architecture, ordered both speed and size, which were antipathetic to one another.

Different kinds of steam yachts were developed. They began with long, thin, open and deckless launches from 40 to 60 feet in length. For a great many years, the New York Yacht Club did not recognize any vessel below 40 feet as being a yacht and refused to admit little boats to its membership lists. So, on the East Coast, where the club counted for a great deal, no one with serious pretensions to being a yachtsman would be caught dead with a 39-foot steam launch. Launches were used chiefly for commuting, never for cruising, although the more elaborate ones might have enclosed, glass-window cabins on deck and a stateroom or two. To accommodate the engine requirements, these launches would run up to 100 feet.

A proper steam yacht with ocean-going capabilities would have a trunk cabin, a flush deck, and a two-masted schooner rig with sails for show and emergencies. Such a yacht would have to be at least 75 feet long and the New York Yacht Club membership did not pay much attention to anything that was under 150 feet.

In the beginning of the steam era, about 1870, almost all yachts were home-built in America. There were no fixed types. Often

J. P. Morgan's CORSAIR *(far left)
had annual crew payroll of $15,000. "Queen
among steam yachts" (left) was
William Astor's 232-foot* NOURMAHAL.

these vessels were incapable of handling seas with any ease because of design deficiencies. The early American steam yachts were planned, rather than designed, by untrained mechanical geniuses looking for speed alone.

The British, on the other hand, had a much sounder background in steam vessels, a fact which rich Americans soon began to appreciate. The British steam-yacht era had begun earlier than America's and it had been greatly stimulated by the construction of the series of royal yachts called *Victoria & Albert.* The first *V. & A.* was a 200-foot paddle-wheeler built in 1843. It could make eleven and a half knots. Queen Victoria watched the *America* win the Royal Yacht Squadron trophy in the race around the Isle of Wight from the deck of this vessel in 1851. The second *V. & A.,* launched in 1855, was a 300-footer which could make a good fourteen and three-quarters knots.

The British steam yachts were well-engineered, safe, and conservative. Speed was not a vital factor. British manufacturing technology was far ahead of American in building steam boilers and engines. Their power plants were strong, heavy, and durable. They might weigh 100 pounds per horsepower, the entire yacht 4,000 pounds per horsepower. (The modern outboard motor weighs 2 pounds or less per horsepower.) On the Clyde in those times, Scottish engineers turned out 1,000-ton yachts which would make a good twelve knots pushed by 500 horsepower. The horse of plough power, the giant Clydesdale, was their standard.

Sunbeam, Sir Thomas and Lady Brassey's famous three-masted steam yacht which traveled all over the world, could make good only eight knots under steam. That was not nearly enough for the United States.

Americans liked the seaworthy qualities of the British yachts and soon began importing them. George Watson was the favored designer-builder. Watson patterned his yachts after the Scottish clippers and he turned out truly handsome vessels with graceful clipper bows. No one in America could match him. But many an importer of a British yacht immediately put the vessel in an American yard for "alterations." The goal was to change the engines to achieve respectable speeds, and to install plumbing up to American standards. This meant ripping out the interior of the vessels—and the costs exceeded the savings inherent in original British shipbuilding.

What kind of men treasured the great steam yachts? There were all kinds, from eccentrics like M. Bayard Brown to dedicated enthusiasts such as Jacob Lorillard. Brown, a millionaire recluse, owned *Valfreya,* a 150-footer. The yacht never left its moorings, but the owner ordered that a full head of steam always be maintained just in case he might want to go somewhere without a moment's delay. The *Valfreya,* which went to pot under Brown's ownership, later was bought and refitted by the Maharajah of Nawangar, becoming the *Star of India*.

Lorillard, on the other hand, closely followed Aspinwall, Senior, as a steam enthusiast. This wealthy heir to a tobacco fortune had his first steam yacht built in 1868. "This gentleman," wrote Jaffray in 1886, "has done more to create and foster the fashion for steam yachting than any other person. His plan was to build a new yacht every year, and after using it through the season and getting it into first-rate running order, to sell it, and thus make room for a new vessel the succeeding year. His yachts were thus transferred to other cities, and this way they contributed to spread the fashion for this pastime. It has consequently now become a great national amusement, and is constantly growing in all our seaboard cities."

Lorillard certainly enjoyed himself and became a real authority on the steam yacht. In a letter to Jaffray, he wrote: "I enclose a chart of the dimensions, power, displacements, etc., of some of the yachts I have built. On nearly all of them I have had a series of different screws of different sizes and pitches, and the ones specified were those that gave the best result after many trials. I weighed all the vessels in the screw dock to check calculated displacement, and the displacement given was within a ton or so of the actual weight, as the coal in them was es-

timated and might vary a ton or two at most.

"A careful study of the results, when the model is before you, will convince one of the desirability of curved lines in every direction, and particularly so in the sectional lines. The midship body was very near in the center of the boat in all that gave speed over 13 miles, and I am convinced that this must be moved forward as the rate of speed increases on a vessel of given length.

"I am now [1886] building one 93 x 16, that has midship frame 3½ feet forward of the center of keel. I have filled up both hollow ends to make as regular an arc from end to end as possible, and with rounding frames expect to get a minimum of resistance, and good speed and economy of power."

Much of Lorillard's finagling made good design sense, and his innovations were picked up by the principal manufacturers and incorporated in their future models. The top builders in America were Cramp & Son of Philadelphia; Harlan & Hollingsworth of Wilmington, Delaware; Charles P. Willard Company of Chicago; Ward, Stanton Company of Newburgh, and the Herreshoff Company of Bristol, Rhode Island.

Opposite: Herreshoff three-cylinder, triple-expansion engine of 1905. Below: Model of ARROW, *palatial, 200-foot steam yacht in 1900's, is built to ½ inch=1 foot scale. It is in Mystic Seaport collection.*

Cramp & Sons built *Stranger* for George Osgood in 1881. She was the fastest of all, averaging fifteen knots, until Jay Gould's *Atalanta* came from Cramp in 1883. Osgood liked to breakfast aboard *Stranger* in Newport and have dinner the same day in New York. The first *Corsair,* belonging to J. P. Morgan, was the same Cramp model as Osgood's yacht, long and thin. *Corsair* measured 185 feet over-all and her maximum beam came to only 23 feet. It is a good thing these yachts followed Lorillard's advice about rounded frames for least resistance in a seaway, because their extreme dimensions made them sensitive to the smallest waves.

Harlan & Hollingsworth built *Nourmahal* for William Astor in 1884. Jaffray called her, "A queen among steam yachts." She was huge, her steel hull measuring 232 feet over-all and 30 feet at the maximum beam. Strength in the new material — steel — was provided by five athwartship bulkheads and two running fore and aft. Painted black with gold trim, *Nourmahal* sported a thick black stack amidships and a tall bark rig.

Jaffray was impressed. He wrote of her: "*Nourmahal* is a yacht of grand proportions and rakish beauty, capable of all-around-the-world explorations, and of strength sufficient to laugh at the fitful moods of the ocean. Internally there is a world of room, supplied with every known novelty of approved excellence, while the finish, fittings and decorations are of a very costly nature and magnificent in their exquisite simplicity."

Nourmahal had been designed by Gustav Hillmann of City Island, New York. Hillmann also produced *Electra* for Elbridge T. Gerry in the same year (1884). *Electra* was not as large, being 178 feet long, but she caught a lot of people's eyes because her owner installed a system of Edison electric lights and an electric ice machine which made fifty-six pounds a day. Lights and ice were sensational features.

Electra's propeller measured eight feet

in diameter and had 13 feet of pitch, a huge prop. It turned at only 160 revolutions per minute. (As time went on propellers became smaller and turned faster, particularly with the advent of the steam turbine and the gasoline—or "explosion"—engines.) *Electra* had a compound engine, one which used the steam first in a high-pressure cylinder and then in a low-pressure cylinder almost twice as big. Double use of the steam made for fuel economy; coal bunkers and boilers could be smaller in size, thus saving weight and space, and reducing fuel costs. Still, *Electra's* twin boilers, engines, and bunkers occupied the entire width of the vessel for 50 feet. That was discounting space for the generators to run the fifty-eight sixteen-candle-power lights, the one-hundred-candle-power light at the masthead, and the ice machine. Other features aboard *Electra* were a pipe from the galley connecting with the double smokestack to carry off the odors of cookery, and a blower system to aid in ventilating the

cabins. The Gerry vessel was the flagship of the New York Yacht Club from 1886 to 1892 and an exciting sight on the club cruises for twenty-five years.

Herreshoff in Rhode Island and Willard in Chicago began to lighten the steam engine's load in the 1880's. Willard spread the gospel of the steam vessel through the lakes of the Middle West, and a typical product was a 40-foot stern-wheel launch which drew only 16 inches. This vessel could carry up to thirty people and had a top speed of ten knots. The twin-cylinder compound engine was economical, burning 400 pounds of soft coal in ten hours of operation, and the boiler was only fifty-three inches tall with a diameter of thirty-three inches.

There was real genius in the Herreshoff yards, which specialized in medium-sized fast steam launches rather than the big yachts, although the firm was capable of making almost any kind of boat. John B. Herreshoff began by building steam launches for the

LILLIAN RUSSELL, *details of
which are shown here, is a naphtha
launch built in 1904. She served
as tender for a large steam
yacht until 1908, then was bought
for use as a pleasure craft on
Lake Hopatcong, N. J. She now is in
Mystic Seaport collection.
She is 24 feet long. Her engine
delivered two horsepower. Her top
speed was 5.7 knots per hour.
William Randolph Hearst's* VAMOOSE
(right) could make 27 knots.

Federal government in 1876 and torpedo boats for foreign nations. His younger brother, Nathaniel, or Captain Nat, soon joined him in a business which thrived for forty years.

The typical Herreshoff steam yacht of the 1880's was 85 feet in over-all length. It carried a crew of four—captain, deck hand, engineer, and steward—a complement considered minimal and economical. There were two staterooms and a saloon; the speed was ten to fifteen knots; the engines consumed a thrifty one ton of coal every 150 miles. Although these yachts were notorious rollers in a sea, they were also noiseless, safe, reliable, comfortable, and popular. Between 1879 and 1885, Herreshoff produced twenty-six steam launches.

When it came to engines, Captain Nat went far beyond what others had dared. The two-cylinder compound engine was all very well, but why not expand the steam further? Triple and quadruple expansion engines were tried, and in 1887 one with five cylinders. A triple expansion engine went into *Vamoose,* a racy launch that was built in 1891 for a young man in a hurry—William Randolph Hearst, who was then building his newspaper empire. *Vamoose* could transport him at twenty-seven miles per hour. That was just a bit faster than *Stiletto,* which the Herreshoff brothers had built for themselves in 1885 and later sold to the United States Navy as a torpedo boat.

Nat had a lot of nerve. On a trial run of a fast launch called *Say When,* he screwed down the safety valve adjustment in the interests of an uninterrupted trial. The boiler tube burst when the fire door was opened. Steam and fire erupted and asphyxiated one fireman. Steamboat inspectors for the government took away Captain Nat's steam-engineer's license for his negligence, and he never got it back.

The naphtha launches which came along in the late 1880's and 1890's proved more practical than steam launches in providing power propulsion for smaller hulls. The naphtha engine burned a colorless, volatile liquid which produced steam for a small, simple steam engine. The naphtha was piped from a tank in the bow of the boat to a light coil boiler where some naphtha was burned under the coil while some was vaporized simultaneously within the coil. This boiler could produce steam very quickly; it took only two minutes for the boat to achieve full headway.

The naphtha device had many advantages. Its small size and light weight could fit into boats as small as 12-footers and the operation was considered simple. A two-horse-power naphtha engine weighed 200 pounds, an eight horsepower 600 pounds, which was one fifth the weight of equivalent steam machinery. A 21-foot naphtha launch could carry ten to fifteen passengers at six to eight knots for six cents an hour. And unlike steam vessels, naphtha-powered boats were free from government regulations.

STEAM YAC

The Property of

NAMOUNA.

Gordon Bennett, Esq.

Length over all	226 ft	10 in.
on water line	217	
Breadth of Beam	26	4
Depth of Hold	15	4
Tonnage 545.64		

NAMOUNA.

Gordon Bennett, Esq.

Length over all	226 ft 10 in
on water line	217
Breadth of Beam	26 4
Depth of Hold	15 4
Tonnage 545 s

The starting directions for a naphtha launch may have seemed simple to the young enthusiast in 1880, but they would perplex today's youth, who is accustomed to opening the fuel line and pulling the starter cord of a small outboard. A typical instruction sheet reads:

"Light the alcohol lamp. Turn air valve B from left to right. Give air pump 10 or more strokes to force gas from the tank through outlet pipe to burner. Open wide naphtha valve D. Give 5-10 strokes on pump F which pumps naphtha from tank to retort on top of engine. Open injector valve C which supplies fuel to burner. Turn reverse wheel G from right to left a few times until engine runs itself. Extinguish lamp."

Naphtha launches were popular as tenders for the big steam yachts such as William K. Vanderbilt's *Alva,* which was named for his wife. This massive steel vessel originally was turned out by Harlan & Hollingsworth in 1886 for Cornelius Vanderbilt's grandson. It cost $500,000, but Willie Vanderbilt could afford it. *Alva*—the yacht, not Vanderbilt's wife—was 285 feet long and carried a three-masted schooner rig. Its engines could move it at fifteen knots and there were bunkers for 300 tons of coal. The yacht had a dining saloon, a library, a nursery, sixteen staterooms, a copy of *Electra's* ice-making machine. The owner and his wife were snubbed by Mrs. William B. Astor, the ruler of society in Newport and New York, but it was hard to snub the yacht.

The Vanderbilts went on a West Indies cruise in the winter of 1887, visiting Nassau, Havana, and Port-au-Prince, cities then untroubled by tourists. Coming home, the family got off in South Carolina, but Willie K. stayed aboard while his vessel steamed through a hurricane. In July of the same year came a voyage to Europe, similar to *North Star's* thirty-five years before. When *Alva* reached Athens the crew went on strike for higher wages, and Willie's reaction would have made his grandfather, the Commodore, proud. He fired them all. In Alexandria, the yacht unwarily took on 300 tons of inferior coal which then had to be unloaded, and Mrs. Vanderbilt, Alva, went ashore until the yacht's rugs could be cleaned. The Vanderbilt marriage later dissolved and when the time came for a new yacht, Willie named her *Valiant* rather than *Alva II. Valiant* cost $1,000,000. *Alva* was later involved in a collision and sank off Martha's Vineyard. Fortunately, however, no lives were lost.

Henry Morrison was captain of the crew of the *Alva,* and he had fifty-three men under his command. The principals were a chief

Opposite: View of NAMOUNA'S *deck.*
Yachts sail past masts of William Astor's ALVA
(below), which sank off Martha's Vineyard
in 1892 in a collision. No lives were lost.

mate, second mate, engineer, two boatswains, four quartermasters, and a surgeon. Although wages were low, crews of this size made the upkeep of a steam yacht comparable to that of a navy warship. James Gordon Bennett's *Namouna* had fifty in the crew and the payroll was $2,500 a month. It cost $1,500 more to feed the men. Townsend Perry, of the New York *World,* writing on November 8, 1885, reported that, "Coal and supplies, repairs and the lavishly supplied table and wine locker of Mr. Bennett, who entertains large parties on her, regardless of cost, make $150,000 a moderate estimate of *Namouna's* annual expenses."

Perry wrote that Edwin D. Morgan's world tour in his yacht *Amy* cost $50,000 in five months. He supposed that J. P. Morgan's annual payroll for *Corsair* was $15,000. Sailors and firemen drew $30 a month, and that was better than merchant-marine wages. So was the housing and the food, so yacht captains had the pick of the seamen, most of whom were Scandinavian. Captains made from $100 to $200 a month, but, said Perry, the chief cook's salary was a secret, "the cook too discreet, the master too ashamed to admit it."

Even a 50-foot steam launch had a sizable overhead. Such a vessel required a pilot-captain and an engineer, each at $60 per month; a deck hand at $30; provisions $75; coal $75; miscellaneous matters $50. The total came to $350 a month, or $1,750 a season, plus $750 for crew uniforms, making an annual grand total of $2,500.

In somewhat larger steam launches, the crew had to be increased by a stoker at $40 a month; a cook at $40; a steward at $50; another deck hand at $30; plus a more capable pilot-captain and engineer at $80 each. The total came quickly to $10,000 a year. Even if the elder J. P. Morgan never in actual fact made his often-quoted remark—"Should you have to ask how much it costs to maintain a yacht, you cannot afford to have one"—it is easy to understand where the inspiration might come from. Perry, the *World* reporter, made this cogent point: "I don't know what will eat a man up the quickest—an extravagant wife or a steam yacht. But think of a man with both!"

No one could think of Jay Gould with any sympathy. A part of his millions, made from stock speculations in railroads and telegraph companies, went into estates and yachts. There was Lyndhurst, 500 acres on the river at Irvington-on-Hudson and the locale for 8,000 of Gould's orchids. He was a fancier. The estate had a swimming pool so large that a lifeguard tended it in a rowboat.

And there was *Atalanta,* an immense, black iron steam yacht. She was built in 1883, and among the big ones of her time she ranked second. *Alva* at 285 feet was the largest. *Atalanta* was 248, Astor's *Nourmahal* 233, and Bennett's *Namouna* 226.

Gould was the son of a country-store clerk in Delaware County, New York. In 1857, at twenty-one, he had saved $5,000 and became a speculator in New York, specializing in small railroads. With the aid of Jim Fisk and Daniel Drew, he wrested control of the Erie Railroad from Cornelius Vanderbilt. With Fisk he attempted to corner the gold market in 1869, causing the Black Friday panic. Colonel Robert G. Ingersoll, a noted orator, lawyer, and agnostic, said, "I do not believe that since man was in the habit of living on this planet anyone has ever possessed the impudence of Jay Gould."

In the face of public outrage, Gould

Frederic Cozzens print shows Hudson River scene of 1883. Jay Gould's steam yacht ATALANTA *passes* STRANGER *(left) and cargo sloop (rear). Launch puts downstream.*

moved his interests out of the Erie and into the western railroads and the Western Union telegraph company. He also began to spend his millions. His first yacht was *Rosamond,* in which he commuted to the city from Irvington-on-Hudson. For his next one, Gould went all the way and ordered what for one year was the largest and fastest yacht in America, the 248-foot, seventeen-knot *Atalanta,* built by Cramp in 1883.

The yacht's compound steam engines mustered 1,750 horsepower delivered to a four-bladed propeller with a 10½-foot diameter and a 16-foot pitch. Gould was no party-giver like Bennett (he had few friends), but even

so the cost of maintaining *Atalanta* came to $6,000 a month. The sailors dressed in uniforms of the Gould colors, blue and white, and Captain Shackford ran a taut ship with navy-style discipline. A rowboat manned by eight sailors ferried the owner from Lyndhurst to *Atalanta* and back, and once under way the short, slight Gould liked to stand silently in the wheelhouse beside the man at the wheel. That was where the power of

*Jay Gould (below) liked to stand in
the wheelhouse where control was exercised.
Opposite: Steam-yacht trophies included
American Yacht Club Challenge cup.*

control lay and Gould was never far from
that point in all his dealings.

To the Astors, certainly to the New York
Yacht Club membership, and even to the
Vanderbilts, Gould was a bounder, a cad, a
villainous outsider. He had no chance of
membership in the club, although it must be
acknowledged that the N. Y. Y. C. holds no
grudges from one wealthy generation to
another. After Jay died, his son and heir,
George, and another son, Howard, became
members, prominent ones who were partners
in syndicates formed to build defenders of
the America's Cup.

After Jay Gould had been refused membership in both the New York and Eastern
Yacht Clubs, he formed his own. This was
the American Yacht Club which, at its founding, attracted other "black balls" who had
money and big steam yachts. This was in
May, 1883, and within two years there were
over one hundred members from Boston,
Philadelphia, and Pittsburgh, as well as New
York. In 1886, the club bought, for $6,000,
a beautiful twelve-acre site at the tip of
Milton Point at Rye, New York, on Long
Island Sound. A clubhouse was erected and
opened in 1888. Women were barred from
the clubrooms at first because the members
were known as a "fast" crowd and it would
be shocking for someone's wife to see chorus

girls from a Broadway show come ashore
from a yacht. A few years later a lady named
Ethel Barrymore created a sensation by
smoking a cigarette right out in public on
the club grounds.

The hack drivers of Rye figured that if
Gould and his gang could afford steam yachts
they could afford to pay fifty cents for a ride
from the railroad station out to Milton
Point. They figured wrong. The club bought
its own horses and conveyances and charged
its members only twenty cents.

Shortly after *Atalanta* had been commissioned, she served her master well. Gould,
then forty-eight years old, had been wheeling
and dealing with the Kansas-Pacific Railroad,
which had outstanding bonds in the possession of Dutch investors. In the consolidation
of the railroad with the Union Pacific there
had been a gain of $3,000,000, but this sum
did not show on the corporate reports. It had
disappeared, the Dutch bondholders believed, and they complained to the district
attorney of New York, who was urged to
seek indictments before the grand jury.
Captain Shackford received the word from
Gould's downtown office and *Atalanta* was
secretly provisioned for a sea voyage. Suddenly the big black yacht was gone from New
York. Gould was aboard, standing silently
by the wheel for hour after hour, watching
the sea and free from any plans the district
attorney might have.

The year 1884 was a critical one for
Gould, who became overextended in his se-
curity dealings as the bottom went out of
the Wall Street market. The embezzlements
of Ferdinand Ward, U. S. Grant's partner,
and the subsequent failure of the former
president's firm undermined public confidence in the stock market. Gould's bitterest
enemies combined to drive him off the street.
They were Addison Cammack, James Keene,
and Charles Woerishoffer.

The New York *Times* said of Gould's position, "An impartial view of the present crisis would indicate that the boys had not only got him under, but were walking up and down his prostrate form." The financier, sickly and apprehensive, still had his nerve, however. On the last Sunday in May, 1884, he stepped aboard *Atalanta* and steamed down to Long Branch, New Jersey, a resort favored by Woerishoffer and his joyful colleagues. When they saw the huge yacht riding offshore, they thought their rival had come to capitulate. He had not. A small boat was lowered and the smartly uniformed crew rowed ashore with a Gould emissary bearing not a plea but an ultimatum. Woerishoffer and his associates were shown a document that caused panic within their hearts. It was an assignment of property executed by Gould which would throw him into bankruptcy, but preserve all his unencumbered holdings for his seven heirs. The bankruptcy of Gould would cause a far worse panic on Wall Street than that existing at the time, and would drag them all down to ruin.

The quiet, determined man, sitting out there alone on his big yacht, had decided that if they wanted to ruin him, he would take them all with him. And he had judged correctly that they would back down.

Back to *Atalanta* came the emissary, carrying with him an agreement to Gould's proposal. Woerishoffer and his group agreed to buy 50,000 shares of Western Union stock at $50 a share. This purchase propped up the falling price of the telegraph company which Gould controlled, and averted a collapse of his empire. Now he had some time to plan a recovery.

The *Atalanta* steamed back up the Hudson that night to Lyndhurst, Gould's world preserved. There would be no panic and the era of the steam yacht, the mightiest symbol of great wealth, would continue.

SMALL
BOATS
AND
FARAWAY
PLACES

6

SMALL BOATS AND FARAWAY PLACES

---

*Sandbaggers,
catboats, sailing
canoes, and
scows give boating
new popularity
and encourage
skippers
like Joshua Slocum
to sail to the
ends of the earth.*

Preceding pages: Model of SUSIE S., *champion
racing sandbagger, rests on deck of* ANNIE, *Mystic
Seaport's superb sandbagger sloop.*

His name was Captain Horatio Hawkes and his home port was Oyster Bay, on the north shore of Long Island. He knew the bay's every square yard of water and shore line. The idiosyncrasies of its tides and current were comfortably familiar to him. And when it came to racing sandbaggers, he was the local champion.

The sandbagger was a shallow, wide-beam, centerboard sloop carrying a tremendous amount of sail, and the resulting problem of ballasting gave the craft its name. Canvas or burlap bags of sand, weighing fifty pounds each, were carried on deck and shifted from side to side by the crew as the boat tacked. The sandbags prevented the boat from tipping over and the technique required a strong, numerous, and indefatigable crew. The sandbagger was the national type of small sailboat in America in the last half of the nineteenth century, and its kind spread from the northeast coast into southern waters and the lakes of the Middle West.

One day in 1886, Hawkes was asked to defend the honor of Oyster Bay by taking on Mr. C. Oliver Iselin from across Long Island Sound at New Rochelle. Mr. Iselin was no shellback like Hawkes, but a distinguished and wealthy clubman who later played a major role in managing four America's Cup defenders — *Vigilant, Defender, Columbia,* and *Reliance* — between 1893 and 1903.

The Oyster Bay summer families, such as the Townsends, the Weekes, the Beekmans, and the Roosevelts, as well as the townspeople, supported Hawkes and wagered heavily on him. They had plenty of takers from New Rochelle.

The start and finish were off Moses Point, within Oyster Bay, and the course took the yachts into the sound and around the Center Island and Lloyds Neck buoys. The breeze was blowing strong from the southwest and the Oyster Bay entry took an early lead. On the beat back to the finish, Captain Hawkes stayed close to the Center Island shore, where the ebb tide was not so strong, and he held his scanty lead by making a series of short tacks. His last tack brought him under the tidal lee of Moses Point and close to the red spar marking the finish line. In fine style, he pushed his sandbagger first to the line, where it received the cannon shot signifying victory and the cheers of the spectators. But as the boat skimmed by the red spar, an enthusiastic member of the crew who was jumping up and down on the sandbags piled along the weather rail, gave it a friendly kick. It was a fatal boot for the Oyster Bay sailors, who were not so well acquainted with the rules of yacht racing as C. Oliver Iselin.

The New Rochelle skipper promptly protested the winners for breaking a fundamental rule: Neither boat nor crew may touch a mark of the course. The protest was sustained, Captain Hawkes disqualified, and Mr. Iselin declared the winner. A lot of Oyster Bay money went home to New Rochelle that evening.

There was something about the speedy sandbaggers that inspired wagering. They were raced for stakes around New York as early as the 1840's, and their huge sails, on hulls only 20 to 30 feet long, made capsizing a constant risk. As large a crew as could fit into the boat was assembled and each man had his own bag of sand to shift at each tack from the old weather rail to the new one. The too-large expanse of sail on the little hull and a sandbag-laden crew scrambling about in the cockpit made for a colorful, competitive sport. The sandbaggers were especially popular on the water front of New York City, and racing skippers built up considerable reputations. Boats represented different clubs, commercial ships, and even saloons. The crews were made up of longshoremen and other water-front characters,

E. Z. SLOAT, *a racing sandbagger, is
shown in 1896 with full crew aboard. Note the
tremendous base of the sail plan and
the 50-pound sandbags stacked to windward.*

tough yachtsmen who settled many a dispute
begun on the water in a bar or on the pier
with their fists.

The sandbagger was the first small-boat
type that found wide popularity among people who were not necessarily "swells," or
yacht-club members of means. Wealth and
yachts do complement one another, but there
also are ways to find pleasure on the water
at a minimal expense. Sandbagger sailors
were among the first Americans to discover
this—and to reap the benefits.

The sandbagger was directly related to a
work boat, the so-called New York sloop
which was used as a fishing vessel for almost
half a century. The New York boats were
developed in the 1830's, once the centerboard had been accepted as a safe and sane
feature for craft sailed in shallow waters.
The model spread rapidly. By the 1880's,
with the growth of the fisheries, the shoal
centerboard sloop—New York style—could
be found all along the Atlantic Coast, in
the Gulf of Mexico, and in San Francisco
Bay. Only to the east of Cape Cod, where
the catboat held supreme, did it fail to become popular.

The sandbagger rig was simple: a jib, a
gaff-rigged mainsail with a long, long boom
reaching far beyond the square stern, and a
bowsprit almost as lengthy. Half of the hull
was decked over and the cockpit had a U-
shaped bench around the sides and across
the stern to provide sitting room for the big
crew. The beam was great; there was plenty
of room for pleasure sailing or racing on
protected waters. *Annie,* the well-preserved
sandbagger at the Mystic Seaport has a hull
29 feet long, but the measurement from the
end of the bowsprit to the end of the boom
is 68 feet. *Annie's* total sail area comes to an
enormous 1,313 square feet.

The sandbagger, then, was the ancestor of
today's small, inexpensive boat, such as the

sailing dinghy or the outboard runabout. And among those Americans who had little time or money for pleasure boats, the sandbagger prospered because it served two purposes: fishing and yachting. Many a vessel with shortened rig spent its weekdays oystering or tending fish lines, and its weekends as a well-backed racing machine.

The catboat, another popular small sailboat and a type existing to this day, had similar work-boat origins. The catboat first appeared on Narragansett Bay and flourished in New England waters, notably on Cape Cod, beginning in the 1870's. The catboat differed from the sandbagger in having a sensible rig: a single, moderate-sized mainsail providing the propulsion. It was so simple that the thick, strong mast had no shrouds for support and just a single headstay. The hull was fat, and centerboard equipped, like the sandbagger, but considerably more rounded and not nearly so beamy. This made for a more seaworthy vessel, a safe, practical sailer for the workingman. The cat rig enables a boat to sail closer to the wind than a sloop rig, but it does not do so well in light airs. This handicap was seldom noticed in the environs of Cape Cod, where the ocean winds are usually strong. So Horace S. Crosby, who began a fifty-year family tradition of building fine cats at Osterville, was a very busy man.

Other noted builders were M. S. Roberts of Edgartown, on Martha's Vineyard, who completed almost one hundred cats; Barzillai Burdett of Nantucket Island, famous for the seaworthiness of his models, and Charles Beetle of New Bedford, Massachusetts, on the mainland. The Beetles, like the Crosbys, were boatbuilders for generations. The modern Beetle Cat, a class of 12½-foot catboats found principally on Narragansett and Buzzards Bays, was designed and first built by Beetle descendents in 1921. Charles Beetle's

original cat, *Matty,* was the first one to go from New Bedford to Oak Bluffs, on Martha's Vineyard, where it became a famous party boat.

The Mystic Seaport has a Crosby cat in its small-boat collection. This is the *Nantucket,* built in 1900. She is 20 feet, 10 inches long, with a 10-foot beam and a draft of only 2 feet with the centerboard up. She has a cabin with two bunks and room for a stove; a fair-sized cockpit with a high coaming; a deep rudder; an able hull, and no provision whatsoever for a motor. Cost? About $250. Cats like these have been the favorites of youngsters for more than fifty years.

A traditional difficulty of the yachting fraternity is its constitutional inability to let well enough alone. The sight of something inherently good often stirs an impulse to improve it. So it was with the catboat. Objections centered on its slowness in light air, and the speed-up remedies were numerous. The cats began to take on the vicious sailing characteristics of the older sandbaggers. Beginning around 1900, more sail was added, resulting in taller masts and longer booms and gaffs. In extreme cases, the main boom extended so far beyond the stern that the boat had to be brought alongside a pier or another vessel in order to reef the mainsail. It was the only way the outermost reef points could be reached and tied. The graceful curves gradually disappeared and "catboat" came to mean a powerful box-shaped hull with a large outboard rudder. It was an extremely swift sailing craft on protected waters, but look out when a squall came! Capsizing was common and sailors occasionally drowned.

Sailing soon acquired a poor reputation and was viewed as a dangerous sport by non-nautical people. The catboat fell into disrepute and around 1925 began a decline in popularity that has continued unabated.

*Catboats appeared in New England waters in the 1870's.
A Crosby cat (below, left) was typical product of noted builders in
Osterville, Cape Cod. Sketches show Cape Cod catboat lines.
Bottom: In light air, catboats were never in a hurry.*

There is nothing wrong, however, with the kind of catboat that follows the sensible Crosby kind of design: moderate beam, round bottom, small sail area, and small rudder. This breed of catboat will always have friends who swear by it.

A third type of small boat popular in America over the last thirty-five years of the nineteenth century was the canoe, and for that we owe thanks to a retired British army officer, Captain John Macgregor, who was a courageous sailor and a prolific writer on the subject of his accomplishments afloat. In 1865, he built the first of a long series of canoes called *Rob Roy*. This one was a 15-footer of the Eskimo kayak type, and Macgregor paddled her about the English Channel to the surprise of many who expected he would drown.

Macgregor found a ready publishing market for his adventures and he expanded them, traveling in various *Rob Roys* through the rivers and canals of Europe. His trips and his prose enjoyed a big following and when the captain paddled through town he attracted large, cheering crowds. He was widely read in America, and the popularity of canoeing shot upwards in the 1870's and 1880's. Adventure and economy seemed to be the appeal. In *Forest and Stream,* the leading outdoor magazine of the era, yachting-editor W. P. Stephens wrote that one could "cruise under sail or paddle, according to weather, carrying stores, a tent, bedding, to a canoe club rendezvous." Sail and paddle races were the attraction at the rendezvous, followed by a cruise home.

Stephens was an avid canoeist and supporter of the New York Canoe Club, which was founded in 1871, six years after the Royal Canoe Club inspired by Macgregor in England. Like Macgregor, Stephens found an audience for articles on the sport. *Forest and Stream* and Stephens published page after page of build-it-yourself plans and advice, and the double-ended, 15-foot sailing canoe with twin masts and sails enjoyed a vogue. *Forest and Stream* told how it could be built out of wood and canvas for $15.

The popularity of canoeing established a rapport between British and American yachtsmen, a communication that resulted in the founding of a racing event for small boats that gained wide renown. The prize was the Seawanhaka International Challenge Trophy, a $500 silver cup that became to some yachtsmen every bit as important as the America's Cup.

In 1895, William Willard Howard of the New York Canoe Club learned through correspondence that J. Arthur Brand of England's Minima Yacht Club planned to bring to this country his small sailboat, *Spruce III.* Howard and several of his friends thought it would be fitting to entertain Brand with a series of races. Members of the Seawanhaka Corinthian Yacht Club at Oyster Bay obliged and put up the challenge trophy. The series would be on a match basis, the prizes going to the boat winning three out of five races. Alternate windward-leeward and triangu-

Captain John Macgregor, heading to sea
in ROB ROY (opposite), was inspiration of the
canoe craze. Yawl-rigged canoes (below)
were raced before feminine admirers.

lar courses, each twelve miles long, were to be run by competing boats.

By the late 1880's, there had developed on England's Solent a full range of small yachts that raced and were rated by a simple formula: L x SA ÷ 6,000. L equaled the boat's water-line length and SA its sail area. The formula separated different boats into classes called half-rater, single-rater, twin-rater, and 2½-rater. The general dimensions of the half-rater were a boat with a water-line length of 15 feet and a sail area of 200 square feet since L (15) times SA (200) divided by 6,000 equaled ½. By this formula, Brand's boat, *Spruce III,* was a half-rater.

There were no comparable small sailing craft in America and six new boats were built for the Seawanhaka Cup Races under a rating rule similar to the English one. Class designations in accordance with this rule were worked out as follows: the sum of the water-line length plus the square root of the sail area divided in half. For example, a boat with a 15-foot length and a sail area of 225 would have a rating of 15, based on the equation $\dfrac{15 + \sqrt{225}}{2} = 15$. Consequently, instead of "half-raters," the American boats were referred to as "15-footers."

By the summer of 1895, when he finally appeared on the scene, Brand had supplanted *Spruce III* with a new contender, *Spruce IV,* which was also a half-rater. After some trial races, a shoal, centerboard yacht called *Ethelwynn* was chosen to race the English invader. W. P. Stephens had designed and hastily built *Ethelwynn,* and she won the Seawanhaka Cup, three races to two.

Seawanhaka Cup competition was thus launched and it quickly bloomed, even though a Canadian, G. Herrick Duggan, was to dominate it through the first decade of its existence. (The deed of gift for the Seawanhaka Cup followed that of the America's Cup and

a recognized yacht club of any foreign nation could challenge.) Duggan challenged in 1896, the year following the cup's inception, and he represented the Royal St. Lawrence Yacht Club of Montreal. His yacht was *Glencairn* and it won the prize by taking three straight races from the defender, *El Heirie,* designed and sailed by Clinton Crane, a twenty-three-year-old naval architect two years out of Harvard.

The trials to select the defender were run off Oyster Bay, and the entry list showed how rapidly the club system had grown. There were twenty-eight original starters in the trials representing seventeen different yacht clubs spread from Fall River, Massachusetts, to Brooklyn, New York. (Founding dates of significant yacht clubs were: New York, 1844; Southern of New Orleans, Louisiana, 1849; Boston, 1866; San Francisco, 1869; Eastern of Marblehead, Massachusetts, 1870; Seawanhaka Corinthian, 1871; Larchmont, New York, 1880; Chicago, 1882.)

Once *El Heirie,* a wide, flat scow with a sharp bow, had won the trials, Crane had a finisher from the Steinway piano company

and never won. Duggan was a very bright engineer who appreciated the speed potential in the flat, scow hull.

The original scows were copied from the bateau type of hull, with its flat floor and sides, and square bilges. It soon became evident that if the flat floor were given a rocker shape from bow to stern, the water-line length might be made very short. But if the boat were inclined in the water on one edge, by means of such movable ballast as a crewman weighing 200 pounds, then the actual water line would be greatly increased. And it was an axiom in boats that the longer the water line, the greater the speed. At the same time, the heeling of the hull on one edge served to reduce the width of the boat that was actually in the water, a condition satisfying another requirement for speed: reduction of the wetted surface of the hull, thereby minimizing resistance. As the hull leaves the perpendicular, immersing the lee bilge, the axis of the water-line plane also lifts. (This axis is a theoretical line, at the water line, between the stem at the bow and the sternpost.) The lifting effect results in a shorter water line, especially at the bow.

The result, with a heeling scow, was a long, narrow, canoe-shaped hull going through the water rather than a wide, square box, as is the case with a conventional hull, such as a catboat's. When a conventional sloop or catboat is at rest on a mooring, the hull's water line is at maximum. Not so with a scow. When at anchor, the rocker-shaped hull has its minimum water line.

Duggan was among the first to appreciate these factors, and others, like Crane, copied his scow designs. Eventually, extreme scows were evolved, boats that could be heeled safely at a much greater angle than desirable in normal yachts. W. P. Stephens, who disapproved of scows as being "unhealthy" types, described the Seawanhaka Cup scows

come out from New York to work on the boat's bottom prior to the cup series. After all, the bottom was mahogany, like the top of a Steinway grand, and Crane hoped for a superlatively smooth, easy-riding finish. The Steinway man did an excellent job, but *El Heirie* was no competition for *Glencairn*. The Canadian scow was shorter on the water line and it carried more sail. Furthermore, the hull was lighter and the sails had better shapes. The result was more speed on almost every point of sailing.

Crane, who later became one of the more successful designers in the United States, took on boats designed by Duggan four different times in Seawanhaka Cup competition

First defender of the Seawanhaka Cup was W. P. Stephens' ETHELWYNN *(below) in 1895. G. H. Duggan took cup to Canada in 1896, winning in his scow* GLENCAIRN *(opposite).*

Designing Seawanhaka Cup entries started Clinton Crane on career as naval architect. But he could never beat Duggan's Canadian defenders. Below: Crane at tiller of EL ANKA, *his unsuccessful Seawanhaka Cup scow of 1897. Use of an overlapping jib on a flat, shallow hull was novel.*

of the late 1890's as "the most grotesque collection of craft ever seen in civilized waters." But his asperity went unheeded. Success commanded respect and inspired emulation.

Duggan managed to stay ahead of the United States challengers as the Royal St. Lawrence Yacht Club successfully defended the Seawanhaka Cup year after year. *Dominion,* Duggan's defender of 1898, had an over-all length of 37 feet, but a water-line length of a mere 17½.

The skimming-dish principle of the scows went beyond Seawanhaka Cup competition. In 1902, designer W. Starling Burgess, son of Edward Burgess, made *Outlook* more than twice as long on deck as on the water line. Her dimensions: LOA 52-7; LWL 20-10; B 16; D 2, and SA 1,800. She was the successful defender of a trophy called the Quincy Challenge Cup.

Another extreme was *Independence.* Bowdoin B. (Bodie) Crowninshield, of the Salem shipping family, designed *Independence* in 1901 for Thomas W. Lawson, a wealthy New York speculator, who, it is said, once made $1,000,000 in a single day. *Independence's* dimensions: LOA 140-10½; LWL 89; B 24; D 20. She was a flat scow with a fin keel, optimistically built as a candidate to defend the America's Cup. Unfortunately, she leaked badly and never passed her own sailing trials. She cost $200,000 to build and after three months she was broken up.

What did *Independence* prove? Not much, except that there were yachtsmen like Lawson who were willing to sink a tremendous amount of money into a fatuous design—even if the outcome proved disastrous.

Seawanhaka Cup racing, even in the freakish scows, had great appeal for the growing legion of small-boat skippers. The trophy stood for international yacht competition which otherwise did not exist except in the expensive, exalted realm of the America's

Cup. For $600, the cost of a scow, an ambitious yachtsman could project his yacht-club colors on the international scene with pretensions equal to those of General Paine or Ollie Iselin.

Aside from their cheap construction cost, the scows were practical. They could be transported in a wagon—the beginning of trailering—and once in the water they could sail almost anywhere. With centerboards up (many had twin boards offset from the centerline and called leeboards), the hull drew only 6 inches of water. With the boards down, the draft was a mere 4 feet.

In terms of fittings, the bigger yachts showed no appreciable progress between 1860 and 1880. The heavy rope shrouds, cast-iron or bronze hardware, and thick spars, all inherited from the merchant marine, carried on. But the do-it-yourself canoe builders had developed lighter cleats and blocks, and stayed their slim hollow masts with thin, lightweight wire. The good features were incorporated into the Seawanhaka Cup scows and soon found their way aboard the larger yachts. Thus the scow period did contribute improvements in the arts of sailing, no matter how grotesque the hull forms may have been.

Seawanhaka members spent their money and effort in building larger and faster freaks to lift their cup from Canada. Their "unhealthy" scow was an exploitation of the basic water-line sail-area rule of measurement in a manner that its authors had never intended. Such "rule beating" would hardly have sat well with such idealists as Robert Center. In 1870, Center had helped to found the club and led the reform movement against the squat schooners. The cup contenders were fostering unseaworthy, uncomfortable sailboats that could not beat the Canadians anyway.

There was the inevitable reaction to im-

practical extremes. It came in the form of widespread acceptance of the 21-foot Knockabout sloop. This had originated at Marblehead in 1892. The firm of Stewart & Binney had built the first pair, *Nancy* and *Jane,* for two members of the Eastern Yacht Club, Henry Taggard and Herman Parker. *Nancy* and *Jane* were prototypes of a kind of small sailing craft that took root and lasted to the fiberglass era of the 1950's.

The dimensions of these sloops were: LOA 25-6; LWL 21; B 7-2; D 4-2. The hull was squared off at the stern with no overhang,

and there was no bowsprit. The ballast was mostly outside in the form of an iron keel weighing 1,070 pounds. The hull was half-decked and had a large oval cockpit and a small cuddy. The rig provided for a mainsail of moderate size and a small jib. The total sail area came to a modest 400 square feet.

The Knockabouts were strongly built and finished in a neat, if not gaudy, manner. They were sound boats that could be sailed safely by a single person even in foul weather, and cost only about $300. They had great appeal and singlehandedly overcame much of the

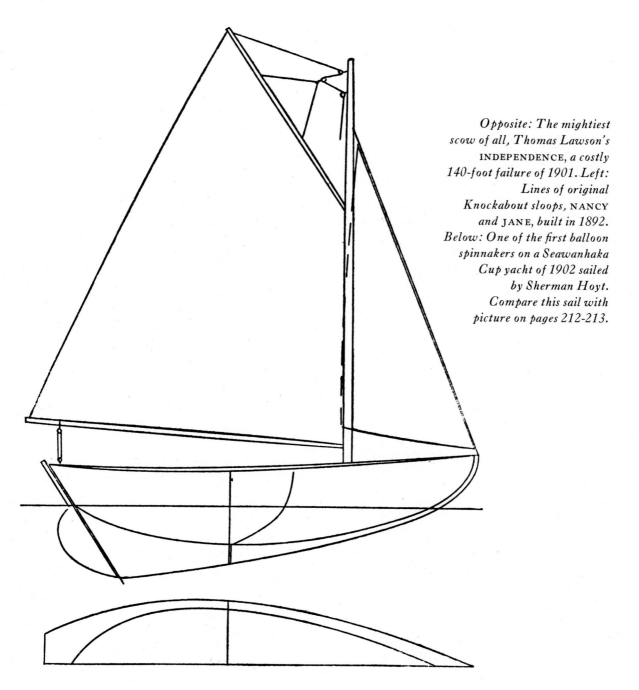

Opposite: The mightiest scow of all, Thomas Lawson's INDEPENDENCE, *a costly 140-foot failure of 1901. Left: Lines of original Knockabout sloops,* NANCY *and* JANE, *built in 1892. Below: One of the first balloon spinnakers on a Seawanhaka Cup yacht of 1902 sailed by Sherman Hoyt. Compare this sail with picture on pages 212-213.*

fear that sailing was dangerous. The Knockabouts spread rapidly from Marblehead and were found all over the eastern United States in the next forty years, bringing recreational sailing into places where either no sailing at all or only adaptations of work boats had existed earlier.

In the years after 1910 the tinkerers and the speed demons did some surgery on the Knockabout, particularly at the site of the boat's birth. More expensive lead keels replaced the iron. Naval architects were called in to add to the sail area. The square mid-

*Captain Joshua Slocum
was born on a Nova Scotia farm
in 1844, left home
at sixteen to go to sea.*

section was reduced, saving weight which went into the keel. The over-all length was raised to 30 feet. And the rule against metal fin keels was dodged by one of the designers, Nat Herreshoff, who built, instead, a deep one of wood. Initial costs, too, went up and up. Eventually, the modified Knockabouts were not Knockabouts at all and, in Marblehead, they made up a splinter class called Raceabouts. The type was short-lived, however, because it had departed so far from the good qualities of the original Knockabout design. The original lived on.

By the turn of the century, sailing in small boats had begun to enjoy a wide popularity. The development of good types helped and so did publicity about romantic, faraway voyages made in small boats. The most famous one of all was made in the years between 1895 and 1898 by Joshua Slocum, a Yankee shipmaster. Shorn of his command by the economics of the time, Slocum sailed around the world all by himself in a 37-foot sloop, the *Spray*. It was a voyage of hazards that ranked with any on record and a resulting book, *Sailing Alone Around the World,* made a celebrity of the skipper.

Slocum was far from original in undertaking a difficult passage singlehanded. Americans had been going to sea in small boats for voyages across oceans for many years. A Captain Cleveland from Salem, Massachusetts, is reported to have sailed alone in 1800 from his home port to the east, going around the Cape of Good Hope to Alaska and the west coast of America. His vessel was a 15-foot cutter. Time has obscured the details of Captain Cleveland's achievement, but if he truly did make such a voyage, his stature is equal to that of Columbus, Magellan, and Captain Slocum. The Gold Rush attracted J. Miller Cranston of New Bedford to California in 1849. He sailed 13,000 miles to San Francisco in a

41-footer called *Toccao,* taking 226 days.

Not everyone made safe landings. On June 26, 1864, two men from Providence, Rhode Island, Captain J. C. Donovan and William Spencer, plus a dog named Toby, sailed down New York harbor pretty as you please in their 15-footer, *Vision,* rigged as a brigantine with foresail, fore topsail, and mainsail flying. Captain Donovan and Spencer had stocked their boat with provisions and carried a lamp to cook by. England was their destination. The pilot vessel *William Ball* passed the *Vision* two days later, forty-five miles east of Fire Island, New York, but that was the last sight anyone ever had of her.

A famous, well-publicized voyage was that of *Red, White and Blue* in 1866. The boat, a 27-footer, happened to be a model of "Ingersoll's Improved Metallic Lifeboat," which imparted a tinny ring of promotion to the enterprise. The owner, William Hudson, had a man and a dog for crew when he left New York on July 12. The little ship was almost lost when a gale tossed her on her beam ends, but she made England in thirty-eight days, and later was exhibited at the Paris Exposition. Some people thought *Red, White and Blue* might have made her transatlantic passage aboard a freighter, but J. D. Jerold Kelly, a former naval officer and a respected yachting writer, saw her in Paris and was convinced that the voyage had been a bonafide one. Nonetheless, said Kelly, "The whole thing was foolish in extreme for it proved nothing except to what ends men will go for notoriety."

How true! Directly inspired by the example of *Red, White and Blue,* a fisherman from the Grand Banks, Alfred Johnson, sailed *Sentennial* singlehandedly across the North Atlantic in 1876, navigating by "dead reckoning" and surviving a knockdown at sea that turned the boat bottoms up.

Captain William A. Andrews, another eager suitor of notoriety, was less fortunate. He made it to England in 1878 with *Nautilus,* a 19-foot dory described by the press as "the smallest yet" to cross the ocean. On two subsequent voyages, however, he was picked up at sea by steamships at his own request after harrowing experiences.

In 1892, on another "smallest yet" voyage, Captain Andrews left Atlantic City, New Jersey, bound for Spain. His boat, *Flying Dutchman,* was 14½ feet in length, a square, flat craft with 300 pounds of lead ballast and no buoyancy. She probably went down like a stone. At any rate neither the boat nor her captain was ever heard from again.

Joshua Slocum was better prepared and more sensible than the notoriety seekers. He did not court fame, although he used it to support himself once his great voyage had been completed. Slocum's life, up to his departure in 1895, had been both a success and a failure—and a preparation for what was to come. He was born on a farm in Annapolis County, Nova Scotia, in 1844 and left home after his mother died in 1860, his life forever after committed to the sea. At twenty-five, he had his first command, an American coasting schooner, and he became an American citizen. Two years later he took the bark *Washington* on a trip from San Francisco to Sydney, Australia, and there he married Virginia Walker. It was a good match. For the rest of her life Virginia sailed wherever Slocum went—Alaska, the Philippines, Japan, the Kamchatka peninsula, China. Between 1872 and 1881, she gave birth to seven children aboard ships commanded by her husband.

Slocum's largest vessel was the *Northern Light,* a full-rigged, three-masted ship of 1,800 tons, of which he owned a share. But the age of steam had arrived and there were

SPRAY *(opposite) was a rugged, high-sided*
sloop, 37 feet long. At sea,
Captain Slocum loved to read (below)
while the SPRAY *sailed herself.*

fewer and fewer cargoes for the sailing ships. In 1884, with *Northern Light* idle and in need of expensive repairs, Slocum sold his interest in her and bought a much smaller vessel, *Aquidneck,* in which he made several voyages to South American ports with his family. During one of the trips, as the *Aquidneck* lay at anchor in the River Plate, which flows between Uruguay and Argentina, Virginia died. She was only thirty-four and Slocum was shaken by the loss. Still, he continued in the South American trade. In 1886, he married a first cousin who had come down from Nova Scotia to Boston, now the captain's home port. Hettie, as she was called, was twenty-four on her wedding day, Slocum forty-two. After their marriage the two went off on another South American voyage aboard *Aquidneck,* taking with them two of Slocum's sons, Victor, fourteen, and Garfield, five.

The *Aquidneck* was shipwrecked at Paranagua Bay, Brazil, for reasons Slocum never made quite clear, although he blamed the Brazilian government. But Slocum managed to get his family ashore and went to work building another boat on the beach. He called the new boat, *Liberdade,* a canoe. It was 35 feet long. The sails sewed by Hettie took the family 5,500 miles to Washington, D. C., where they arrived in December, 1888. It was a testing experience and Hettie never went to sea again.

Slocum now encountered hard times. There were few berths open for sailing captains. Three years later, still at loose ends, Slocum ran into an old friend, Eben Pierce, a wealthy, retired whaling captain. "Come to Fairhaven," Pierce said. "I'll give you a ship." And he added, "But she wants repairs." Slocum the next day was in Fairhaven, a Massachusetts town across the Acushnet River from New Bedford. The "ship" was *Spray,* an ancient oysterman lying high and

dry in a pasture along the river. Captain Pierce had played "something of a joke on me," Slocum later wrote. But the desperate Joshua saw something in *Spray,* and in the spring of 1893 he went to work on the old boat. For thirteen months he rebuilt her from stem to stern. She turned out to be a husky, high-sided sloop, 37 feet in length and weighing 9 tons. After her launching, according to Slocum, "she sat on the water like a swan."

It is difficult to say when or where Slocum got the idea of sailing *Spray* around the world alone. Such a voyage had never been made before, perhaps had not even been contemplated. However, Slocum was as well-qualified as anyone could be. He knew the anatomy of boats and their limitations, having built three with his own hands—*Spray, Liberdade,* and earlier, in the Philippines, a schooner called *Pato.* He knew the sea, having battled it most of his life. "I was born in the breezes," he wrote, "and I had studied the sea as perhaps few men have studied it, neglecting all else." In merchant ships, he had sailed around the world five times and had risen, through merit, to the top of his profession. He was a skilled seaman who knew full well what a singlehanded circumnavigation might require.

To Slocum, such a voyage would be a fitting climax to his lifelong experience. From a practical standpoint, it might make some money through syndication of travel letters that he would write along the way. (In fact they were a failure.) But the truth seems to be that the voyage was the way out of a trap in which the captain had found himself. The circumnavigation had purpose. It was a voyage only a brave and competent seaman would dare to venture. A lesser man might have broken under the disappointments that had stung Slocum. But Joshua was a tenacious Yankee, full of courage. He did not succumb to indolence or alcohol. He continued to battle life as he had battled the elements. He would make the voyage.

Spray and Slocum left Boston on April 24, 1895. The skipper was fifty-one years old. He stood five foot, nine and one half inches tall and weighed 146 pounds. The Boston *Globe* said he was "spry as a kitten and nimble as a monkey."

He took three years, two months, and two days to sail the 46,000 miles, and parts of the voyage were an ordeal. His route took him first across the Atlantic to Gibraltar. There, British naval officers advised him not to enter the Mediterranean because of the danger of pirates in the Red Sea. Slocum thereupon reversed his course and sailed back across the Atlantic, this time in a southwesterly direction, heading for Cape Horn at the tip of South America.

Slocum took his time. He was never in a hurry. He worked out a unique way of sailing *Spray,* so that she steered herself while he stayed below, sleeping or reading. Slocum had a $1 tin clock to help him with his navigational sights, and such was his skill that he made a series of perfect landfalls around the globe.

Just as important, he had learned the disciplines necessary to survive when alone. He never gave in to fear. One day in the South Atlantic, Slocum looked astern and saw a monstrous wave coming on. He quickly dropped the sails and climbed the halyards, leaving the deck to the comber. When the wave hit, *Spray* was awash for a few seconds. "The mountain of water submerged my vessel," he wrote. *Spray* shook off the water and he dropped down to the deck. The incident did not terrify him. Rather it gave him renewed confidence in the ability of his boat.

A few weeks later *Spray* ran aground on the Argentine coast and Slocum, who could not swim, almost drowned while trying to work the ship off with his dinghy.

He had a terrible time sailing the Straits of Magellan, beset by storms and the savage Fuegian Indians. The captain of an Argentine destroyer gave Slocum some tacks and told him how to use them. At an anchorage in the straits, an exhausted Slocum spread the tacks about the deck of the *Spray* before he went below to sleep. During the night a Fuegian canoe stole alongside and a savage stepped onto *Spray's* deck. He also stepped on the tacks and was so surprised that he let

out a cry of terror. The Fuegian leaped into the water and Slocum was not bothered again that night.

Four months went by before the patient sea captain worked his way through the straits. Once in the Pacific, the trip went smoothly. The longest leg of the voyage was a seventy-three-day passage to Samoa. Slocum then sailed serenely to Australia and South Africa, stopping for many weeks on both continents and earning expense money by giving lectures about his travels. His trip had gained the attention of the world press and he was becoming a celebrity.

Heading homeward, *Spray* was becalmed for eight days. Slocum, refusing to become anxious, read his books at night on deck by the light of a candle. Then came another gale and the headstay broke. The skipper went aloft to make repairs as *Spray* sailed on by herself.

The voyage had two endings, the first came at Newport on June 27, 1898, the second was a few days later when Slocum took *Spray* back to Fairhaven and the Acushnet River, "where I secured her to the cedar spile driven in the bank to hold her when she was launched. I could bring her no nearer home."

Century Illustrated Monthly magazine ran Slocum's account of his voyage in serial form, and in 1900 his book, *Sailing Alone Around the World,* was published.

The book was a success and it served to impress Joshua Slocum's mark on the world of men, ships, and the sea. Joshua inspired many others to take to sea on long, romantic voyages, and in every decade since there have been Americans scattered all over the world, sailing about in small boats. Most profess to have read Slocum, but few have been as able seamen as he. A number have lost their lives trying to be. Ira C. Sparks was one.

Sparks was a farmer from Indiana with no nautical background. He left Honolulu one day in 1924, sailing alone in a 16-foot craft which was little better than a flat-bottomed rowboat. The little ship came ashore in excellent condition some months later at Zamboanga, in the southern Philippines. But Sparks was not aboard and no one ever learned what happened to him.

Slocum, alas, had a similar end. He drifted about in *Spray* for several years, scratching out a living by putting himself and his boat on public exhibition. It was an unhappy life for him. Finally, in 1909, he planned another voyage, one to South America to explore the headwaters of the Amazon River. He left Vineyard Haven, on Martha's Vineyard, in November, 1909. Slocum was then sixty-five, and he and *Spray* had worn down considerably since their circumnavigation.

In a petition to a court a few years later to declare Slocum legally deceased, his widow said, "He sailed away on November 14 . . . encountered a very severe gale shortly afterwards and has never been heard from since."

THE DAYS OF THE GIANTS

7

THE
DAYS
OF
THE
GIANTS

*The biggest racers
ever built
successfully
defend America's Cup
five times,
while millionaires
acquire ocean
liners
for family outings.*

Preceding pages: SEA CLOUD, *a 316-foot,
four-masted bark costing $900,000, was the most
spectacular of all yachts.*

The years from 1893 to 1903 were a golden age for yachting. The America's Cup was defended five times, a sustained competitive effort unequaled at any other period in cup history. The contenders were the largest boats ever to race for the cup; they were capable of spectacular speed and cost a fortune to build. Best of all, they were brilliantly, overwhelmingly successful. In fifteen cup starts during the five challenges the Americans never lost a race.

Size, speed, money, and success were touchstones guaranteed to stir public interest. The races attracted a great following, so that for the first time the spectator fleet became a nuisance and even a hazard to the racers. Among the observers, too, were the first of the giant, million-dollar steam yachts which became perhaps the most ostentatious symbols of great wealth ever devised by man.

In the eyes of this avid audience the professional sailors who achieved the cup victories—men like Charley Barr, who captained three of them—became heroes. And even the frosty aristocrats of the N. Y. Y. C. who made up the syndicates and footed the bills earned a measure of public regard. One such was C. Oliver Iselin, who, having beaten Captain Hawkes in a sandbagger, went on to bigger things as manager of four of the five successful syndicates. A real favorite was the perennial challenger, Sir Thomas Lipton, who eventually became America's most-beloved loser. In fact, although there were touchy moments under the stress of competition, almost everyone connected with the races acquitted himself well, with the exception of Lord Dunraven, who was ungentlemanly and unsporting.

A participant who lent color and style to the show was Mrs. Iselin, the former Hope Goddard of Providence, who was a member of her husband's afterguard. Her role was a bold one, for the sportswoman was almost unknown at that time. At sea she took her station in the yacht's companionway and served as a timekeeper. She wore gloves and a heavy brown veil to shield her skin. In those days a sun tan was not at all chic. Her costume was demure: full skirts reaching to the deck. Ankles were not supposed to show, Mrs. Iselin recalled a few years ago, "but of course they did." Sailing at her side was Dandy, a dog who began a life at sea as mascot of *Defender* in 1895.

During that decade the first momentous occasion of a cup season came in the springtime at the Herreshoff yacht yard at Bristol, Rhode Island, when the new defender was launched: *Vigilant* in 1893, *Defender* in 1895, *Columbia* in 1899, *Constitution* in 1901 (she lost out to *Columbia* in the precup trial races), *Reliance* in 1903. The launchings were widely celebrated, Mrs. Iselin performing the christening rites with a champagne bottle wrapped in ribbons of red and black, the Iselin colors. The yachts were launched at eight in the evening, accompanied by muffled explosions as the press photographers made their own light with magnesium powder in flashpans. At the *Columbia* launching, one spectator was killed by exploding flash powder.

The season went on to fitting-out weeks, shakedown cruises, the New York Yacht Club cruise in midsummer, trial races thereafter, and finally the cup races themselves in the early fall. In tonnage, the 1903 club cruise resembled an armada. There were forty-eight steam yachts in the fleet, sixteen schooners over 100 feet in length, and twelve sloops, seven of which exceeded 90 feet. The cruise began at New London, went to Newport, then over to Martha's Vineyard, and back to Newport. In New London, Mrs. Iselin recalled, the hotel orchestra played until dawn, and in Newport there was a ball every night.

The cup yachts were huge sloops that grew larger almost every year. *Vigilant* was 124 feet long and *Columbia* 131. *Reliance* at 143 feet was more than twice the length of the 1881 winner, *Mischief,* and the longest America's Cup defender of all time. The reason for the increase in size lay in the New York Yacht Club rule of measurement.

In building a yacht, the three design factors that have a bearing on speed are the vessel's length, its sail area, and its displacement, meaning the size of the mass that must be driven through the water. The N. Y. Y. C. rule rated only two of these factors: the water-line length when the boat was on an even keel, and the sail area. The result-

ant rating was the basis for assigning handicaps—the number of seconds per mile a yacht would give or get when racing. As only two factors were taxed, the designers took all the liberties possible with the third one in an effort to build speed into the hull. They lowered displacement by cutting away the underbody of the hull and they extended the ends to give greater water-line length when the boat was heeled over by the wind. The result was a long, flat hull with a deep, thin keel, carrying a big chunk of lead ballast at its very end, and towering masts of steel to support tremendous sail plans.

These yachts—racing machines, really— were fast in smooth water but useless in any

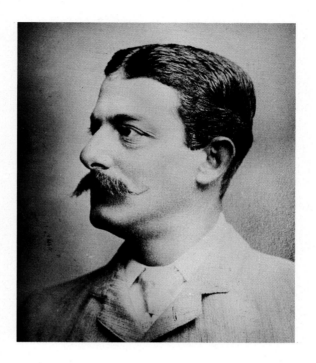

RELIANCE, *143 feet long, was the largest single-masted yacht ever built. She is shown going down a marine railway with the crew on deck ready to sail. This bronze racing machine was the work of Nathaniel G. Herreshoff, her designer and builder. It belonged to a N.Y.Y.C. syndicate whose manager was C. Oliver Iselin (above), a winner in four cup series.*

kind of a sea because the spars could not support their mass of canvas when a breeze came up. *Constitution* lost her first steel mast and the next one buckled. When members of the crew heard a snap or a groan aloft, they took cover, fearing that the yacht's rig was about to drop on them. With this kind of construction it was imperative that no cup races be sailed in heavy weather.

America, however, was not only successful at building these huge freaks but at racing them. No challenger was able to break the long string of American victories, although Lord Dunraven, in 1895, felt his defeat had not been achieved entirely on the water. It was a tense and unpleasant series, with each

race marred by incident or dispute. The dramatic finale came when Lord Dunraven withdrew *Valkyrie III* from the third and final race, and two months later, in a magazine article, charged that lead ballast had been added surreptitiously to *Defender* after she had been measured for the series. Iselin, who was in charge of *Defender,* wrote the New York Yacht Club: "I stand before the world solemnly charged by Lord Dunraven with an offense as base as could possibly be imputed to a sportsman and a gentleman, and which I indignantly resent and repel." An investigating committee found no basis for Lord Dunraven's charge and he was asked to resign his membership in the N. Y. Y. C.

When he failed to do so, he was expelled.

Then came Sir Thomas Lipton, whose sportsmanlike efforts "to lift the cup," as he put it, removed the bad taste of the Dunraven affair. Lipton's *Shamrocks* challenged in 1899, 1901, 1903, 1920, and 1930. Unlike Lord Dunraven, who concluded his cup efforts as a villain, Sir Thomas wound up a hero. After his final effort in 1930, the old man said publicly, "I cannot win, I cannot win." And, Ring Lardner wrote, "there was hardly a dry eye in any American speakeasy."

Lipton came from a poor Irish family and began life as a grocer's clerk. By ability and perseverence, he became a successful tea merchant and built up a world-wide business which was not hurt by publicity regarding his yachting efforts. Sir Thomas had owned large steam yachts before his first challenge, but knew nothing about sailing yachts or racing. His humble beginnings, his acquired fortune, his sportsmanship, and his graciousness over losing made him a sympathetic and popular figure in the United States. He enhanced the America's Cup.

Captain Barr kept the cup safely in the possession of the New York Yacht Club. He was the most famous professional captain of his time and he teamed well with Iselin, the wealthy sportsman who represented the owning syndicates and shouted Barr's orders to the professional crew through a megaphone. The aggressive Barr steered *Columbia* in 1899 and 1901, *Reliance* in 1903. The hull of *Reliance,* which cost her wealthy syndicate $175,000, was an immense flat platform of bronze with a fin keel attached. She was a "skimming dish," if not a scow. She carried the greatest mass of canvas ever seen on a single-masted vessel: 16,160 square feet of sail, which was four times the size of the ballroom in New York's Plaza Hotel.

The rules in 1903 still required that the challenger be sailed rather than shipped to America, but a compromise was made so that *Shamrock III* could be towed. She was, by

Lipton's steam yacht *Erin*. He also brought over *Shamrock I* to serve as a trial yacht. There were racing crews of forty-one men each for the two yachts, plus the group on *Erin* and a fourth crew on the tug that towed *Shamrock I*. It took a lot of tea to pay for their upkeep.

Lipton's efforts were in vain because *Reliance* beat the challenger easily in three straight races off Sandy Hook. *Reliance* was Nat Herreshoff's fifth successful America's Cup design.

Captain Nat excelled at the feats of engineering required to build and stress these giant yachts. Supporting the steel planking of the deck and hull was a complex inner basket of steel: deck beams, diagonal straps, floor beams, gussets, stringer plates, sheer strakes. And because the defenders were built in his own yard, Herreshoff saw that his designs were followed precisely.

Herreshoff's early successes had been with steam launches, but just one yacht made his reputation in sailboats. This was *Gloriana,* built for Edwin D. Morgan, a prominent New York Yacht Club member, in 1891. With this yacht, Herreshoff boldly changed the shape of the yacht hull. The forefoot below the water line was entirely cut away, the sweep from the stem to the keel being almost a straight line. This greatly reduced the displacement and shortened the water line. *Gloriana's* water-line length was 46 feet, but her over-all length was 67 feet because of her long forward and stern overhangs. When heeled in a breeze, the long ends gave her considerably more wetted surface and thus more speed. Her deep keel

drew 10 feet and that helped carry a big spread of sail—4,100 square feet. Furthermore, Herreshoff designed a spoon-shaped bow which was widely copied thereafter. Instead of the customary hollow, concave lines, Captain Nat drew full, convex ones which caused *Gloriana* to ride over the waves instead of pushing through them. The yacht was made of a light composite construction— steel framing and wood planking—that had been highly successful in his steam launches. Critics called *Gloriana* a masterpiece of original thought and designing skill, and after she won every start—nine straight races— during her first season, Captain Nat succeeded Edward Burgess as the naval architect most in demand by yachtsmen. Burgess had died of typhoid fever the year before at the

age of forty-six, never knowing that his latest 46-foot water-line yachts would be made obsolete by *Gloriana.*

Besides cup defenders, Herreshoff was called upon to design several classes of racing sloops, such as the Newport Thirty-sixes, Larchmont Thirty-fours, and the New York Seventies. There were four Seventies built at great expense in 1900 for men who could afford any whim: August Belmont, William K. Vanderbilt, Jr., Cornelius Vanderbilt III, and Herman Duryea and Harry Payne Whitney, who shared one. These were the largest sailing yachts ever built to a single design: 106 feet in over-all length, 70 feet on the water line. They incorporated the *Gloriana* principles, but Herreshoff built them rather lightly and after one season they had to be rebuilt at more expense. The owners had hoped they would get fast cruising yachts suitable for competition. Instead, the Seventies were outright racing machines requiring large crews and large bank accounts. By 1904, their owners had tired of them.

The experience of the Seventies, as well as the impracticality of such giant America's Cup yachts as *Reliance,* led the powers that be in the New York Yacht Club to seek a new rating rule. Herreshoff, with *Gloriana* and her successors, had exposed the deficiencies of the old rule which measured only water-line length and sail area. The yacht club wisely turned to the exploiter, Herreshoff, for help in writing a new rule. The result was the Universal Rule, adopted by the N.Y.Y.C. in 1903. This rule took into account displacement as well as length and sail area. The mathematical computations gave a premium to displacement and thus encouraged a sharper, fuller-bodied hull, instead of the fast freaks that had grown up under the old rule.

Herreshoff could design and build yachts to any rule, expensive ones or cheap ones, large ones or small ones. His New York Thirties of 1905, 43 feet in over-all length, cost $4,000. His New York Fifties of 1913, 72 feet over-all, cost a mere $17,000 and required a professional crew of only four—a captain, two sailors, and a steward—which was truly Spartan for that era.

However, Herreshoff's last cup defender, *Resolute*, built for Lipton's 1914 challenge, was neither inexpensive nor small, with an over-all length of 106 feet, 3 inches. The beginning of World War I in Europe that summer forced the postponement of that series until 1920, when *Resolute* defeated *Shamrock IV*. Significantly, both yachts were skippered by amateurs for the first time in America's Cup history—Sir William Burton aboard *Shamrock IV* and Charles Francis Adams on *Resolute*.

It also was the last time the cup yachts sailed on a handicap basis, with one giving the other a time allowance. Sir Thomas' final challenge, in 1930, was sailed by boats built to the J class of the Universal Rule, which listed rating limits alphabetically. Yachts whose ratings fell within certain limits belonged to a class designated by a letter, and the closer the letter to the beginning of the alphabet, the larger the class. An M boat, for example, was about 80 feet in over-all length, a J from 119 to 135 feet. It was customary for yachts within a class to race boat for boat, without handicaps.

There were three America's Cup series involving the giant J boats, with Harold S. Vanderbilt defending on each occasion. He sailed *Enterprise* to victory over Sir Thomas' *Shamrock V* in 1930, *Rainbow* over T.O.M. Sopwith's *Endeavour I* in 1934, and *Ranger* over *Endeavour II* in 1937. The three triumphs established "Mike" Vanderbilt as one of the most talented racing skippers in yachting annals. A great-grandson of the old Commodore, "Mike" was a man of keen intelligence, endless patience, and driving force, all of which were clearly demonstrated in his conduct of the three series. In 1930 and 1934 it took particular effort to beat out *Weetamoe* and *Yankee* in the trials and to

"There is many a slip 'twixt the CUP and the LIP(ton)," jibed JUDGE *in 1901 cartoon on Sir Thomas' second loss. Below: Captain Nat Herreshoff, a little man, was a giant among designers. Bottom: His New York Fifties, shown off Larchmont in 1913, were a departure—inexpensive to build and requiring minimal paid crew.*

The spectacular J boats continued America's Cup yachting on a grand scale. Above: RAINBOW of 1934 was not as swift as challenger, ENDEAVOUR I, but she won anyway because of the skills of skipper Harold S. Vanderbilt. Opposite: Vanderbilt (with pipe) and J-boat designer Starling Burgess. Entire 1937 defense, which included building of RANGER (top), was financed by Vanderbilt. With him at helm, RANGER trounced T.O.M. Sopwith's ENDEAVOUR II, 4-0. Some believe RANGER was the fastest sailing yacht of all time.

be selected as the cup defender. In 1934 it also was generally acknowledged that *Endeavour I* was a faster boat than *Rainbow,* and that only Vanderbilt's superlative sailing skill made the four-to-two victory possible.

Enterprise and *Rainbow* were the creation of W. Starling Burgess. *Ranger,* in 1937, was a combined effort of Burgess and the up-and-coming Olin Stephens. Her hull form was tested in water tanks at Stevens Institute of Technology, and she emerged as the swiftest J boat of all time. *Endeavour II* took some of the worst boat-for-boat beatings the series had ever seen.

Being first had long been a Vanderbilt family trait. Apart from his cup triumphs, Harold Vanderbilt was the source and fountainhead of contract bridge, having developed the game in 1925. And it was his father, William K. Vanderbilt, Sr., who acquired what was said to be the first million-dollar yacht—*Valiant.* She was built in Scotland in 1893 by Laird Brothers and was steam powered with a gross tonnage of 1,823. Imitators came thick and fast, the most prominent ones being J. Pierpont Morgan's *Corsair* (1899) 1,136 tons; James Gordon Bennett's *Lysistrata* (1900) 1,942 tons, and Anthony J. Drexel's *Margarita* (1900) 1,780 tons.

Drexel, a Morgan partner in organizing the lucrative steel-industry combines, had a crew of seventy-three for *Margarita,* and his own frank appraisal was that only three other men in the world were rich enough to maintain this miniature ocean liner. Drexel later owned *Sayonara,* which had carpeting at $15 a square yard and a rose garden installed on an afterdeck. The sea air killed the plants, however, so Drexel ordered roses of imitation India rubber to decorate the trellis. It was an equally poor idea. The coloring washed all over the deck.

A contemporary of Drexel's housed a live cow on the afterdeck of *Flying Cloud* for a voyage to Mediterranean ports where milk supplies were questionable. The cow attracted flies, which reduced the milk output, so the owner rewarded the members of the crew with one cent for every dead fly they produced. The cow thereafter had a most enjoyable cruise.

What one rich man did often inspired another. Morton F. Plant of New London sold his interests in railroads and steamships for many millions and spent much of the money on all kinds of boats, from gasoline launches to steam yachts. And while commodore of the Larchmont Yacht Club in 1904, he wished to do something of note, so he had Nat Herreshoff build *Ingomar*, a 126-foot steel schooner, and he hired Charley Barr to race her. Barr took *Ingomar* to Germany and won twelve out of twenty-two races. He said he would have won more, but the Germans did not respect the right-of-way rules. They gave him room after Barr hit one of their yachts.

Five years later, Barr was in the employ of another wealthy yachtsman, Alexander S. Cochran. Barr reminisced so fondly about his days abroad with *Ingomar* that Cochran decided to undertake a similar venture. He had built at the Herreshoff yard a 136-foot steel schooner, *Westward,* and under Barr's command she had a spectacular winning record in Germany and England during the summer of 1910.

Plant in turn admired *Westward* and had Herreshoff build him a duplicate, *Elena.* Not to be outdone, Cochran in 1913 ordered two yachts from the designs of William Gardner. One was *Sea Call,* a three-masted schooner, the other *Vanitie,* an unsuccessful America's Cup contender. The George Lawley yard in Boston built both. *Sea Call's* hull was made of plated Monel metal, *Vanitie's* of manganese bronze.

Cochran spent a fortune on these yachts,

*Opposite: An impressive gold-plater
was* HI-ESMARO, *267 feet long, built by the Bath
Iron Works in 1929 for H. E. Manville.
Below: Upward view of* SEA CLOUD'S *rigging.*

but he was disappointed with *Sea Call*. The schooner's Monel plating was supposed to do away with the necessity of painting her, but when she showed slight signs of corrosion forward, Cochran ordered her scrapped. Someone offered to buy her at double her scrap value, but Cochran refused. He blamed Gardner for the corrosion, and although it could have been easily remedied, he destroyed the yacht as a way of injuring the designer's reputation.

Following World War I, the wartime luxury tax on the over-all length of yachts was lifted and diesel power came to replace steam at a great saving of space and weight. No longer would the wealthy have to suffer the limited deck space, the cramped quarters, and the soot of the smoky coal burners. A new diesel yacht became a status symbol and the larger the vessel the more satisfactory the status. A kind of competition arose in the 1920's and early 1930's. A listing of America's largest yachts in 1931 found Julius Fleischmann's *Camargo,* for instance, way down in twenty-fifth place. *Camargo's* length was a mere 225 feet.

The champion yacht builder of all was Mrs. Emily Roebling Cadwalader of Philadelphia, granddaughter of the man who built New York's Brooklyn Bridge and an heiress of the Roebling family fortune. The names of her yachts were *Savarona I, II,* and *III*. *Savarona I* was a modest 174 feet long. *Savarona II,* delivered in 1928 at a cost of $2,000,000, was 294 feet long and carried a crew of forty-one. Annual upkeep? About $200,000. There were accommodations for seventeen guests. The bathrooms, done in black Italian marble, had gold fixtures. Mrs. E. T. Stotesbury, a friend, explained that gold was economical for fixtures. "You don't have to polish it."

Mrs. Cadwalader enjoyed entertaining guests by having the yacht's gyrostabilizer turned on when in a quiet harbor. This device, found on ocean liners to minimize the roll in rough water, had the opposite effect in calm waters. It rocked the big yacht.

Mrs. Cadwalader soon found *Savarona II* outbuilt by such yachts as Julius Forstmann's *Orion*. Forstmann, a woolen manufacturer who had come to America as an emigrant from Germany in 1909, wanted to show how well he had made out, so he had the German builder, Krupp, turn out *Orion*—all 333 feet of her. *Savarona II* was sold to a copper king, William Boyce Thompson, in 1929 for $1,800,000. A good price, and Mrs. Cadwalader gave an order to William F. Gibbs, one of the nation's leading big-yacht designers, for *Savarona III*. She was built in Germany, was 407 feet long, and cost $4,000,000. She could cruise 6,000 miles at eighteen knots and had a crew of eighty-three. She was the largest American yacht ever built. Mrs. Cadwalader had *Savarona III* in commission for only two seasons, and never in America to avoid duty taxes. In 1938, she sold the yacht to the Turkish government for $1,000,000. The vessel then was presented to the country's leader, Kemal Ataturk, as a gift from the people.

Among Mrs. Cadwalader's prominent competitors was J. P. Morgan whose *Corsair,* completed in 1930, was 343 feet long. She had a crew of fifty-five and her captain, William Porter, was reputed to be the highest paid seaman in the world. *Corsair's* maiden voyage took her from Glen Cove, Long Island, to Cowes in seven days, seven hours, at a speed of eighteen and five-tenths knots. The Morgan family debarked there and Porter took her back to Glen Cove.

Vincent Astor's *Nourmahal* was a bargain vessel, a 263-footer which cost only $600,000. Its predecessor of the same name had been equipped with machine guns to guard against pirates in Mediterranean and Caribbean waters. The new *Nourmahal,* built in 1928, became well-known because Franklin Delano Roosevelt was often a guest aboard her in the early years of his presidency. On one occasion in 1935, he told Astor that the short cruise would hardly justify putting the yacht in commission. Astor replied somewhat testily that *his* yacht was always in commission. Roosevelt quipped, "I guess we'll have to increase the taxes on the rich." Astor did not find the remark funny.

Henry Ford had a yacht, *Sialia,* a 202-footer for Great Lakes cruising. The owner did not think she was big enough so he had her cut in half and added a twenty-one-foot midsection. The bill was $650,000, which exceeded the original cost by $50,000 and Ford's eventual sale price by $400,000.

George F. Baker, Jr., chairman of New York's First National Bank, built *Viking,* 272 feet long, at a cost of $1,500,000. His eighty-eight-year-old father, who had made millions as a Morgan banking partner in railroads, liked to save his money. When *Viking* was launched, Baker, Senior, explained, "My son can afford it. He has a rich father."

William K. Vanderbilt, Jr., at one point had two large yachts, the 211-foot *Ara,* on which he had cruised more than 150,000 miles, and the new *Alva,* 264 feet. *Alva* was built abroad and when Vanderbilt registered her in the United States, he had to pay $267,000 in customs levies. David Rockefeller, as a youth, was asked why his family did not own yachts. He replied, "Who do you think we are? Vanderbilts?"

The stock-market collapse of 1929 did not have an immediate impact on the big yachts, but the depression and the resulting changes in American economic life eventually wiped them out. An early concession to the times was made by J. P. Morgan in 1930. The usual ostentatious launching of a new yacht—in this case his new *Corsair*—would be in bad taste, he decided. So the public was excluded when she slid down the ways at the Bath Iron Works, at Bath, Maine. A tug boat was provided, however, for the press.

Edward F. Hutton, an investment broker and the husband of the General Foods heiress Marjorie Post, reasoned that it was fitting for yachtsmen to keep their large vessels in commission, because the upkeep expenditures of $100,000 or more each year would help the economy. Hutton went ahead with the launching of *Hussar* in 1931 in Germany. This was the most spectacular of all the big yachts, 316 feet long and rigged as a four-masted bark with thirty towering square sails measuring 30,000 square feet.

Following her divorce from Hutton and marriage to Joseph P. Davies, Marjorie renamed the yacht *Sea Cloud* and kept it in commission for many years. She helped the economy.

Sea Cloud carried a crew of seventy-two to work all those sails, and the monthly payroll amounted to $20,000. Mrs. Davies liked to have her crew change uniforms twice each year and she spent an additional $20,000 on that item. The yacht's annual expenditures came to something over $200,000, which

seemed reasonable for a vessel that had cost $900,000 to build, even at depression prices. *Sea Cloud* had everything. A wag claimed that even the lifeboats had lifeboats.

Gradually, however, as the depression deepened, the big yachts were decommissioned, one after another. Even Morgan, who did not make enough money to pay an income tax in 1931 or 1932, was forced to lay up *Corsair*.

In another few years there was war. The armed services were willing to pay fair prices for laid-up yachts, and many a floating palace went on active duty, never to return to civilian life. Morgan gave *Corsair* to the British navy in 1940. Baker's *Viking* joined the United States Navy and went down with all hands when rammed by a tanker in 1943. *Orion* also went to the navy, *Nourmahal* to the Coast Guard.

Sea Cloud escaped military service, but was sold after the war to one of the few people who could afford her—Rafael Trujillo, the dictator of the Dominican Republic. *Corsair* became a cruise ship after the war, first around Trinidad and then on the West Coast. She was wrecked outside the harbor of Acapulco, Mexico, in 1948. Her remains were visible there for many years afterward.

In a way it was sad to see them go, although life on their afterdecks was often dull. Owners like William K. Vanderbilt, Jr., who spent more time at sea than on a mooring, were the exceptions. Desirable guests who had the time to spare for extended cruises were hard to come by. And there often were crew troubles such as those experienced in 1928 by William P. Bell, president of the American Cyanamid Company. In 1926 he had bought Morton Plant's 136-foot schooner *Elena,* which had been out of competition for ten years. When the ocean race to Spain came up in 1928, he entered. He hired Charley Barr's brother John as captain and en-

listed a paid crew of forty-five, following the customs of the past. The afterguard were passengers coming along to enjoy the race, but not to work the boat. These were the owner; his wife; his young daughter, Helen; her friend, Marion Walters, and two dogs, Nip and Tuck.

On the eve of the race, sixteen of the crew struck for higher wages, asking double the agreed bonus of $75 starting money and $75 additional if *Elena* won the race. The sailors were dismissed and substitutes found overnight—substitutes who knew little about sailing. They went through the race being told to "pick up that" and "pull this."

The second steward got drunk before serving dinner the night of the strike. He, too, was dismissed. Once the boat was under way, the dogs became seasick, but not the passengers, who feasted royally on such delicacies as squab, duck, alligator pears, caviar, paté de foie gras, and one hundred bottles of ginger ale. Meanwhile, the thirty-eight sailors of the two watches were sharing nineteen bunks forward and being fed for eighty-seven cents per man per day.

Yachting has never been that way again. There were two fleets in that race to Spain in 1928, one consisting of large yachts, such as *Elena* and *Atlantic,* manned almost entirely by professional crews. The other included four small yachts, all below 60 feet in length and carrying only one paid hand apiece—a cook. The big yachts were closing out the past, while the small ones were setting standards for the future.

Elena won the King's Cup and Bell sailed her to Cowes that summer, where he left her. She was never in commission again and slowly deteriorated, being broken up for scrap during World War II. *Niña,* victorious among the small yachts for the Queen of Spain's Cup, was still active and winning races thirty-six years later.

REVOLUTION
ON
TWO
FRONTS
—
8

REVOLUTION
ON
TWO
FRONTS

---

*"Pop" Corry's Star
boats introduce
one-design
classes, and the
music of
Ole Evinrude's
outboards
attracts a new
crowd of yachtsmen.*

*Preceding pages: Pacesetters, 1924. Skiff
with outboard tows Star-class sailboat. Above: 1909
Evinrude cost only $1 per pound.*

The year? It must have been around 1905. "Pop" Corry did not remember exactly. The race was to be a free-for-all. No rules applied other than right of way. "That meant you didn't have to go around any government buoys. You could cut corners as you pleased," said Corry. "The first boat in was to be the winner."

The race was for Swampscott dories and other small centerboard boats, and the course ran from Cow Bay (now Manhasset Bay on Long Island) out to Long Island Sound and to a finish within Hempstead harbor, the next bay to the east.

The starting cannon fired and one of the boats that crossed the starting line suddenly turned and sailed back to shore. The boat was beached and the mast was struck. The crew jumped overboard, picked up the craft and hauled it to a waiting farm wagon. They hoisted it aboard, made it secure, and urged the horses onward. Passing through the village of Port Washington, the voyagers enlisted a four-piece German band which was playing in front of a saloon. Overland, Hempstead harbor was only a short distance away. The farm wagon went down to the shore, the boat was launched, the mast stepped, and the four bandsmen taken on board. The vessel was so crowded that it almost sank, but the wind was light and the finish line was only a short distance offshore. With the band playing, *There'll Be a Hot Time in the Old Town Tonight,* the boat completed the race, winning handily.

"Having complied with all the conditions of the race, the triumphal procession started home with the cup before the first sail was sighted in the mouth of Hempstead harbor," said Commodore George A. Corry, as he told the story to his friend and biographer, George W. Elder, many years later. The boats involved in the free-for-all cost about $50 apiece and the race demonstrated that small, cheap craft could be as much fun as huge, expensive ones.

Corry had a lot of fun on and off the water in a long lifetime associated with boats. He left his mark, too. He was the founder of the Star class which, if it was not the first one-design class of sailboats, certainly became the most significant and most imitated. At the instigation of Corry and his friends around Port Washington, a man named Francis Sweisguth drew the lines for the Star in 1911, generally copying and enlarging on the Bug, a little sloop introduced in 1907. Sweisguth was a designer in the naval architecture firm of William Gardner, and although Sweisguth's name is not associated with any other notable yachting designs, he did nobly with the Star.

The hull was 22 feet, 7½ inches long and its characteristics were a low freeboard, hard chines, a slightly rounded bottom, and a thin fin keel with a cast-iron bulb at the base weighing from 860 to 900 pounds. The hull is the same to this day, and Stars are raced all over the world in greater numbers than ever before. Other dimensions are a beam of 5 feet, 8¼ inches (4 foot, 6 at the chine), and a draft of 3 feet, 4 inches.

The rigging has been modernized twice. Originally, Stars had a gaff mainsail. This was changed in 1915 to a short Marconi rig, eliminating the gaff, and in 1930 to a taller Marconi rig. The boom overhanging the stern was cut down, and the rig brought entirely inboard. Two hundred and eighty square feet of sail is now supported on a slender wood mast stayed with the lightest stainless-steel wire. The Star has a tiny cockpit for the helmsman and single crew. In heavy weather it is a wet boat, and it has never been anything except a racing machine.

But what a racing machine! It became universally popular with serious sailors because of its fascinating sensitivity and delicate bal-

ance. Its advocates soon discovered that the boat would almost sail itself, requiring only finger-tip pressure on the tiller. And it could handle a sea. Many Star races have been held on ocean waters.

For the first few years, the Star was confined to waters around New York City, Corry winning most of the races on Long Island Sound and Gravesend Bay. Pop was an individualist with strong opinions. He stood on his head for five minutes every evening, claiming that the brain needed the added blood circulation, and he ate a tablespoonful of Vaseline every day for his digestion. He also could take a joke: One day in Larchmont harbor he heaved an anchor overboard with his foot in the center of the anchor-rope coil. The sinking anchor took

him overboard, and after a while Corry thought it was pretty funny, too.

He may have been right about the Vaseline and the headstands. Corry raced in Star regattas until he was well into his seventies. His boat, *Little Dipper,* was battle scarred, the sails patched and baggy. But out he came, weekend after weekend, sailing from Port Washington to the starting lines off Execution Rock in Long Island Sound. After Corry died, *Little Dipper* stood on a cement block like a statue in the Manhasset Bay Yacht Club's parking lot until it disintegrated.

As commodore of the Star class, Corry had the executive's good sense to delegate. His friend George Elder was the class secretary and its promoter, effectively describing the Star as a "poor man's racing yacht."

Early Star-class regatta on Long Island Sound included the first boat, No. 1. Note the original gaff rigs. Commodore George A. Corry (above, left), the class founder, and George Elder, its promoter, in 1930.

(Early Stars cost only $250. By 1960 the price was $3,000.)

The Star Class Association of America was founded one night in 1915 at Mouquins restaurant in New York City, and that meeting marked the beginning of intersectional yachting. Corry, carried away with what he had wrought, called up the commodore of the California Yacht Club on the new, transcontinental telephone and challenged the Californians to build some Stars, come east, and race. They ignored him.

Between 1911 and 1922, 111 Stars were built and raced on the sound, Narragansett Bay, Lake Erie, the Detroit River, and, for the first time in 1922, on the West Coast at Los Angeles. The class organization had been perfected largely by Elder. The boats

were divided into local fleets. A measurement rule was written. A monthly magazine and a yearbook were published. And the class provided its own organization in running regattas, taking over from yacht clubs which up to that time had never had to cope with running races for dozens of evenly matched yachts.

The first national championship between winners of local fleet eliminations was held in 1922, and Stars became international with the establishment of a fleet at Vancouver, British Columbia, in 1923. Soon there were fleets at Havana, Cuba; New Zealand; Pearl Harbor, Hawaii; England's Solent, and Cannes, France. By 1931, Stars were also racing in Venezuela, Algeria, Germany, the Scandinavian countries, Switzerland, Spain, Portugal, and Italy.

The principle of one design had been known since the 1890's, but now it aroused interest and was given support. Yachtsmen began to agree that racing was more competitive if it matched crews and skippers in boats exactly alike, rather than opposing designers' notions and owners' bank accounts in boats that had different characteristics and different speeds. Sailboats all of one design cost less because many could be built at once. They did not become obsolete like open-class yachts that might be outbuilt within a year. A one-design class organization made possible more and better-run races among participants from different geographic locations. Finally, the one-design

principle did away with disputed systems of handicapping boats to obtain fair competition for prizes.

A summer resort town in Maine—North Haven—was where one-design yachting began, and in a very modest way. Dr. Charles G. Weld of Boston drew lines for a 14½-foot open dinghy in 1884 and a local North Haven carpenter built two of them.

The cost was probably no more than $20 per boat. More were built and the first race was held in 1887. In 1957, a fleet of twenty-seven North Haven dinghies raced in the seventieth anniversary regatta. The class survived because it was kept strictly one-design —no gadgety fittings, revolving masts, adding of ballast, or rule beating of any kind.

One-design classes multiplied after 1900. Even the wealthy yachtsmen came to see that they made sense. Rich and famous yachtsmen like Cornelius Vanderbilt, E. D. Morgan, Harry Payne Whitney, W. S. Gould, and

James A. Stillman owned Newport Thirties, sloops 30 feet long on the water line and 42 feet over-all. Nat Herreshoff designed these boats and also the New York Thirties, which were 43 feet over-all. The New York Yacht Club promoted this "small" class because many members believed there was a need for a less expensive yacht. The first order, placed with Herreshoff in February, 1905, was for eighteen boats, and they were raced hard and often that season, the club running fifty-one events for them.

The New York Thirty was the smallest boat a N. Y. Y. C. member could own to be eligible to vote on club business. There is a story about a member who had sold his much larger vessel and temporarily found himself without a yacht to his name. But he wanted to vote at the annual meeting. A friend suggested that an inactive New York Thirty might be purchased for a pittance. The member bought one, sight unseen, only to find out

later that it was a derelict in a shipyard and incapable of floating. His friends never let him forget it.

The New York Thirty could not have been one of Nat Herreshoff's better conceptions. The boat was wet, narrow, and uncomfortable, with a tiny cockpit and a long tiller that got in the way. The cabin accommodations were best suited for midgets. But the design was successful and some Thirties lasted for fifty years.

The Barnegat Bay Sneakbox was an early one-design class. It evolved from the early nineteenth-century Sneakboxes used for shallow-water gunning by duck hunters. The name probably came from the term "sink

Opposite: A pair of Stars beat to windward. Their rig is early Marconi with a long boom. Below: New York Thirties were successful racers for more than forty years. Herreshoff designed them in 1905.

Top left: Long skirts to leeward, 1895. Top right: Skirts were not so long on 1925 bathing queen. The boat is a sailing canoe. Left: Early canoeists stayed upright on the hiking board. Right: Hiking had become more acrobatic by 1940. Below: Women eventually were allowed to sail. All-girl crews are third and last in 1904 race among Herreshoff 15's at Beverly, Mass.

box," meaning a floating duckblind which, when camouflaged with marsh grass, could be used to "sneak up" on unwary ducks. J. Howard Perrine produced a formal design in the early 1900's, a 15-foot, gaff-rigged centerboard sloop that weighed only 350 pounds and could sail in as little as six inches of water. In subsequent years over 3,000 boats of this type were sold, but no national association was ever formed to promote them. The successor boat, the 14-foot 8-Ball Sneakbox, is a modern one-design class on New Jersey's Barnegat Bay.

The American Canoe Association, founded in 1880, established rules for decked sailing canoes and some uniformity of design. In the early 1890's, a man named Paul Butler developed some features for canoes, which later became standard on many small one-design sailboats. He invented the thwartship sliding seat for hiking, so that the weight of the helmsman could serve as stabilizing ballast when projected outboard of the hull. He put a crosshead extension on the tiller so the boat could be steered at the windward end of the hiking seat. He developed an "automatic" jam cleat that eliminated the slower and somewhat clumsy technique of tying half-hitch knots to secure sheets. And he made the cockpits self-bailing, so that water taken inboard ran out of the boat.

Nat Herreshoff, who could produce an excellent design for any type of vessel, drew the lines and built the Herreshoff Twelves, fat little gaff-rigged sloops that came out in 1914 as a one-design class. They were 15 feet, 8½ inches long (12 feet on the water line). The Twelves became popular on Buzzards Bay. Their modern successor is known as the Bull's Eye class, and it carries on as a $2,000 fiberglass boat.

Another early class boat that still survives is the Wianno Senior, a 25-foot, gaff-rigged sloop. The Crosby Boatbuilding Company at Osterville built the first one in 1914 and all the successor boats; the total had reached 116 in 1962. Some sixty are still being sailed and raced on southern Massachusetts waters, and in 1962 the very first boat was still active in the hands of its original owner, James G. Hinkle, of the Wianno Yacht Club. *Victura* of Hyannisport, Massachusetts, belongs to the Kennedy family and it was sailed often, but not raced, by the late President Kennedy.

Who won the first race among one-design boats? It was a girl, Miss Ellen Hayward, and she was ahead of her time. The race was held in Maine in 1887 among the North Haven dinghies. Accounts indicate that two of the leaders in the race, one of whom was the class designer, Dr. Weld, became embroiled in a personal luffing match. Miss Hayward, sticking to her knitting, sailed through the leaders and won. The name of her boat, borrowed from Alfred Bowditch, was *Guffin*.

Pop Corry, ever an individualist, opposed the Victorian philosophy that a woman's place was in the home, or at best on the piazza of the yacht club. He installed Mrs. Corry on his boats as his crew, first aboard his Bug-class sloop, later on his Star. They were among the first husband-and-wife yachting teams in the United States and forerunners of many others, notably in the Star class. By 1924, there was a sufficient number of women skippering small boats in the area of Massachusetts Bay to inspire an intraclub race. This was the Hodder Cup affair begun by the Boston Yacht Club. Within a few years the competition was nationwide, the prize was called the Mrs. Charles Francis Adams Trophy. It became symbolic of the women's national sailing championship.

The development of small, inexpensive sailboats also brought many more youngsters to the sport. Although the *America* had a thirteen-year-old cabin boy, George Steers II, in her complement, there had been no organized effort to encourage juniors who liked to sail. Commodore Herbert Sears of the Eastern Yacht Club made a notable move in 1922 when he offered a prize for a regatta among boys fifteen to eighteen whose parents belonged to Massachusetts yacht clubs. This trophy, the Sears Bowl, in 1930 became a national award for the United States junior championship. Today girls may also compete for it, as skippers or crew.

The organization of junior programs is a good example of the growing importance of yacht clubs to the sport. By the 1920's, there were hundreds of yacht clubs, most of them operating independently and occasionally bending the sport's rules to suit local whims. The North American Yacht Racing Union was founded in 1925 as a national organization of clubs and their regional associations, such as the Yacht Racing Association of Long Island Sound and the Inter-Lake Yachting Association of Lake Erie. The N.A.Y.R.U. hoped to encourage the sport and maintain some standards for it. In the latter role, the N.A.Y.R.U. became a substitute for the New York Yacht Club, which had been the source and arbiter of the racing rules for seventy years.

These rules were first drawn up by the New York Yacht Club in the 1850's. They were copied largely from the British and revised from time to time by club committees. This made sense because only the New York club conducted regattas at the start. In 1906 the club members saw fit to ask the opinions of others, and a conference on rules was held, delegates from a selected list of other eastern clubs were invited. Fifteen years later yacht races were being held all over the country and it made no sense for the New York Yacht Club to dominate the sport. With that club's blessing, the North American

Yacht Racing Union was created. All the yacht clubs that joined were grouped into regional associations. Rules likewise became the province of the N.A.Y.R.U., which in turn sanctioned delegates to the International Yacht Racing Union, long dominated by the British. And the Sears and Adams cup competitions came under the N.A.Y.R.U.'s jurisdiction.

Out of the N.A.Y.R.U. also came a U.S. Olympic yachting organization. Participation in yachting events of the Olympic games began in 1928 at Amsterdam. The classes there were eight meter, six meter, and monotype, a heat sailed by a single participant. The Stars joined the Olympics in 1932.

The success of the Star has inspired other one-design classes in the years since 1911. In 1921, the Cape Cod Shipbuilding Company of Wareham, Massachusetts, began producing an 18-foot, centerboard sloop called the Cape Cod Baby Knockabout. It was designed by the founder of the company, Charles Gurney, and it proved to be a good performer and a safe one. The Knockabouts were almost impossible to tip over. When a gust hit, they would heel far enough to spill the wind out of the sails, then come up again and head into the wind. Small rudders helped. They came out of the water when the boat heeled over, so that it naturally headed up to wind. The materials were excellent. The hull was framed of white oak and planked in white cedar. Nothing was fancy about these sloops, not even the price. The company turned them out by the hundreds, the price at one point going as low as $175. And

Top: Cape Cod Knockabout, a safe sensible 18-footer. Below: Comets were called baby Stars because of similarity. Right: Early Snipe. Thousands were home built at $200 or so. Bottom: Jam at the mark during an international Snipe regatta among world's champions in 1961.

if the purchaser wished to sail down Buzzards Bay from the factory, he was given a "sail-away" box lunch, gratis.

The most popular one-design class of all, the Snipe, appeared in 1931 and boat number 14,700 was built in 1963. The beginning came at a meeting of the West Coast Racing Association at Sarasota, Florida, in March, 1931. The delegates decided the time had come to introduce a small boat which could be trailered about the state much the same as outboard racing hulls were. William F. Crosby, of *Rudder* magazine, was present and he promised to deliver such a design. In the July issue of the magazine the plans appeared and the boat was called the Snipe in keeping with *Rudder's* policy of naming all boats it introduced after sea birds. Crosby received credit for the design and the issue in which it appeared was soon out of print.

A fourteen-year-old boy named Jimmy Brown, of Pass Christian, Mississippi, built the first Snipe with the help of his father and was given Number 1. The Snipe was intended to be home built for under $100. It is 15½ feet long with a centerboard, weighs 440 pounds, and has a sail area of 116 square feet in a sloop rig. When racing, it is sailed by two people. The Snipe design spread rapidly, and by 1963 there were more than 500 fleets in thirty nations. Snipes have been sailed in some odd places. Ted Wells, one of the early champions of the class, learned his yachting in a Snipe at Wichita, Kansas, on a man-made pond whose purpose was to provide water for the Santa Fe railroad's steam engines.

The Comet class began the year after the Snipes, in 1932. C. Lowndes Johnson of Easton, Maryland, was asked by Mrs. Elliott Wheeler to design a small sailboat for her sons, one that would be inexpensive, easy to handle, and competitive enough for the handicap races at nearby Oxford. Ralph Wiley built the first one in Oxford for $120.

Yachting magazine published the plans and Dr. John Eiman and Dr. Wilbur Haines introduced the boat to their summer resort, Stone Harbor, New Jersey. They also founded the national class organization and helped promote the popularity of Comets, increasing their number into the thousands.

The Comet is a small Star (except that it has a centerboard instead of a keel) and was called in its early days the Star Junior. Its over-all length is 16 feet, sail area 130 square feet, weight not less than 300 pounds.

Sailing in Knockabouts, Stars, Snipes, Comets, and other one-design classes became very popular in the early 1930's, and many a boatowner wished that the season could be extended beyond the traditional closing date in the fall. It was several such die-hards, gathered in the men's bar of the Larchmont Yacht Club on a hot July afternoon, who planted the seeds of the first frostbite regatta. One yachtsman challenged another to a race in sailing dinghies on New Year's Day and was accepted. As the months passed and word of the event went around, others clamored to be let in. They were. The first regatta took place on January 2, 1932, off the Knickerbocker Yacht Club in Manhasset Bay. No one drowned. No one froze.

William H. Taylor, who was then the yachting editor of the New York *Herald Tribune*, raced his Ratsey dinghy that day and realized what a good idea the event was. He enlisted a fellow worker, James Robbins, the yachting editor of the New York *Times*, and with the promotional force of those two newspapermen winter dinghy racing soon became a regular affair on the north shore of Long Island. Publication of the racing results in the *Herald Tribune* and the *Times* did nothing to discourage the undertaking. The participants were soon the subject of many feature stories in newspapers and magazines. The theme was always the same:

How crazy can people be to go sailing in the wintertime? Frostbiters they were called, and the Frostbite Yacht Club was soon founded. Its burgee shows a polar bear sitting on a cake of ice.

In later years, under pressure, Taylor and Robbins confessed to a selfish motive. True, they were altruistic in promoting a pleasant activity, but they were also looking for something to write about in the winter in order to avoid onerous chores, such as covering basketball games.

In time, special dinghies were designed to put frostbiting on a one-design basis, and the sailors found the weather to be no handicap provided they dressed sensibly—that is, if they came prepared for rain, sleet, or snow. Cancellations due to weather were few.

A development that paralleled the growth of small-boat sailing—and one that eventually would dwarf it—was the gasoline outboard motor. Once it had arrived, the pleasures of boating were no longer the aristocrats' exclusive privilege, but available to everyone. Two worlds of boating now existed: sail and power. The sailors belonged to yacht clubs, the outboarders to the cult of the spark plug and the shear pin. They were destined never to have much to do with one another, on or off the water.

The first practical outboard motor, a purely American conception, came on the scene in 1903. Its birthplace was an unlikely one—a student's room in a boardinghouse in New Haven, Connecticut. The student was Cameron B. Waterman of Detroit, then aged twenty-six and attending Yale Law School. "I had an air-cooled bicycle engine that I was cleaning in my room," Waterman recalled fifty-three years later. "I clamped it on the back of a chair and started it for a test. Suddenly the thought struck me, 'If it runs on a chair, why not on a boat transom turning a propeller?'"

It beat rowing. A Waterman outboard motor takes a pair of fishermen across a lake. A gas tank was welded on top of the motor. The manufacturer claimed a gallon would last four hours. The Waterman weighed 40 pounds, put out two horsepower, cost $75. Sales were slow, never topped 3,000 in any year.

159

Waterman took the thought back to Detroit and in 1905 the first engines were offered to the public. They were cumbersome and heavy, but they did work and had the marvelous outboard advantage of being portable. You could take them off the boat for repair, storage, or transport.

Were the Waterman motors immediately popular? "No, not at all," Waterman explained. "I guess people thought they were a freak, because in our top year we sold only 3,000, at $75 apiece."

A 1909 copy of *Motor Boating* magazine carried the following advertisement: "Make a motorboat of any boat in five minutes. Here's a little 2 horsepower marine motor (40 pounds complete) that you can attach to the stern post of your boat in five minutes without any tools. Drives an 18-foot rowboat 7 miles per hour (runs four hours on one gallon of gasoline). Can be detached from boat just as quickly and stored in box in which it is carried. Simplest motor made, does not get out of order. Money back guarantee. Write for full description and price. Waterman Marine Motor Company, 1520 Fort Street, Detroit, Mich."

In 1916, Cameron Waterman sold his outboard engine interests to the Arrow Motor and Marine Company of New York, which in turn went out of business in 1924.

The man who popularized the outboard and founded a company that made millionaires of his heirs was Ole Evinrude, a second-generation Norwegian toolmaker from Wisconsin. Evinrude, who had a natural aptitude for mechanics, built his first boat in his father's barn at Cambridge, Wisconsin. The father discovered the boat and took an axe to it. Boats, he thought, were frivolous toys. Ole built his next boat in secrecy in the woods.

As a young man in Milwaukee, Evinrude manufactured four-cylinder, air-cooled automobile engines, but went bankrupt. One hot day in 1908, Evinrude, his girl friend Bess Cary, and some friends went on a picnic. What happened has become a part of American folklore. The site of the picnic was an island a mile or so offshore in a Wisconsin lake. Rowing out to the island down wind was no problem, but after the sandwiches were consumed Miss Cary said out loud that ice cream would taste awfully good. The gallant

Evinrude volunteered to row back to town to purchase some. The row upwind blistered his fingers and the row back melted the ice cream. There must be a better way, Ole told himself.

In his spare time at his little pattern shop near the Kinnickinnic River in Milwaukee, Ole worked on the first Evinrude Detachable Rowboat Motor. After nine months it was done, and Miss Cary, the shop's bookkeeper, said it looked like a coffee grinder. In April, 1909, Evinrude took his motor down to the river and tried it on a rented rowboat. The homemade iron and brass engine worked. That fall a friend borrowed an improved Evinrude Number 2 and took it on a fishing expedition. He came back enthused and with orders for ten more. Ole was in business.

The first ten Evinrude motors were hand-built and each weighed 62 pounds. Ole charged a dollar a pound, so they sold for $62. Miss Cary became Mrs. Evinrude and played an active role in the business, especially in advertising. Her first slogan was "Don't Row! Throw the oars away! Use an Evinrude Motor!"

Like Waterman, the Evinrudes did not

Far left: Publicity shot for "original Evinrude Fleetwin," considerably improved, 1925. Left: Outboard fleet in early days. Above: Racing was an important promotional device for powerboating. A Chris-Craft, foreground, won this race among stock runabouts at Baltimore in 1927.

immediately prosper in this seasonal business. An order of 5,000 motors exported to Norwegian and Scandinavian fishermen in 1912 saved the firm from bankruptcy. In 1913, Mrs. Evinrude's health failed and the couple sold the company to a partner, Chris Meyer, for $137,500. By 1920 Evinrude had $40,000 left and with that he started again, producing the Elto. His wife had coined the name. It stood for Evinrude's Light Twin Outboard. The new motor was made of aluminum and weighed 48 pounds as compared with 72 for the Evinrude being produced by Meyer. It also had two cylinders and three horsepower while Meyer's Evinrude was a single-cylinder and two-horsepower model.

Evinrude's new business flourished and grew into the multimillion-dollar Outboard Marine Corporation. The lightweight, inexpensive, and fairly efficient motor put people on the water all over the United States. In 1929, the major models—Evinrude, Elto, Lockwood, and Johnson—sold a total of 55,000 motors. The majority of them was used by fishermen, but the impact was general. The outboard has become a leading force in making boating one of the nation's major recreational sports.

Another was the inboard gasoline engine —the "explosion motor," as some called it— which had been accepted for boats as readily as it had for automobiles. By 1904 it had made the naphtha engine obsolete and cut heavily into the use of steam engines. "It does away with fire and is compact and light," W. P. Stephens reported enthusiastically. "The gasoline engine is by far the most convenient power yet put in a vessel."

Gar Wood, at wheel of MISS AMERICA X, *was first man to go 100 mph on water. Orlon Johnson is the mechanic. Bottom: Wood's* MISS AMERICA VI *and* VII *finishing first and second in 1928 Harmsworth Trophy race.*

It was inevitable that speed-minded Americans would start racing gasoline-engine launches. And those alert to the opportunity began to supply the need. A mechanic in Algonac, Michigan, began in 1908 to build three dozen race boats a year, which he sold for $550 apiece. His name was Christopher Columbus Smith, his nickname was Chris, and in time it was the front half of Chris-Craft, the famous trade name of the world's largest boat company. By 1910, founder Smith was also producing hydroplanes, boats with a step in the underside of the hull. This raised the boat out of the water, reduced drag, and increased speed. His inspiration for the planing hull was water bugs skating on the surface of a pond.

The uniquely American urge to test everything to the limit now came into play. Every time the twentieth century invented a new gadget or improved an old one—an automobile, an airplane, a speedboat—everyone asked: How fast will it go? How far will it go? How much can it take? Motorboat enthusiasts hurled themselves into the pursuit of answers. Some became national heroes, like Garfield Arthur "Gar" Wood, the lean, gray-haired daredevil who was the first man to go faster than one hundred miles per hour on the water. Others are less familiar, although they, too, are part of the brave company that in every decade, in every field of endeavor, tries to stretch the limit of the possible. Such was Captain William C. Newman, who made the first successful transatlantic voyage in a motorboat. Captain Newman performed the feat in 1902 in a 38-foot launch named *Abiel Abbott Low* with his sixteen-year-old son as crew.

The voyage was a frightening ordeal and a heroic tale of survival, which also suited America's tastes. It was a promotion of the New York Kerosene Engine Company, which built the boat and equipped it with one of their products, a ten-horsepower kerosene-oil motor installed in the cabin. The hull was a typical one for the time—round and narrow. That shape was all right for sheltered waters, but in the ocean the *Abiel Abbott Low* rolled ferociously and Captain Newman and his son were often seasick.

When the seas built up, Captain Newman could not continue to run the launch so he shut the motor off and lay to a sea anchor for hours on end as the round hull rolled with the waves. Fumes from leaking kerosene could not have helped the health of the crew. "It is a bad night," Captain Newman wrote despondently in his log on August 1, the twenty-fourth day at sea. "I do not know what will become of us." Other entries were similar. August 2: "The man who made those kerosene tanks ought to be with me. We are swimming in kerosene, the tanks leak so." August 3: "Our clothing is all saturated with kerosene and we have not tasted food in 30 hours. I am very ill, bleeding and very tired." August 6: "I am worn out and sick." August 7: "My health is very poor; I am losing ground fast."

Fortunately, everything improved after August 7: the weather, Captain Newman's health, and the motor, which turned out to be a rather good testimonial for the kerosene people after all. Despite the prolonged periods on the sea anchor and the endless leaks, the motor never failed to start up. The harrowing voyage ended safely and successfully on August 14, when the *Abiel Abbott Low* touched Falmouth, England, after a thirty-seven-day passage.

The little boat's amazing feat inspired no confidence in the English pilots, however. Seeking a guide through the coastal waters to London, Captain Newman found no takers. Despite the fact that his craft had survived a 3,000-mile ocean voyage, the pilots were afraid to board her.

YACHTING'S
COMPASS
POINTS
WEST
—
9

YACHTING'S
COMPASS
POINTS
WEST

*The Great Lakes,
the Pacific Coast,
and points
in between follow
a traditional
path—and
add some wrinkles
of their own.*

*Preceding pages: Scows went from East
to West and stayed. Class E scows on Lake Okoboji,
Iowa. Above: A "Mackinaw" boat.*

By eastern standards, San Francisco was a crude, raw city after the Civil War. When measured against the New York Yacht Club set, the San Francisco Bay yachtsmen were uncouth laborers. Take C. L. Place, for example. This transplanted Yankee owned the *P.M. Randall,* a huge scow-shaped sloop 110 feet long, which he normally sailed in commercial haulage about the bay. The *Randall* was the fastest craft around and Place took on all comers—for money. In 1870 a man named Hughes decided to test the *Randall* with his *Herald,* a new scow sloop that sailed awfully fast when alone. The following conversation is said to have taken place between the two adversaries one day in the Bank Exchange, a noted San Francisco saloon.

"Place," said Hughes, "you offered to match your scow against mine over the Fourth of July course last week."

"I did," replied Place, "and I'm ready to do it again."

The Fourth of July course was the one used on that holiday when the Master Mariners' Benevolent Association staged its annual regatta. The course began on the east side of the San Francisco water front, running south to a stake boat at Hunters Point, then across to the Oakland stake boat, north to Fort Point, and home to the finish at Meiggs Wharf, on the city's north water front.

Place and Hughes put down $500 each as a forfeit against a default. If the race was sailed, the winner would take all. "Now," said Hughes, "I'll bet you $1,000 I win that $500." "I'll take you," Place answered. "Come again, happy days." Before they parted, the two men had bet another $1,000 on the outcome.

The day before the race, Place went along East Street in a buggy with a bag full of $20 gold pieces. He bet against anything offered, $20 against a side of beef, $40 against a ton of potatoes. The next day, one hour be-fore the race, he walked into the Ocean Pearl saloon and made eight bets from $60 to $100. "If I lose," he said, "I'm going to carry a hod, like a Greek, for the rest of my life. I don't know any easier way to get this money except to knock Hughes and his friends in the head with a club and take it away from them."

A pistol shot started the race from a stake boat off Vallejo Street, but not before Place made five final bets. "That'll do me," he said. He had almost $3,000 riding on the outcome. There was no need to worry. The *Randall* won by sixty yards, and a contemporary account said that afterwards "Place was full of gin and glory and ordered a big champagne supper for Hughes and the backers of the vanquished vessel." The *Randall* burned up in Suisun Bay while hauling a cargo of hay the next year.

In eastern yachting circles around 1870, there was no comparable person to Captain Place nor a vessel similar to the *Randall.* But yachting in the West had its origins in work boats like Place's scow, just as it had in the East thirty and forty years before. In yachting, as in many other matters, the West learned from the East.

The first people to sail for pleasure on the great expanse of San Francisco Bay were commercial boatmen. The Master Mariners' July 4 parade and regatta was the city's first notable sports event. Members of the association raced their scow sloops for such prizes as a ton of coal or a cord of wood.

The first true yachts were imported from the East, starting a habit which continues on the West Coast to this day. The importations began in the 1850's with the *George Steers,* a craft modeled by and named after the builder in New York, and the *Restless,* a 31-foot sandbagger sloop. The latter was said to be a Mystic racer with origins in that Connecticut seaport, and she came West aboard the clipper ship *Andrew Jackson.*

Restless belonged to Captain Edwin Moody, an enthusiastic sailor who made some creditable sketches of yachting scenes. Moody even took on Place's *Randall* and the lumber schooner *Sarah Adelia* when these two had a match race in 1859. *Restless* sailed the course with them and did well, in spite of a leak in her hull. She had been strained by carrying too much ballast as a sandbagger back East and took in so much water that one of the crew suggested to Captain Moody that they run the boat ashore. "No, sir," said Moody. "She's got to go over this course and show those other boats what she can do if she has to do it chuck full of water." *Restless* did complete the course, but lost the race to *Randall.*

By 1869 Moody had found enough kindred souls so that the formation of a yacht club could be undertaken. The San Francisco Yacht Club was the name chosen, and the first regatta was held on October 16, 1869. J. L.

Eckley's sloop *Emerald* won the prize, thanks to her time allowance, over Richard L. Ogden's big schooner *Peerless,* sailed by Captain Moody.

That event launched yachting of a somewhat formal type on the West Coast and set San Francisco on its way to becoming the leading port for the sport beyond the range of New York and Boston. San Francisco was to hold this eminent position for at least eighty years, until challenged by the surging yachting movements in Southern California and Florida in the 1950's. The city was influential in the eventual spread of yachting to other western areas well after 1900: Puget Sound, Washington, and Santa Barbara, San Diego, and the twin Los Angeles ports—San Pedro-Long Beach and Newport-Balboa—in California.

The use of boats for pleasure was also slowly being discovered between East Coast and West, beginning about 1870. Chicago

169

and other cities in the Middle West generated the semblance of a leisure class that began to establish resorts on hundreds of nearby lakes. This was ripe territory for sandbaggers and Rob Roy canoes from the East.

Chicago's yacht club was founded six years after San Francisco's. On Lake Michigan, as elsewhere, wagering seemed to be on the minds of the early boating enthusiasts. The club's first events were stake races among a mixed bag of small sailing craft, with entrance fees building prize pools to $500 and $1,000. One fifth of the total paid judges and timekeepers. The winner got two thirds of the remainder, the runner-up one third.

A tribute to a hero of the Civil War inaugurated a famous yachting event on Wisconsin's Lake Geneva in 1874. The hero was General Philip H. Sheridan, then commander of the Department of Missouri, with headquarters in Chicago, and the Sheridan Cup was the prize. It is still in competition.

The first race brought together seven sandbaggers from 18½ to 27 feet long. The sandbagger was an ubiquitous craft in this era. In anticipating the first race, a newspaper account said, "Several hundred invitations have been sent to the most distinguished citizens of Chicago to be present at the race and picnic dinner at Kaye's park afterwards." Invitations included "a free pass on a special train from Chicago." And the writer promised, "If the weather is at all decent, it will be the toniest affair of the season."

The weather was fine, if breezy. A news story said of the big day: "The wind blew heavily and, in fear of some accident, the steamers *Gertie* and *Arrow* accompanied the race, and it is well they did, or we fear the splendid result would have been saddened by the dark shadow of the death cloud."

Several mishaps inspired this supposition. Two of the sandbaggers capsized, the steamers rescuing the crews. Another "carried away her foreboom" (presumably lost it), and a fourth ran aground when the tiller was damaged. *Nettie* "carried away her stud sail and shrouds and sprung her mast, but proceeded as soon as she could clear the wreckage." She was the winner on corrected time, the race being handicapped according to the water-line length of the boats. *Nettie's* owner was Julian M. Rumsey, the Civil War mayor of Chicago. In 1892 he decided that *Nettie's* racing days were over, so he loaded her full of rocks, took her out on Lake Geneva, and drilled holes in her hull.

Boats like *Restless* and *Nettie* were yachting's pioneers. The milestones of the movement are the founding dates of various yacht clubs: Buffalo, New York, 1860; St. Augustine, Florida, 1872; Michigan (Detroit), 1876; Mobile, Alabama, 1882, and Ohio (Toledo), 1882.

Around San Francisco's Golden Gate, yacht clubs came and went in the early years. The first one lasted through three seasons, then underwent a temporary collapse. The problem was financing. The first year, 1869, "life memberships" were solicited for $50, and the proceeds went toward erecting a small clubhouse at Long Bridge. But almost everyone was a "life member," so that annual income from dues amounted to very little. In addition there was misapprehension as to the nature of the new yacht club. Active sailors complained that those who came to the clubhouse to eat chowder on Sundays thought the boats were free for any member's use.

The club folded in 1871 with a flourish. A grand clambake was held at Sausalito and executed in such style that, when the bills came in, the club was bankrupted beyond hope of recovery. The next year the property was sold to the Central Pacific Railroad, and the year following, the club was organized anew by thirteen old members, Captain Moody included. The new outfit was an inactive one,

failing to hold any regattas. But at least it did not have life members.

The membership was stirred into action and enlarged in 1876, inspired in part by the desire of local yachtsmen to participate in the Master Mariners' big Centennial Regatta on the Fourth of July. The event was a smash, with twenty-nine boats participating. The schooner prize went to the 71-foot *J. C. Cousins,* the sloop prize to *Emerald.* The revival put the S.F.Y.C. on a sound footing and the next year there were fifty members and eighteen yachts—eight schooners, five sloops, two yawls, and three steamers.

A splinter group formed the Pacific Yacht Club in 1876, and it sponsored popular schooner races during the 1880's. But the membership was ostentatious, more inter-ested in parties ashore than cruises afloat. The Pacific died quietly in the 1890's.

The Corinthian Yacht Club, founded in 1886, attracted a rougher, water-front crowd and its "socials" became infamous stag parties. One dinner featured bear meat. The club chef had been bitten by a somewhat tame bear that hung about the place and he retaliated by cooking the animal. The Corinthian survived that affair and is with us today, on Corinthian Island at Belvedere.

Mining and railroading were producing millionaires in the West during the last forty years of the century, but few of the new rich turned to yachting as an outlet for conspicuous consumption. Gingerbread mansions on San Francisco's Nob Hill were preferred. An exception, however, was William C. Ralston, a member of the Bank of California combine that controlled that great vein of silver, the Comstock Lode. His vessel was the *Brisk,* a steam yacht built locally by Domingo Marcucci, who constructed many California river steamers in the 1850's and 1860's. The *Brisk* was expensive, originally costing $57,000. But her boilers did not work very well and Ralston had Marcucci make alterations in 1868. The craft was cut in two and 25 feet were added in the middle for new boilers. This made her over-all length 100 feet, an impressive size for San Francisco Bay. Of the refitting, Marcucci said "Two tubular boilers were put in her and she went all right, except that she was never very brisk." The owner's time with his steam yacht was short. The Bank of California failed in 1875 and Ralston drowned while swimming at North Beach five days later.

A lesser figure in finance, but one with a longer yachting career was Isidore Gutte. He emigrated to California from Germany at the height of the Gold Rush in the 1850's and went into the draying business, afterward becoming a commission merchant and, finally, an insurance broker.

Gutte's yacht, *Chispa,* was an exception to the run of eastern imports. This 61-foot centerboard schooner was modeled and built in 1879 by Matthew Turner, a busy San Francisco shipbuilder. A maritime historian, John Lyman, credits Turner with launching more wooden hulls than any American builder of the nineteenth century. He was noted particularly for his South Sea traders and lumber schooners. Gutte, a commodore of the San Francisco Yacht Club, sailed *Chispa* for thirty years. His yacht was a floating clubhouse in which he entertained countless visitors with his unique collection of musical instruments. One, a trick flute, was loaded with flour. With the player's first breath, the flour discharged in his face. The victim, the

source of a laugh, was then given a raffle ticket, Gutte explaining that on his death *Chispa* would be raffled off. "You may win the yacht," he would say. "Then you'll have the laugh on everyone."

After Gutte's death in 1908, there was no raffle. The *Chispa* was sold into the Mexican freighting service and ended as a wreck on the shores of Lower California.

Turner, the builder, had a healthy influence on San Francisco yachting. His short-ended yachts were no beauties, but they took into account wind and water conditions on San Francisco Bay, something the eastern imports did not do. During the summer months, strong westerly breezes of at least fifteen knots blow almost everyday. Such consistent winds are ideal for wide-beam yachts with short, modest rigs. Centerboards in shoal hulls are preferred because much of the bay is shallow.

When Turner was building beamy schooners, like *Chispa, Nellie,* and *Lurline,* between 1879 and 1883, the East was responding to the British influence and turning toward narrower, deeper sloops and cutters. Many of the eastern yachts brought west at that time were competitive failures. They carried too much sail for the strong westerlies, and when the rig was cut down, they slowed down. Turner's beamy yachts had the necessary stability with outside ballast in shallow lead keels. But San Franciscans, looking always to the East, were not entirely convinced and the importations never ceased.

The *Lurline* was an 80-foot keel schooner, belonging to Adolph B. and John D. Spreckels, sons of the sugar and shipping magnate, Claus Spreckels. She was built for the ocean as well as the bay, schooner racing down the California coast to Santa Cruz and Monterey being a popular and brilliant addition to the Master Mariners' regatta. The *Lurline* outlasted those events, which ceased

after 1891. In later years she went on to win three Transpacific Races to Honolulu.

The Transpacific Race, the West Coast's leading yachting event, had a timorous beginning. Its founder was Clarence W. MacFarlane of Honolulu, a yachtsman so enthusiastic that he was called the Lipton of Hawaii. He was often seen sailing around Honolulu harbor with King Kalakaua, the islands' last monarch, or Governor Sanford Dole as his guest.

MacFarlane hit upon the idea of inviting the San Francisco fleet to race to the islands, a proposal that had been tossed about as early as 1883. There was no difficulty in sailing down wind to Hawaii, pushed by the gentle trade winds, but the West Coast yachtsmen wondered how long it would take them to beat their way home after such a race. MacFarlane decided he had to prove that the west-east trip was not so difficult.

He planned to sail his yacht, *La Paloma,* to San Francisco, and once he had proved his point, he felt sure that a transpacific race would follow. *La Paloma* left Honolulu on April 14, 1906. Aboard were MacFarlane; Mosher, a navigator from the steamships; Spinnine, an Irish first mate; Pangelly, the Spanish cook, and two deck hands, a Samoan named Bill and a Hawaiian lad named Jimmy Grube.

The trip took a month. On May 15, *La Paloma* tied up at Meiggs Wharf. There were no boats in the harbor, not even the ever-present fishing boats. No carriages were in sight, nor any streetcars. Army tents were up at the Presidio. The crew took no particular notice. The port physician, Dr. Hobson, came by and while clearing the vessel he said to MacFarlane, "Where do you plan to stay, Clarence?" The skipper was tired and salt-encrusted after his long voyage. He replied, "I think I'll go up to the Occidental Hotel, take a hot bath, eat a steak, and go to sleep."

The doctor was taken aback. He told MacFarlane, "You'll go a hell of a long way to find the Occidental Hotel." It was then that the crew of *La Paloma* learned of the San Francisco earthquake and fire which had struck the city four days after their ship left Honolulu.

MacFarlane was not easily discouraged. Realizing that it was a bad time to promote anything but the Red Cross in San Francisco, he sailed down to San Pedro, the harbor town for Los Angeles. There he found two takers for his race. One was *Lurline,* which by this time belonged to Captain H. H. Sinclair, commodore of the South Coast Yacht Club, a predecessor of the present Los Angeles Yacht Club. Another was the 112-foot schooner *Anemone,* belonging to Charles Tutt of Colorado Springs, a member of the New York Yacht Club. The three began their 2,400-mile race from San Pedro on June 11, 1906. After fifteen days at sea, MacFarlane found himself looking in vain for Diamond Head. Mosher, the navigator, suggested

Above: An Oregon stock outboard racer.
Opposite: Yacht parade into Union Bay opens
the Seattle boating season every spring.

darkly that perhaps the Hawaiian Islands had sunk. All of them had been formed upon a range of volcanic mountains, remember. MacFarlane was just about to turn around and head for California when Jimmy Grube sighted Kealia harbor on Kauai. *La Paloma* was only slightly off course. *Lurline,* completing the passage in thirteen days, won the race. *Anemone* took one day longer and was second. *La Paloma* was last.

San Francisco recovered from its fire with the help of L. A. Norris. He was in the construction business and profited greatly in the rebuilding of the city. Norris also had a nautical background and spent a lot of his

money on a series of fine yachts imported from the East. His first, in 1910, was *Seafarer.* Norris ordered it from Bowdoin Crowninshield. The 92-foot schooner was delivered to him in Boston, and he and his crew set sail for San Francisco, going the long way around the world—east to west via the Mediterranean Sea, the Red Sea, the Indian Ocean, and then across the Pacific.

The Transpacific Race, begun in 1906 by MacFarlane, was sailed with some regularity until the outbreak of World War I, and *Lurline* beat *Seafarer* in the 1912 event. This prompted Norris to order a new yacht. This one was *Seaward,* a 106-foot schooner which later was bought by movie director Cecil B. de Mille.

For a third yacht, Norris turned to W.

From left: Light air on an Illinois lake; a breeze indeed on Seattle's Lake Washington; an Ohio lake

Starling Burgess, who in 1922 turned out *Mariner,* a magnificent 120-foot schooner that held the Transpacific Race record for twenty-six years and won the 1925 race to Tahiti. She was later sold to John Barrymore. The last Norris yacht was *Navigator,* an 80-foot schooner. Five times Norris sailed his own or others' yachts from the East Coast to the West, a much-admired feat called "bringing 'em around." He told an interviewer in 1929, "There's nothing to it. You just bring 'em around. The only way to learn about the sea is to go to sea. Ship before the mast on a square rigger like I did. But nowadays young fellows don't do it—too hard work." In 1929, however, Norris came to a tragic end. He drowned after falling overboard from a small boat in front of his home at Sausilito.

Norris was a patron and a pacemaker for yachting. His expectations were high, and his deeds of sailing yachts from East Coast to West again and again showed the way to others. Norris was one of the men who helped to make yachting a noble sport in America.

Another was a onetime mayor of Cleveland named George W. Gardner. Yachting in the Great Lakes states originally was found in limited areas around Chicago, Lake Geneva, or White Bear Lake, Minnesota. Clubs were formed and then regional associations of clubs, which brought a better understanding of rules, an introduction of sound boats, and the establishment of well-run regattas. Cleveland's Gardner was the founder of one of the largest and best regional associations, one which has done much to foster yachting throughout the Lake Erie region.

Gardner was aboard a sloop, Henry Gerlach's *Lu Lu,* sailing from Cleveland to Toledo in the summer of 1884. The sloop stopped at Put-in-Bay in the islands off Sandusky, Ohio, in the southwest part of the lake, and Gardner admired the pleasing surroundings. He thought what a wonderful place this would be for a regatta, bringing together boats from all parts of Lake Erie. At that time it was hard for yachtsmen in that area to be cosmopolitan. There were only five yacht clubs within hundreds of miles.

Gardner tested his idea for a common regatta at Put-in-Bay on his companions and then on the officers of the Toledo clubs and on boatowning friends back in Cleveland. The proposal met with such a good response that he called a meeting in Cleveland the following winter. On January 17, 1885, the Inter-Lake Yachting Association was born. The first regatta was held at Put-in-Bay the next summer. In the almost eighty years since the inaugural affair, this regatta has grown to be one of the major social-sporting events on the national yachting calendar. And the Inter-Lake association grows and grows. At a recent count, it had eighty-six member clubs stretching from Bay City, Michigan to Buffalo, and including many clubs situated on inland lakes of Michigan, Ohio, and northern Pennsylvania. The clubs in turn have 21,000 members who own some 9,000 boats.

regatta; cruising-yacht race on Lake St. Clair, Michigan; class sloop on Michigan's Little Traverse Bay.

The regattas at Put-in-Bay have reflected the changing tastes of yachting. In 1904 the craze for powerboat competition began, and a professor from the University of Michigan, H. C. Sadler, was called upon to write a handicap formula. The races were run and the professor announced that the winner among boats with cabins was the *Kitchell. Georgia* won the open class. Sadler never divulged his handicapping formula, and no one seems to have questioned him. Five years later the Inter-Lake regatta was the occasion for the setting of a world's speed record on the water: twenty-eight miles per hour, made by a White-powered steam launch from Cleveland.

The most elaborate of these regattas took place in 1912. It lasted for thirty days and the prizes had a value of $25,000. The occasion? The one-hundredth anniversary of Commodore Oliver Hazard Perry's victory over the British in the Battle of Lake Erie during the War of 1812.

In the 1930's, as sailboats won increasing favor, powerboat racing faded away. And in more recent times the regatta has been dominated by the smaller one-design classes, with skippers bringing their boats to the islands by automobile trailer. Facilities are so crowded that 300 visiting boats are moored on the shore line, side by side, with crews sleeping in the bilges or on shore nearby, hopefully under the stars.

Farther west, a comparable event is the Inland Lake Yachting Association's annual regatta, which rotates among the lakes of Minnesota and Wisconsin: Minnetonka, Mendota, Winnebago, and Green. This regatta is for the Inland Lakes scows, the flat-bottomed, shallow, rectangular craft that go as fast on smooth water as any boat powered by sail. The scows go back a long way, and in performance, if not in lines, they take after the early sandbaggers which found their way west in the 1870's and 1880's. There are six scow classes now, ranging in size from the 38-foot Class A boats, slowly dying out, down to the 16-foot M's and X's.

The scows are representative of the regional yachting development in America. They suit their lake environments. Their adherents swear by them over all other kinds —and their creator was Nat Herreshoff. The same Nat Herreshoff who built cup defenders and steam yachts in his plant at Bristol, Rhode Island, turned out *Alfreda,* a large flat-bottomed scow, in 1896 for Milton Griggs of Minneapolis and Lake Minnetonka. Using *Alfreda* as a take-off point, local "designers" and builders did some improving in the decades that followed, and the present-day scows evolved.

Some of the in-between models were outright busts. James H. Kimberly, a member of the Kimberly pulp and paper empire of Neenah, Wisconsin, had one which he described as being "deep-bellied." It refused to sail. So Kimberly, with typical middle-western inventiveness, moved the mast from the forward part of the hull toward the stern. He then sailed her backwards and she went fine.

RACECOURSES
IN
THE
SEA
—
10

RACECOURSES IN THE SEA

Bermuda, Europe,
Transpac,
and other events
challenge
younger generations
of racing
skippers in
handsome sloops
and yawls.

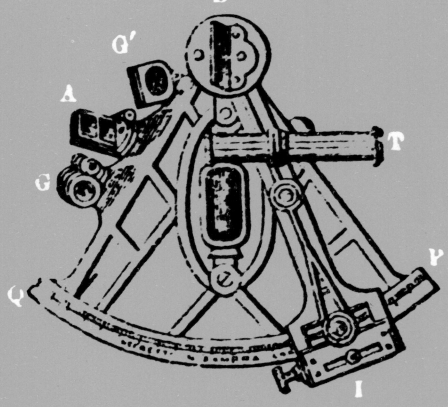

Preceding pages: SIRIUS II, *an 81-foot*
sloop, nears the end of the 1961 Transpacific Race
to Honolulu. She finished first.

Six days out of Sandy Hook they had sighted icebergs in the distance off to the north. The *Atlantic,* a three-masted schooner 185 feet long, was south of the Grand Banks en route to England, racing ten competitors from three nations for a solid gold cup put up by the German emperor, Wilhelm II. It was May 23, 1905.

The yacht passed to windward of the ice as the wind backed around to the south, placing her on a reach, her fastest point of sailing. The *Atlantic's* professional captain, the famous Charley Barr, ordered on more canvas, and the yacht soon carried almost all of her 18,500 square feet of working sails. Barr knew how to win yacht races. He had defended the America's Cup three times for New York Yacht Club syndicates and he believed in driving a boat, carrying as much sail as was prudent. The limit of his prudence was a dismasting.

Atlantic roared on, across the ocean for which she was named, through the night and into the following day. When the noon sights were taken on May 24, it was discovered that in the preceding twenty-four hours the *Atlantic* had sailed 341 miles. Frederick M. Hoyt, one of the passengers, described the moment in his log:

"May 24th, Wednesday: Of all days, to-day is the day which will ever be fixed in our minds with greatest pride and joy, for the good yacht *Atlantic* broke the record held by the old *Dauntless* since 1887, for the greatest day's run on the passage from New York to England, traveling . . . 341 miles, or 14.2 miles per hour, the former record being 328 miles.

"Our good southerly breeze kept up all night and this morning going on deck, it was blowing a fresh breeze and quite a good sea was running. In fact, the skipper said that he hoped the breeze would not increase any more, for he did not want to delay by having

to reef. But we were fortunate and were able to drive her through it till noon. The fine run was soon known forward and the men were as pleased with the ship's performance as ourselves. Also, they had a double allowance of grog served out in celebration of the event."

Atlantic went on to win the race, reaching the finish line off the Lizard on the southwestern tip of England in the elapsed time of twelve days, four hours, one minute, and nineteen seconds for 3,014 miles. No sailing vessel has ever beaten that for a transatlantic passage. *Atlantic* made several daily runs of 280 miles or more, and one of 270 miles with reduced sail and a whole gale blowing. This was on the twenty-sixth, when the decks were awash and two helmsmen were lashed to the wheel. Barr carried only two square sails and a fore trysail, but the *Atlantic* flew. Nothing less than one of Donald McKay's long-departed clipper ships could possibly have stayed with her.

All eleven yachts completed the race and they were widely hailed for having withstood the ocean's wrath. The smallest, *Fleur de Lys,* was a schooner 108 feet long, and one of her crew, James B. Connolly, later wrote in *Harper's Weekly* about an incident at Falmouth following the race. Two Englishmen rowed out to have a look at the yacht, which had stove in her dinghy and lost the services of one sailor due to broken ribs.

"Is this the yacht busted in the man's ribs and the boat in?" one of the rowers called to the mate. "You must 'ave 'ad it something rough?" The mate did not reply. The question was repeated, "Must 'ave 'ad 'eavy weather, sir?" Again the mate did not reply, but he addressed a passing member of the crew loudly enough for the sightseers to hear. "Oh, Dominico," he said, "draw a bucket of fresh water and go aloft and wash the salt off the mastheads."

Wilson Marshall, *Atlantic's* owner, re-

The three-masted schooner ATLANTIC
*won the Kaiser's Cup in 1905 by crossing the ocean
for which she was named in twelve
days—a record never equaled under sail.*

ceived the Kaiser's solid gold cup, and when World War I came along, he donated it for a war-bond auction. The cup was melted down and the solid gold proved not to be. It was a thinly plated base metal.

The Kaiser's Cup Race, as it came to be called, was the first ocean race in American yachting—except for two match events—since the "Great Ocean Race" held thirty-nine years before. The exceptions were the victory of Ashbury's *Cambria* over *Dauntless* in 1870, and *Coronet* over the same *Dauntless* in 1887. Against *Coronet*, Caldwell H. Colt, owner of *Dauntless*, not only lost his race, but a $10,000 bet to owner Rufus T. Bush.

The racing of yachts across the ocean during these years was considered to be an extremely hazardous operation. Overcoming this fear took many years and many thousands of words, a great number of them written by that sulphuric and outspoken editor, Thomas Fleming Day, of the *Rudder*.

Day had no fear, on land or sea. He drove a motor vessel across the Atlantic Ocean from Detroit, Michigan, to St. Petersburg, Russia, in 1914, and often went to sea in small sailboats. He sailed his 25-foot yawl, *Sea Bird,* from Providence, Rhode Island, to Gibralter with two companions in 1911, and in 1904 he organized and sailed in a race from Brooklyn to Marblehead. Six small yachts, the largest with a water-line length of less than 30 feet, raced one another for some 330 miles out in the ocean—an unprecedented feat.

Day wrote: "I cannot praise too highly the courage and skill of all those who engaged in the race. It is all very well for me to go outside. I have been doing it for years. But it was different with the other yacht crews. Many of these had never been to sea before. Several had not been out of sight of land. All praise to you, boys! It made my old heart glad to see the way you all, like the comrades of Ulysses, 'Ever with a frolic took the thunder and the sunshine.' "

Day provoked yacht owners into sailing offshore and he had twelve starters and finishers in his next promotion, the 1905 race from Brooklyn to Hampton Roads, Virginia. Many had been inspired by the Kaiser's Cup Race in May of that year, as well as by Day's caustic prose. When the newspapers pondered the advisability of racing small yachts offshore, Day counterattacked in the *Rudder:* "Newspaper men ought to know better than to consult a lot of grey-headed, rum-soaked piazza scows about such racing. What do those miserable old hulks, who spend their days swigging booze on the front stoop of a clubhouse, know about the dangers of the deep? If they make a voyage from Larchmont to Cow Bay in a ten-knot breeze it is the event of their lives, an experience they never forget and never want to repeat. What does the average yachtsman know about sea sailing? Absolutely nothing! Then let him hold his tongue."

Day was right. American familiarity with the sea, so pronounced from colonial times to the Civil War, had slacked off. In the last quarter of the nineteenth century, the United States merchant marine had diminished to minuscule size, and the youth of the country no longer turned to the sea, but rather to new opportunities in the West where the railroad was king. In yachting circles, at the turn of the century, owners were pressed to find professional American seamen, and many hired on foreign-born crews. The term "Swedish steam"—meaning "elbow grease" or physical effort—came into vogue as a result of employing hard-working Scandinavian crews.

When Day organized the first Bermuda Race in 1906, he got only three entries— *Tamerlane, Gauntlett,* and *Lila.* Yet his persistence and scorn and encouragement eventually paid off. Some fifty years later the

*Breeze catches smoke from starting
cannon as 1905 ocean race for Kaiser's Cup begins.*
ATLANTIC, *the winner, is second from left.
White, square-rigged ship, partly obscured,
is 245-foot* VALHALLA *from England.*

Bermuda Race would involve approximately 1,000 sailors, ninety-nine per cent of them amateurs. By then it had become one of yachting's greatest events, with so many would-be entries it had to be limited to 135 boats.

The race that began it all, however, was hardly promising. The three contenders left Gravesend Bay in Brooklyn on May 25. *Lila,* a 40-foot yawl, was dismasted in a squall shortly after the start and put back to refit. *Tamerlane,* a 38-foot yawl, returned with her, but not *Gauntlett. Gauntlett* was a 28-foot cutter sailed by a crew of three—Mr. and Mrs. George W. Robinson and John W. Dunlap. The threesome failed to see the dismasting and so pressed on to Bermuda, 675 miles to the southeast.

Tamerlane and *Lila* started out again three days later, but *Lila* quit after two days. Surprisingly enough, *Tamerlane* won the race, finishing a whole day ahead of *Gauntlett* which had experienced a hard, stormy passage. *Tamerlane's* time was 126 hours, nine minutes. Incidentally, the Bermuda Race record — set in 1956 over a slightly shorter course by *Bolero,* a 73-foot yawl—is seventy hours, eleven minutes, forty seconds. In fifty years, the track record was lowered by fifty-six hours.

Twelve entries responded to the second Bermuda Race in 1907, but it did not catch on as an annual event. And finally after the 1910 race, which showed only two starters, it was abandoned. In 1923 the race was revived and the response was good. From then on it flourished as no other ocean race has.

The 1923 Bermuda fleet enlisted seventeen schooners, three yawls, one ketch, and one cutter. All were gaff-rigged except a New York Forty called *Memory,* which had the relatively new and untried Marconi rig. Many were sure she could not stand a good blow and that her mast would come down before she cleared the Gulf Stream. It didn't.

The winner was *Malabar IV,* a schooner designed and owned by John Alden, a naval architect from Boston. Alden sailed in thirteen Bermuda Races—his first in 1910, his last in 1954—and won three outright: with *Malabar IV* in 1923, *Malabar VII* in 1926, and *Malabar X* in 1932. In all, he built thirteen *Malabars* for himself, each of which was sold to one of a crowd of eager customers at the end of the season.

Alden, or "John o' Boston," as he was known, was all but deified by yachtsmen for the style and integrity of his product, and from his board before he retired in 1955 came designs for some 2,000 boats. In the beginning, he followed a distinctive design—

and it was a healthy one, thank heaven, for many a customer did not know right from wrong. The "Alden type"—a husky, round, full, high-sided hull with a bowsprit and a gaff rig carrying a moderate amount of sail—was based on the New England commercial-fishing schooner. And like the fishing schooners, these vessels were built to go to sea and to come back. Alden had a good reason for favoring the fisherman-schooner design. In 1908, as a young man of twenty-four, he had worked as a naval architect in Boston for Bowdoin Crowninshield. As a side line to his design firm, Crowninshield owned several fishing schooners. One, *Fame,* was stuck in Halifax, Nova Scotia, without a crew until Alden and some friends volunteered to sail the 124-foot vessel back to Boston. They very nearly did not make it. *Fame* was blown out in the Atlantic and found at last by the Coast Guard off Mantoloking, New Jersey. But Alden was impressed with *Fame's* sea-worthy character, and it was later reflected in many of his designs.

Alden gave his customers good value. He contracted with small shipyards in Maine to build his boats for moderate prices, and held the yards to his high standards through a system of rigorous inspection and quality control. When the stock market crashed in the fall of 1929, Alden had sixteen schooners on the stocks of the Maine shipyards, all of them being built on speculation. Thanks to

his reputation, he sold every one of them.

In smaller boats, Alden liked simplicity. He expected them to be amenable to single-handed sailing. One day off Newport, sailing *Malabar III* alone, John fell overboard. The yacht came up into the wind by herself and Alden, exaggerating only slightly, later explained, "She turned around and came back to get me."

With larger yachts, like *Mohawk,* Dudley Wolfe's 58-foot schooner, the rig was not so simple. In the 1928 ocean race to Spain, she carried balloon jib, spinnaker, gaff-topsail, flying jib, queen staysail, balloon staysail, raffe, a square sail with bonnet, and, in addition, her orthodox working sails. John Parkinson, Jr., who sailed on her, recalled "The myriad of halyards, lifts, braces and outhauls around the foremast formed a cat's cradle that took a smart man to find his way around on a dark night. Of course, there were no spreader lights. All lighting was kerosene. Oh yes, there were two nested dories on deck. It makes one think of Magellan."

Alden's taste-maker role with influential yachtsmen was on the wane by 1935. There was little demand for his gaff-rigged schooners. More "modern" designs were coming into style—sloops and yawls with tall Marconi rigs. Alden knew his days of eminence were over. Once, while walking about the Henry Nevins shipyard at City Island, New York, during the winter of 1935, he spotted

a yacht whose identity was obscured by a tarpaulin covering her deck. His practiced eye nonetheless recognized excellence. To a companion he said, "A better design would be impossible to achieve." The boat was *Stormy Weather,* a 53-foot yawl built for Philip LeBoutillier the previous year. Her designer was Olin J. Stephens, whose brilliance had manifested itself early.

In 1930, Stephens had produced the precedent-shattering *Dorade.* He was twenty-two, and this was the third boat he had created. His father, Roderick Stephens, had put up $28,000 to build her, hoping that she would further his son's career as a naval architect. She did, indeed. She was a slim yawl with a deep keel and a tall Marconi rig—quite a departure from Alden's fishing schooners. She was beautifully balanced and sailed very fast under the hand of her designer-skipper and his younger brother, Roderick, Jr. Her launching at the Minneford shipyard at City Island was inauspicious. She settled three inches above her planned water line. Undaunted, young Stephens ordered a new water line painted three inches higher.

Dorade placed third in the fleet in the 1930 Bermuda Race. Schooners designed by Alden took the first four places in Class A that year. In 1931, however, *Dorade,* sailed by Olin and Rod, won the transatlantic race to Plymouth, England, by a margin of two full days over her closest competitor. After that she took the English classic, the Fastnet Race. Upon their return to New York the Stephens boys were given a ticker tape parade up Broadway and orders poured into the design firm of Sparkman & Stephens. (Under different ownership, *Dorade* later won the 1936 Transpacific Race from San Pedro, California, to Honolulu.)

Stormy Weather was somewhat broader in the beam than *Dorade,* but just as successful a racer. With Rod Stephens as guest skipper sailing her brilliantly, she scored a triumph in the 1935 transatlantic race from Newport to Bergen, Norway, a straight-line distance of 3,050 miles. The route was threatened by icebergs, but Stephens followed the advice of Grand Banks fishermen and took a chance. He sailed her inside of Sable Island, south of Cape Breton, Nova Scotia, which none of her five competitors dared to do. It gave him an edge, for he was sailing a shorter great-circle route—even as he and Olin had done with *Dorade* in 1931.

Rod Stephens was considered to be extremely courageous, and he was, but he also used his head. He listened to the radio broadcasts and plotted the icebergs being tracked

187

thus duplicating *Dorade's* double of 1931.

The fame of the Stephenses and *Stormy Weather* spread far and wide. When the 1936 Bermuda Race came around, there were a dozen new yachts of Stephens' design in the fleet, all of them looking more or less like *Stormy Weather*. The schooners were on the way out. There was nothing wrong with them and no one could impugn their sea qualities. But they did use a lot of sails, which required a sizable crew, they were often expensive to build and operate, and they were not "modern"—and yachtsmen follow fashion's dictates as closely as handsome women.

The *Stormy Weather* type has continued in yachts with ocean-going capabilities to this day. The versatile easy-to-handle yawl rig, with its ability to balance a boat in the foulest weather, is favored in equal proportion to the sloop. Schooners and ketches are rarities.

An exception would be *Niña,* a 59-foot schooner, designed by W. Starling Burgess, which won the Queen's Cup Race to Spain in 1928. Seven years later she was bought by DeCoursey Fales. He has modernized her sail plan from time to time, taking advantage of the improvement in sails, and *Niña* has won more than her share of races. In 1962 she surprised yachtsmen by winning the Bermuda Race at the advanced age of thirty-eight. With that victory, her seventy-four-year-old skipper, Commodore Fales, showed several younger generations a thing or two.

Older ketches and schooners have lasted longer on the West Coast than the East because of the nature of the Transpacific Race, 2,225 miles from California to Hawaii. Given the prevailing winds, most of the course to the islands is down wind, and Cali-

by the United States Coast Guard for the benefit of commercial ships in the North Atlantic shipping lanes. From the reports, he found a track fifty miles wide that would take him sixty miles south of Cape Race, Newfoundland. The boat bored right into the track, and since she was sailing in fog for most of three dangerous days, the pressure on the crew must have been tremendous. Were the radio reports right? Could the Coast Guard have missed maybe one iceberg, a little one but big enough to sink the yacht? What's that ahead in the fog?

Stormy Weather never touched a thing and almost beat *Vamarie,* a 71-foot ketch, boat for boat to Bergen. The over-all prize was *Stormy's* on corrected time, and later that summer she won the Fastnet Race,

fornian yachtsmen have surpassed their eastern friends in the knowledge and use of spinnakers, spinnaker gear, and spinnaker staysails. Ketch and schooner rigs on large hulls have provided great opportunities for flying yards and yards of light sails.

The "Transpac" Races of the 1950's displayed such vessels as *Goodwill,* a 161-foot schooner, and *Morning Star,* a 98-foot ketch. (These yachts would be ineligible for the Bermuda Race, which has an over-all length limitation of 73 feet.) *Morning Star* set the course record in 1955: nine days, fifteen hours, five minutes, ten seconds, for an average speed of 10.23 knots.

The yacht, built in Italy in 1927, came to a tragic end in 1963. She was sailing in the Caribbean Ocean, 150 miles east of Nicaragua, en route to Newport for the transatlantic race. Her owner, Fuller E. Callaway of San Francisco, was steering and closely watching the fathometer, which continually registered "no bottom." It was nighttime and the yacht was under power, working against a strong current, which, in conflict with the hydrographic tables, continued to set *Morning Star* to the west without Callaway's knowledge. To the skipper's horror, the depth finder suddenly showed two fathoms. He threw the engine into reverse, but *Morning Star* hit hard on a coral reef. She hit six times before grinding to a halt, her port side under water. Next morning the ship's boat, a 14-foot outboard hull, was found trapped in the coral a short distance away and the crew of five recovered it and paddled to a nearby island. The yacht was a total loss.

The year that *Morning Star* set the Transpac record was also the year of the record

fleet: fifty-three starters. That was a creditable showing considering that preparations for the race, sailing it, and returning to California might consume six weeks' time for an owner and his crew.

The Transpacific Race began the same year as the Bermuda—1906—and like the Bermuda it did not survive at first. There was a hiatus between 1913 and 1922, and the event was not put on its regular biennial basis until 1926.

However, there was one interlude—a race to Tahiti from San Francisco in 1925. This was a course of 3,700 miles, the second longest ocean yacht race of all time. The longest —4,200 miles each—were the races from Havana, Cuba, to San Sebastian, Spain, in 1951 and 1955.

The Tahiti race started at lunch in the San Francisco Yacht Club one day in November, 1924. L. A. Norris made the proposal and by dessert there were three entries. A fourth was added later and away they went on June 10, 1925. The competitors were the 107-foot Norris schooner, *Mariner; Eloise,* an 85-foot schooner; *Idalia,* a 75-foot schooner, and *Shawnee,* a 73-foot ketch. Norris, who had sailed to Tahiti many times, took issue with the pilot charts that recommended sailing to the east of the Pacific's feared doldrums. The latter is a vast area of calm and cat's-paws, broken by occasional thunder squalls, that overlaps the direct route to Tahiti. Instead of bearing east to avoid it, Norris sailed *Mariner* right through the doldrums, thereby gaining the advantage of the shortest great-circle route. He reached Tahiti in twenty days, eleven hours—a full week ahead of the second boat, *Idalia.*

The Middle West's "ocean" race, from Chicago to Mackinac Island, 333 miles up Lake Michigan, is even older than the Transpacific or Bermuda events. The first one was held in 1898. As with the Transpac, the

Welcoming parties provide some
of the best moments of the Transpac Race.
Opposite: Start of one of the classes
in Chicago-Mackinac Races. This Lake Michigan
classic dates back to 1898.

yachts in the early years were imports bought from eastern owners, at first large schooners and sloops. In the 1890's, Chicago yachtsmen often cruised to Mackinac Island and the islands adjacent to the Straits of Mackinac. In the winter of 1898 several skippers were sitting around a potbellied stove at the Chicago Yacht Club and boasting about how fast they could sail to Mackinac. Challenges and counterchallenges brought about the

first race that summer. There were two sloops and three schooners, and the winner was William Cameron's sloop *Vanenna*. The event was sailed on a boat-for-boat basis without handicaps, and *Vanenna's* elapsed time came to fifty-one hours.

The race was not run again until 1904, when the Chicago Yacht Club made it an annual affair. The big topsail sloops won most of the prizes, particularly *Vencedor*, owned by Fred Price of the Columbia Yacht Club. *Vencedor* had a disastrous ending, however, running aground on Fisherman's Island, off Charlevoix, Michigan, during a whole gale in the 1911 race. A powerboat took the crew off safely. That also was the year the

100-foot schooner *Amorita* set an elapsed time record of thirty-one hours, fourteen minutes, thirty seconds.

The 1911 passage, which saw the wind reach a measured hurricane velocity of eighty-two miles per hour, dampened the ardor of Lake Michigan yachtsmen and the entries fell off after that. Only five boats competed in 1914 and seven in 1916. The race was suspended during World War I and revived in 1921, continuing each year since, and even running through World War II.

The Chicago-Mackinac and its sister race in Lake Huron—the Port Huron, Michigan-Mackinac Island event—have presented to yachtsmen every variety of weather from long calms to exasperating squalls and damaging gales. Only eight of forty-two starters were able to finish the 1937 Chicago-Mackinac Race, owing to a seventy-five-mile-per-hour storm. Those who have sailed in the oceans and on the Great Lakes say that they cannot tell the difference when the wind blows up, except for the taste of the water slamming into their faces.

On the southern ocean-racing circuit the water is definitely salty, but it also can be warm. The original race, organized principally for northern yachtsmen vacationing in the South during the winter, was from St. Petersburg, Florida, to Havana, first run in 1930. This 284-mile event was climaxed by a gala welcome in Havana, but the coming of Fidel Castro's government has changed all that. Since 1960, the race has been run around the Florida peninsula, through the Keys, then north to Fort Lauderdale, a distance of 403 miles.

An event claimed by many yachtsmen to be the best ocean race of all is the 184-mile Miami-Nassau contest. Instead of a straight-line course, such as those run in the Bermuda and Transpacific Races, the Miami-Nassau has three legs to it, with turning marks at Great Isaacs light and Great Stirrup light to add zest. The Miami-Nassau event was first run in 1934, and like the St. Pete-Havana competition, almost all the contenders were yachts from the Great Lakes or the Northeast that were wintering in the South.

Yachtsmen attracted to offshore races can count on the regularly scheduled events, such as the Transpacific, the Bermuda, the Mackinacs, and the southern circuit. But trans-

*Opposite, at top: Double-ended,
wooden-hull cruising yacht of the 1930's.
Deck layout shows double cockpit,
cabin doghouse, gallows frame, skylight,
and midships hatchway.
Fiberglass yawl of 1960's (left) has
cleaner deck, stronger
standing rigging, bigger winches, roller
reefing gear. Top: Mighty yawl*
BOLERO, *rigged as sloop this day for
better handicap rating, leads
N.Y.Y.C. fleet at 1953 spring regatta.
Above:* CRIOLLO, *a handsome, pre-Castro
Cuban yawl, was an American design.
Right: Yawl* FINISTERRE *won Bermuda
Race unprecedented three times.*

atlantic races seem to come along only when the right spirit moves enough of the right people at the right time. Kaiser Wilhelm's "solid" gold cup inspired the 1905 race and His Majesty Alfonso XIII of Spain donated the prizes that brought about the race to Spain in 1928. With the impoverishment of royalty, however, it has been necessary for yacht clubs to assume responsibility for prize offerings, as well as for the organization and supervision of the race.

Following the race to Norway in 1935, there was no transatlantic event from American shores until 1955. That year a race was run from Newport to Marstrand, Sweden, under the auspices of the New York Yacht Club, and it was so successful that another— Newport to Santander, Spain—came along in 1957. Richard S. Nye's *Carina,* a 53-foot yawl from Greenwich, Connecticut, won both times, and also the following Fastnet Races in England for a grand sweep.

Nye, a middle westerner by birth, who never did any kind of yachting until he was approaching middle age, seems to have been a spiritual descendent of a Charley Barr or a Dick Brown. He crewed *Carina* with strong youths of college age and drove his yacht without letup. In the 1957 Fastnet, *Carina's* decks were lifted and she broke three ribs in a gale. On the last day the boys on the pumps had to work hard to keep ahead of incoming water. Once Nye had crossed the finish line he said, "Okay, boys, you can let her sink." Of course, they wouldn't and she didn't.

Ocean sailing, to be sure, is not without danger. Storm, fire, disabled men, or a disabled boat—all are lurking hazards. And, perhaps, most ominous of all is man overboard. On the other hand, many safety devices have been worked out to reduce the risk —lights on life jackets, safety harnesses and belts, double-strand life lines, and bolted stanchions. Furthermore, the over-all safety

record has been good. Only four lives have been lost in American ocean racing in the twentieth century. In the nineteenth there were the six men scooped out of *Fleetwing's* cockpit in 1866, and two sailors aboard *Dauntless* who went overboard while furling a jib during an 1870 race with *Cambria.* There were no life lines or safety belts in those days.

The worst tragedy in modern times took place during the 1935 transatlantic race to Norway. *Hamrah,* a 55-foot, gaff-rigged ketch, was 600 miles east of Cape Race, Newfoundland, on the morning of the race's ninth day. Charles F. Tillinghast, Jr., a twenty-one-year-old college student, was at the helm, with the yacht's owner, Robert R. Ames, fifty-two, sitting in the cockpit with him. The others were below: Richard A. Ames, twenty-three, the owner's son; Henry A. Ames, twenty, a second son; Roger Weed, twenty-three, and Sheldon Ware, twenty. Around nine in the morning "an unusually large sea broke over the windward port side." Tillinghast reported later in his matter-of-fact account.

The sweep of water down the deck took Ames over the life lines and into the sea. "I yelled for the men below," wrote Tillinghast, "and started to jibe. Before the sail came over, however, Richard had come on deck, seized the emergency line and jumped from the starboard side. The line was too short for him to reach Mr. Ames, as the vessel was still going away from his father who was just above the surface, but obviously close to sinking, weighted down as he was with boots and oilskins. Richard let go the rope and swam to his father."

The others managed to jibe the ship and bring it back to the men in the water. When they were within fifteen yards, a steep wave pushed Ames and his son out of reach. *Hamrah* was jibed again for another attempt. Tillinghast wrote: "On the second jibe the main boom broke, therefore making it impossible to bring her about. We immediately put the mizzen on her (it had been furled), but still she would not come about, or work to windward. While we were putting the mizzen on her, Henry launched the small rowboat and reached his brother whom he got aboard. His father by this time was possibly drowned. At any rate, I did not see him."

The rowboat swamped as *Hamrah* drifted off to leeward. The three who were left aboard had an arduous time cutting away the mainsail and rigging of the broken boom, while still controlling the boat in gale-force winds. Of course, they lost sight of the upset dinghy during their labors. When the ketch was able to come about and work to windward, the remaining crew of three sailed back and forth for five hours, looking for the Ames men. They had no luck. The wind increased all the time and for the next fifty hours, the crew hove to, under staysail alone. Then Tillinghast, Ware, and Weed turned back and sailed 900 miles in nine days to Halifax, Nova Scotia, reaching that port on June 30 with their terrible story.

Three years earlier the *Adriana* had caught fire off Montauk Point the first night out in the Bermuda Race of 1932. Fire from a tile stove had worked into a locker loaded with oilskins, and the interior of the ship was burning beyond control when discovery was made. A flare was lit and a nearby boat, Robert H. Somerset's *Jolie Brise*, answered the distress signal. Somerset laid his yacht alongside the burning schooner and the crew jumped. All made it save the man at the helm, Clarence Kozlay, who jumped short of the rescue vessel and fell into the water. Weighed down by heavy clothing, he sank immediately.

Not all mishaps end in disaster. There also have been some remarkable escapes. Quick

Top: CARINA, *winner of transatlantic races to Sweden in 1955, Spain in 1957. Above:* HAMRAH *before start of 1935 race to Norway. The owner, Robert Ames (at the wheel), was drowned, as were his sons, Richard and Henry (second, third from left).*

thinking saved the life of Alexander Troonin, *Vamarie's* professional skipper, in the 1935 race to Norway. He was knocked overboard by a spinnaker pole and passed under the keel of the big ketch which drew 10 feet of water. When he came up on the other side, Troonin grabbed the lightweight line of the patent log, but it tore out of his hands. C. Sherman Hoyt, a first-rate skipper, was on the helm and he managed to bring *Vamarie* back to Troonin in two tacks. It was daylight and crew members had been able to keep the skipper in sight. He was on board again eight minutes after going over the side.

Ted Sierks also got home free, but only after thirty hours in the Pacific Ocean with a ring buoy and an occasional shark for company. In the 1951 Transpacific Race, Sierks, a forty-year-old photographer and foredeck man, was aboard *L'Apache,* a 72-foot cutter. On the morning of the seventh day of the race he leaned far overboard in an attempt to fix broken tackle on a spinnaker pole. A wave rolled the yacht and Sierks went into the sea. He too grabbed the log line, but it parted. Then someone on deck tossed him a big ring buoy. *L'Apache* searched for three hours, but could not find him. He was 2,400 miles from San Pedro, the start of the race, and 840 from Honolulu, its finish. North of his position were the Aleutian Islands, to the south Antarctica.

As Sierks pulled off his heavy boots and dragging pants, he figured the odds on his rescue were 1,000,000 to one. He had cut his fingers and the blood attracted a shark almost right away. The shark made a pass at Sierks' feet and he jerked away just in time. He next kicked the shark, hitting its tough hide with his shins. Then he took a knife that had stayed in his belt and sank it twice into the fish, the second time ripping the underbelly of the shark. "How I did that I'll never know," he said later.

The navy laid on a large-scale search operation utilizing an escort carrier, four destroyers, and three destroyer escorts, plus six yachts and a B-17 plane. During the night Sierks was about to pass out when, he said later, he heard a voice saying, "Don't give up, you weakling." He took the advice.

He then saw a flare and knew the navy was looking for him. In the morning two destroyer escorts approached in line and Sierks shouted at them. A man on the foredeck of one of the ships, who was looking in the opposite direction, heard him, turned around, and saw him. Sierks was rescued.

Despite hazard and the occasional tragedy, ocean racing goes on. Sailing far offshore against the challenges of wind and water, as well as against competing boats and crews, is an exhilarating experience that draws yachtsmen back again and again. In his *Memoirs,* C. Sherman Hoyt, who in sixty-five years sailed hundreds of races and all of them well, sums up the feeling that yachtsmen have about it:

". . . for anyone who really loves the sea (and if you do not come by this feeling naturally and instinctively, avoid ocean racing) there is the fascination of the ever-changing open ocean; the sequence of calms, with their exasperating rolling and slatting; the ideal sailing weather when your craft, with everything set and straining, slips sweetly along like a high-powered car on a perfect road (at a rate you fatuously suppose must be putting you miles ahead of your competitors); the thrill of the storm; the anxiety about the proper sails and extent of sail to be carried. There is the lift, shoot and swing of the seas; the excitement of parted gear; the necessity for intense application to the helm, when a false motion may bring disaster; often the fights to shorten sail, and the feeling of elation, pride and deep affection for one's shipmates when a hard job has been well done."

THE
GREAT
WHITE
FLEET

---

*New designs,
new materials,
and livelier yacht
clubs make
sailboating a
favorite
sport wherever
there is
water enough
to float a hull.*

*Preceding pages: The 12-meter yacht
VIM in the 1958 America's Cup trial races with
Emil Mosbacher, Jr., at the helm.*

Junior Day comes on Wednesday during Larchmont Race Week, a Wednesday in mid-July that has the importance of Christmas for 500 fortunate boys and girls. It is a day at one of America's biggest and most famous regattas set aside exclusively for the seven-to seventeen-year-old crowd. The youngsters are fortunate because their families belong to economic classifications said to be middle or upper-middle comfortable. This permits membership in a yacht club, which in turn means participation in a junior sailing program for sons and daughters. For the especially privileged, it means ownership of one's own boat. Since the good health of the American economy has brought about an expansion of yachting eligibility, there are thousands of kids in boats in the United States.

Elders say the juniors also are fortunate because sailing a boat teaches so many virtues: self-reliance, sportsmanship, integrity, the value of observation, and the worth of experience. The children care little about these qualities. The soda fountain near the swimming pool at the Larchmont Yacht Club serves jumbo-sized malts and they will put chocolate chips on top of the fudge sundaes if requested. Should the committee have to postpone the races because of too little wind, an excellent opportunity for a water fight arises. But the more competitive youngsters anticipate the opportunity to finish ahead of a rival from another club, and the more skillful weigh their chances of winning one of those prizes displayed in the club's foyer. A marine knife with blade, marlin-spike, bottle opener, screw driver, can opener, and shackle key would be a fitting reward.

Junior Day begins in the morning, when the suburban mothers drive up to various yacht clubhouses adjacent to the western end of Long Island Sound in Westchester, Nassau, or Fairfield Counties, and empty their station wagons of skippers, spinnakers, crew, and coolers. Many juniors proceed directly to the Larchmont club and have an early run at the soda bar. Their boats are already in the harbor, having been in use in the prior contests of Race Week.

The Larchmont clubhouse is a big, rambling affair that makes marvelous creaking noises. It is almost seventy-five years old and its architecture is Victorian gingerbread. During Race Week, the old club generates a good deal of excitement.

Nylon spinnakers are taken to the lawn, stretched out, and stopped, meaning that a series of loops is tied around them with easy-breaking thread. The sail then will hold its shape until that breathless moment on the racecourse when it bursts from its halyard like a bubble-gum bubble being blown. Spinnakers are transported in, and set from, cardboard grocery cartons which must be scrounged from stores or club kitchens. Over 1,000 grocery cartons are used up during Race Week, which severely tests the local supermarkets.

When the time comes to go to sea, the crews crowd onto the club piers and are ferried out to their yachts' moorings aboard launches driven by uniformed employees. Almost all yacht clubs have a launch or two, but none has so many so grand as Larchmont's. These long, narrow, open boats, their varnish and brasswork gleaming, belong to a past age of naval architecture and a time when do-it-yourself was unthinkable.

The juniors then rig their craft and sail out into the sound. Those coming from distant clubs line up, one behind the other, in their own harbors and are towed in long strings by the head sailing instructor, a heroic collegian driving a club launch. These tows can be seen coming from many directions and converging on the race-committee boat, a large white vessel populated by adult males, in uniform, who display an array of signals on hoists and fire blank shells from twin signal cannons. The cannonade starts the races and after half an hour of competition, there is a mass of sail spread across the sound, from Larchmont south to Hempstead harbor, from Execution Rocks east to Scotch Caps. The great white fleet is in action.

This fleet is composed mostly of 13½-foot sloops made of plywood and called Blue Jays. What makes this white fleet a great one is its number. On any Larchmont Junior Day there will be some 250 Blue Jays racing, fortunately not all at once. The fleet is divided up into five divisions according to the age of the skippers (midgets are those fourteen and under, juniors fifteen to seventeen) and/or the last digit of the number on the mainsail. All midgets whose sail numbers end in one, two, or three, for example, race together. The divisions start out on their respective courses every five minutes, and one of the year's most difficult tasks begins for adults on the committee boat. For these gentlemen must make an accurate count and identify by sail number each of the competitors according to his or her class.

Such a big fleet is not unusual in yachting's world. At Marblehead Race Week, the vessels are not Blue Jays but Turnabouts. In Clearwater, Florida, the fleet is composed of Optimist Prams, 8-foot boats not much bigger than an orange crate. At Newport Beach, California, the flight of the Snowbirds refers to a regatta involving the 12-foot, cat-rigged dinghies called Snowbirds.

When masses of small boats race together on closed courses, as at Larchmont, the competitive problem is to find the right kind of wind. If it does not blow hard enough, the starts are delayed, the interfleet water fights begin, and the afternoon drags. But if the wind comes on too strong, over fifteen knots, the grownups worry and often cancel the races. When the wind is suitable, there is always the problem of finding a piece of it for one's very own, undisturbed or distorted by other boats. "Clear air" is the cry and the skipper who finds it consistently is on his way to winning the prize knife of many purposes.

A few years back a young man named Johnny Weidenhammer came down to Larchmont from the Pequot Yacht Club in Southport, Connecticut, and won a Blue Jay race in crowded conditions for seven straight days. He threw out many principles of yacht racing and stressed one—find clear air. Weidenhammer tacked away from his competitors and, for a while at least, away from the turning marks in his dedicated effort to get out of traffic and into clear air. He won again and again and again.

Junior Day is not a onetime regatta for its participants. Almost all of them go to sailing school two or more days a week back at their own yacht clubs and participate in club races or in other junior regattas, of which Long Island Sound has more than a dozen. The junior programs turn out competent, knowledgeable sailors by the hundreds each year in just about every port where organized yachting exists. No other nation in the world approaches the United States in the breadth and depth of its junior yachting programs.

This is a comparatively recent development. Larchmont's junior regatta, for example, is the oldest one on Long Island Sound, but dates only as far back as 1925. Before that the youth of a club's membership stayed ashore with mother. An occasional lucky boy went on board his father's big yacht and was told to remain in the cockpit out of the way of the professionals who pulled all those ropes and worked the sails.

Many factors brought a change about. Shifting economic values all but eliminated the hired hands and the jumbo-sized yachts. And in the two decades since World War II

Left: Juniors in Blue Jays rounding a mark at Larchmont. Above: Leeward end of the starting line on Race Week Junior Day.

millions of people have found they can afford to own a boat, for themselves or for their children. Furthermore, the nautical life became a recognized leisure-time activity, widely advertised and endorsed.

In addition to spectacular growth, yachting has undergone a series of technological improvements unmatched in prior history. The improvements have been in synthetic sailcloth (nylon and Dacron), in the hardware of fittings and standing rigging, and in hull materials (fiberglass and aluminum), which permitted greater design and cost flexibility. And the designers became ingenious in exploiting these improvements.

Yachtsmen suspected right away that the duPont nylon going into female hosiery in the late 1930's had possibilities for use afloat. World War II confirmed the suspicions but delayed the availability. Following the war, yachtsmen who had experience with nylon in the services eagerly tried it on their sailboats. It made a fine spinnaker, but did not serve at all for working sails. It stretched.

Under the stress of booms, headstays, and masts, nylon sails soon became shapeless. Free-flying spinnakers, however, retained their shape.

Around 1950, Dacron became available and the sailmakers found that this was the best sailcloth ever made. It was far stronger than cotton, the traditional fiber. It held its shape in much better fashion, lasted longer, did not require washing or other tedious care, and did not rot or fade. Hallelujah! All sailing men were beneficiaries, but the poor more than the rich. Among the wealthy in pre-Dacron days, the habit had been to build up an inventory of cotton sails for competitive use in varying conditions of wind: a light full sail for light air; a smaller, heavier, and flatter one for heavy air, and so forth. The skipper who could afford only one mainsail and one jib for his boat was at a disadvantage. Dacron's uniformity and performance all but eliminated the advantages of multiple sails.

It took the designers a little while to real-

Left: Mold for fiberglass Triton,
Pearson Corporation's popular 28-foot cruising
auxiliary sailboat, produced at Bristol,
R.I., Nat Herreshoff's home port.
Hull is built up inside the mold with
lay-up of glass-fiber mat and
resin, the hardening agent. These simple
methods have replaced the great
woodworking skills of Herreshoff's
time. Right: C. Raymond Hunt, brilliant naval
architect and skilled sailor.
Below: Ted Hood, designer-sailmaker and
extraordinary sailor, at wheel of
NEFERTITI, *Hood-designed 12-meter.*
Bottom: Olin Stephens at the wheel of
COLUMBIA, *the 1958 America's Cup defender*
he designed for syndicate headed by
Henry Sears and Briggs Cunningham.

Lightnings probing for room at a race's start.

ize that the strength of the new sailcloth required a general beefing up of all the standing rigging. Sailors were carrying more sail in stronger winds, knowing that Dacron cloth was unlikely to blow apart as cotton often did. This put new strains on sheets, winches, wire rigging, and such items of hardware as shackles and cleats. Prewar winches sometimes tore out of the decks when asked to sheet in big Dacron genoa jibs. Rod Stephens once applied a dynamometer to measure the strain on the sheet of a number-two genoa jib aboard *Bolero*, a 1949-model, 73-foot yawl. In a fifteen-knot breeze, the dynamometer measured two tons. So the designers and builders put on sturdier winches. Marine engineers devised stronger stainless-steel wire rigging, extruded aluminum spars to replace wooden ones, and lighter but stronger fittings to accommodate the new forces. The performance results were not reflected so much in added speed, but in greater sea-

worthiness. A small sailboat, properly balanced and rigged, can stand up today to a storm that would have torn the sails right out of a vessel of twenty-five years ago.

Speed in sailboat hulls has not increased appreciably. (The fastest time ever turned in for an America's Cup Race was by the schooner *Columbia* in the series of 1871.) The problem is not a scientific one, as Olin Stephens has pointed out. Stephens, the leading yacht designer of modern times, once told an interviewer, "There can be no purely scientific approach to yacht designing, because there are too many variables." Among them are: the angle of heel of the hull, lateral and forward resistance of water against hull displacement, wave-making resistances, changes in the direction and force of the wind, changes in the trim of the sails, changes in the trim of the hull because of shifts of live ballast (the crew).

The chief accomplishment of yacht designers in the 1950's was their quick acceptance and application of the new material, fiberglass. Boats made of fiberglass come from molds and can be shaped in any way, most notably with the compound curves particularly well-suited to sailing craft. The material itself is a blend of glass fibers, woven into mats, and quantities of liquid resin, which provide the hardening agent. In boats, fiberglass construction is characterized by great strength, no leakage, easy repair in case of accident, a minimum of painting, and far fewer maintenance chores than must be faced with wooden boats. Many old hands who predate fiberglass can expound on the virtues of spring fitting-out: chipping old paint, sandpapering the wooden hull, waiting for a clear, dry day to put on new paint. They say they like it. Fiberglass yachtsmen merely vacuum the bilge and launch. They like that, too.

It was fortunate that fiberglass came along when and in the way it did—after 1955 and with a rush. Wooden sailboat manufacturing, custom or stock, had just about disappeared in America because it required such a great deal of skilled and expensive labor. In the good old days before World War I, Nat Herreshoff paid his loyal workers at Bristol twenty-five cents an hour, and they had great pride in their performance. Carpenters working on the two America's Cup yachts of 1964 (which in accordance with the rules must be built of wood) made a minimum of $3 an hour, and nothing was said about pride.

The modern classification of sailing yachts consists of different one-design classes built to race; cruising yachts for racing, cruising, or both; day sailors with neither competitive intentions nor overnight cruising abilities, and the very specialized catamarans. Within these four broad classifications, there is great variety.

The number of different one-design classes is beyond strict accounting. In his authoritative book, *The Sailboat Classes of North America,* Fessenden S. Blanchard listed 127 different classes. The smallest craft on the list is the Dyer Dhow Midget, a 7¾-foot fiberglass dinghy which costs $440. The largest falls into the Twelve Meter class, in which a new 69-foot model runs at least $300,000. The author purposely did not attempt to list all one-design classes, but limited his choices to those which had a distinguished record or, in his opinion, promised to attain one.

The variety of one-design classes in this country is astonishing. Hulls may be of traditional wood planking (Stars, Internationals, Lightnings), of plywood (Blue Jays, Penguins, El Toro dinghies), of molded plywood (Thistles, Ravens, Luders 16's), or of fiberglass (Mobjacks, Flying Scots, Bull's Eyes). Some of the older wooden-hull classes (Snipe, Comet) now permit construction in fiberglass, and the two types race competi-

tively, a compliment to the stringent class rules regarding measurements and weights. Most one-design classes are small in size, with hulls below 25 feet in over-all length; centerboards are preferred to keels. Notable keel classes are the 210's and 110's, the Stars, and the Internationals.

Currently there are several classes for boats with planing hulls. These lift out of the water in a reasonable breeze, thereby reducing drag and increasing speed. Although planing hulls are far from new, they have become popular with speed-minded young sailors of the present generation. The advocates of modern planing hulls, like the Flying Dutchman, 5-0-5, and Finn monotype classes, are vocal and sincere. These last three classes are developments of the 1950's, and since two of them—the Flying Dutchman and the Finn—are certified by the International Yacht Racing Union for Olympic

The 33-foot International comes from Norway.

games competition they seem certain to last for a while.

One-design classes come and go. It is no trick to invent a new class, but quite an undertaking to establish it—on a semipermanent basis, with a broad fleet representation in the different sailing areas, and a national class organization. Pop Corry's Star is more that fifty years old, but the class has issued more new numbers in recent years than ever before. The Star remains fashionable and its magnificent class organization has a lot to do with this fact. The class attracts some of the best small-boat sailors of all, such as Skip Etchells, a former world's champion and a builder of Stars, and Lowell North, a sail-

and the Lightnings, in their third, continue to grow on a world-wide basis, too, and have withstood the challenges of the modern planing classes. The longevity of the Stars, Snipes, and Lightnings seems to make this point: A good class organization run by dedicated officers attracts the best kind of competitive sailor, who in turn perpetuates the class.

One-design yacht racing against skilled competition means, under ideal conditions, an event of one to three hours' duration, sailed around a course from four to ten miles long, and including three to five legs. This can be enjoyable and rewarding fun, although the demands on the racing skipper are many. He must concentrate throughout the race and constantly re-evaluate several factors that bear upon his next tactical decision: wind shifts, tide or current influences, sail trim, centerboard adjustment, crew placement, competitors' positions, the relevance, if any, of similar situations in past races, the choice of future moves and each one's probability of success or failure.

Emil "Bus" Mosbacher, Jr., the America's Cup defending skipper of 1962, cites his days of one-design racing in Internationals on Long Island Sound as the most intense competition he has ever known. This class collected a brilliant group of competitors in the 1950's when Mosbacher won six straight fleet championships. Among its members: Cornelius Shields, Sr., the first winner (1952) of the Mallory Trophy for the national sailing championship; Bill Luders, a noted racer in cruising and class yachts of his own design and an America's Cup designer-builder; Arthur Knapp, Jr., a winner for forty years in everything from frostbite dinghies to the J

maker who to date has won three Star world titles.

There are over 4,700 Stars racing actively, 3,100 of them in the United States. The old adage of the class still applies: "No matter where you go, it's not difficult to find someone who can beat you."

The Snipes, now in their fourth decade,

Largest and most expensive of the five Olympic classes is the 5.5-meter sloop. Tank testing, competitive designing, and building bring cost of this 32-foot boat to about $10,000. Opposite: Bud Melges, of Zenda, Wis., won Mallory Trophy for North American sailing championship three times (1959-1961). He builds and sails Inland Lake scows.

boat *Ranger;* George Hinman, a former commodore of the New York Yacht Club and president of the North American Yacht Racing Union. Mosbacher said about racing in this company, "Summer after summer, on any given race day, if you made a single mistake in the first five minutes you were out of it for the afternoon. Errors in judgment were just not permissible."

Beyond winning local fleet honors, one-design skippers may aim for national or international championships in their individual classes; Mallory Trophy competition against the best from other classes on a local, regional, or national basis, and the Olympic games. Most classes have national championships sailed at a yacht club where a particular class is strongly represented. In large classes, like Lightning and Thistle, preliminary eliminations are sailed on local waters and winners only go to the finals. In smaller classes, all entries are welcome at the "nationals."

Mallory Trophy competition begins on an association level. The Inter-Lake Yachting Association or the Southern Massachusetts Yacht Racing Association, for example, invites prominent class skippers each summer to sail in a round-robin series held at a local yacht club using a fleet of class boats. The winner then proceeds to a regional elimination involving champions from other associations—Southern Massachusetts, Buzzards Bay, Massachusetts Bay, and Maine, for example. The winner of the regional elimination in turn goes to the finals, which are held at different sailing centers in the United States and Canada each year. There are always eight finalists, and eight races are sailed in a fleet of one-design boats. The crews exchange boats after each race so that any inequity in hull or sails will be shared by all. About 200 skippers try for the Mallory prize, and the most frequent winner has been Harry C. "Bud" Melges, Jr., a builder-designer of Inland Lake scows from Zenda, Wisconsin. He won the Mallory for three straight years—1959, 1960, and 1961.

Olympic yachting, with its international glamour appeal, is attracting more competitors in this country. This facet of yachting finally has achieved a sound basis. American Olympic participation began in 1928 and for many years was open only to wealthy yachtsmen who, if selected, could afford the great expense of shipping their boats and crews to the site of the games. The United States International Sailing Association now raises money to pay the team's complete expenses. A sister organization, the United States Olympic Yachting Committee, conducts the trial series to select the crews. There are five competitive classes in the Olympics: 5.5 meter, Dragon, Star, Flying Dutchman, and Finn monotype. The American record in Olympic yachting is a good one, with a consistent run of medal winners since the postwar revival of the competition in 1948.

The wide category of cruising yachts is generally designed for what the name suggests—sailing from port to port, with facilities on board to house and feed the passengers and/or crew. Theoretically, racing is a secondary consideration, but no aspect of yachting in the past decade has shown a greater growth of popularity than cruiser competition. To qualify as a bonafide cruising yacht, a boat should have a built-in head, berths for at least two, an inboard or outboard motor, a galley and icebox, a cuddy or cabin, and, hopefully, a self-draining cockpit.

With family togetherness rating as highly as it does these days, boat designers have tried to pack as many family aspects into their cruisers as possible, while holding the product to an attractive price level, say, $2,500 to $6,000 in the under-25-foot classification. The results are generally worthwhile, although some boats are more suitable

for a family of midgets than the standard-sized, vitamin-chewing American unit. Of the many cruising yachts displayed at the boat shows, the best seller in recent years has been the Triton, a 28½-footer in sloop or yawl rig, which sells for about $12,000. Carl A. Alberg, of Boston, designed it for the manufacturer, the Pearson Corporation of Bristol, Rhode Island. More than 500 Tritons have been sold since the design was introduced in 1959.

Day sailers, again, are literally named. They are suitable for daylight cruising or racing, but must put into port at nightfall since they lack all the comforts of home. Technically, most one-designs could be classified as day sailers.

Catamarans are not yet fully established, although they are becoming more numerous all the time. And for exuberance and enthusiasm it is hard to match the men who sail these

swift boats. Many claim they have sailed a cat as fast as twenty-five knots. Catamarans are not permitted in the Bermuda Race, or the other major distance events. The powers that be still hold to an old prejudice that the twin-hulled craft are not seaworthy. Still, *Aikaine,* a 46-foot cat, has twice sailed in the Transpacific Race as an unofficial competitor and "beaten" everyone to Honolulu. It would seem that the cats are proving themselves to be entirely seaworthy and practical as cruising boats or day racers.

A consuming American interest in anything can be satisfied only by the widest possible range of products. The ever-increasing popularity of boating, and the special impetus given by fiberglass, has meant a steady demand for new designs—and a considerable stimulus for the normally rather quiet and specialized field of naval architecture. Today there are dozens of successful boat designers across the United States. Four, perhaps, are

the most important, the ones responsible for the most successful yachts. These are Olin J. Stephens, Philip L. Rhodes, C. Raymond Hunt, and William H. Tripp, Jr.

Stephens and Rhodes have large staffs which deal in all kinds of naval architecture: commercial, military, and pleasure yachts from dinghies to ocean racers. Sparkman & Stephens of New York has been responsible for the Interclub dinghy, an 11½-foot cat-rigged craft used for winter frostbite racing; also *Bolero,* the largest ocean racer built since World War II, and the 69-foot *Columbia,* the first Twelve Meter to defend the America's Cup (in 1958). Similarly, Rhodes' firm produced the Penguin, an 11½-foot dinghy; the twelve-meter *Weatherly,* the 1962 America's Cup defender, and Pierre S. du-Pont's *Barlovento,* a 72-foot ketch.

Stephens' yachting background began on Cape Cod in his teens and came to fruition with *Dorade,* the family ocean racer, in the

1930's. In later years he dropped yachting as an avocation and took up painting. He is seen on yachts now only in a professional capacity, as an advisor to a client.

Rhodes, an Ohioan by birth, claims no youthful nautical background other than fooling around with leaky canoes. The sea, however, attracted him and he studied naval architecture, beginning a professional practice in New York in the 1930's. Success came almost immediately, although Rhodes never practiced his vocation in company with other yachtsmen, as Stephens did.

Ray Hunt, by contrast, is a brilliant racing sailor today and has been for a long time. As a youth he won the Sears Cup twice, representing the Duxbury, Massachusetts, Yacht Club in 1923 and 1925. He had a series of successes in the 1950's with *Harrier,* a 41-foot Concordia yawl of his design, and won the world's championship in the 5.5-meter class in 1963. Unlike Stephens and Rhodes,

Action on board the 12-meter COLUMBIA,
the 1958 America's Cup defender. Left:
Genoa jib is trimmed on one of the
pedestal winches called coffee grinders. Above:
Extra sails are stored and made ready
below decks. View is forward, toward sail hatch.
Nine to eleven man crews work 12's.

Hunt operates no design factory. He is an independent, almost casual designer, reputed to have done some of his best work while perched on top of a piano at his farm in Tilton, New Hampshire. The versatility of his designs is shown in his outboard and inboard powerboats; his 5.5-class sloops; *Easterner,* the Twelve Meter he did for Chandler Hovey, and such cruising yachts as *Harrier* and Max Aitken's *Drumbeat.*

Bill Tripp came into prominence with his designs for fiberglass cruising yachts. He made his name with the Block Island Forties, 40-foot glass yawls that won a series of distance and ocean races following their intro-

HARRIER, *a 41-foot Concordia-class*
yacht, was raced by Ray Hunt at various times
with sloop rig (shown here), yawl rig, and
once, without success, as a catboat.

duction in 1957. The Block Island Forties were the first new design in the cruising classification that utilized fiberglass, and the immediate success of such yachts as Fred Lorenzen's *Seal,* the prototype, inspired many others. Tripp's early apprenticeship as a designer and draftsman was accomplished at Sparkman & Stephens, and he struck out on his own soon after World War II. His ability as a deck hand or a watch captain put him in demand as a member of distance racing crews. Tripp is based in New York.

It is not always easy to distinguish one designer's effort from another. The practiced eye, however, can pick out an Olin Stephens 40-footer as opposed to one by Tripp, for example. There is something distinctive about the lines of Olin's larger yachts, the graceful sheer in the after sections perhaps or the small, square ports set in a low-profile cabin housing. Tripp's hulls are easy to identify because of their distinctive, husky, high free-board in the forward sections.

Most of the new designs are under 35 feet in over-all length. Some make an effort to adhere to one-design class rules and operate under class organizations. Others conform to the measurement rules of the Cruising Club of America or the Midget Ocean Racing Club. The C.C.A. rule is generally applied to yachts from 25 to 73 feet in over-all length. The M.O.R.C. "rule," which is a suggested list of requirements more than a specific set of standards, applies to yachts from 18 to 29 feet. Several types of boats are eligible to race under both rules.

Rules have had a hard time of it throughout yachting history, perhaps deservedly so. Their intentions have been good—to find a fair and accurate way of equating unequal boats, so that they can race together—but they always have fallen far short of their goal, and the fall has been attended by loud, endless, prove-nothing argument.

Captain Nat Herreshoff thoroughly exploited the New York Yacht Club's old water-line-length-and-sail-area rule at the turn of the century, and was then prevailed upon to help write the so-called Universal Rule, which lasted for some forty years and governed, among other things, the formula for the J boats. The Universal has now been replaced, in some respects, by the International Yacht Racing Union's rule (the "International") and by the Cruising Club of America's rule.

These rules are mathematical computations to produce a rating in feet or meters which will approximate the water-line length of the yacht. The rating is applied to speed tables which show the seconds per mile each yacht is entitled to have in a given race against a real or imaginary scratch boat. The scratch boat has no handicap, and to win a distance race it must beat all the others, boat for boat, and by such a margin that when the handicaps are applied its time over the course is still the lowest.

The arithmetic for all of the rules is complex. Of the lot, the Universal Rule is the easiest: the rating equals eighteen per cent of L times the square root of the sail area divided by the cube of the hull's displacement. Here L equals the length of the hull measured at one quarter of its beam. The C.C.A. rule fills a dense little book and is entirely comprehensible to very few outside the ranks of naval architects.

The Cruising Club of America, which was founded in 1922, took over the running of the Bermuda Race in 1926 and evolved its rule of measurement thereafter. The C.C.A. members wisely wrote into the rule a purpose for it: to encourage the design and building of sound, seaworthy yachts able to cruise or race offshore with accommodations of reasonable comfort for the crew. That is the spirit of the rule, and it has had a major

Far left: TRITON, *successful, 28-foot
stock fiberglass sloop or yawl,
costs about $11,000. Left: Bill Luders'*
STORM *as a ketch with a cutdown
mainsail. The designer had fun with this
1961 rig which exploited loopholes
in rating rules. Right: Cornelius Shields,
Sr., of Larchmont, N.Y., an avid
yachtsman and patron of the sport. He
has been a winner in a variety
of yachts, from dinghies to ocean racers.
Below: Summertime activity at
Newport, R.I., docks in 1962. A 12-meter
is on the railway (left) at Newport
Shipyard. Black powerboat
with flags, at right, is N.Y.Y.C.
committee boat from which races are run.
Entrance to Brenton Cove, Newport's
great anchorage, is at left
rear. Cove has never been crowded.*

effect on yacht design in this country for some thirty years. Few can quibble with the kind of yachts it has encouraged, despite an occasional furor over alleged "rule beating."

Carleton Mitchell started one furor with *Finisterre,* a 38½-foot yawl that came out in 1954. Mitchell, a photographer and writer in his mid-forties, had a lifelong ambition to build "the perfect boat" and he knew what he wanted. Under his explicit instructions, Sparkman & Stephens designed a shoal draft, centerboard hull of extreme beam (11 feet, 3 inches) and heavy displacement, and one loaded with extras. Mitchell's credo was that any feature contributing to a life of ease and pleasure afloat was a good feature, and so *Finisterre* was given an ice-making machine, a removable fireplace, an automatic pilot, two generators, and a remote control unit with a trailing electric cord which permitted steering from anywhere on deck. (The skipper rejected a suggestion that he install a periscope over his bunk.)

Mitchell had serious doubts about the end result during the design and building of *Finisterre.* He wrote: "She might hobbyhorse in any sort of a sea. She might be impossible to steer with the wind aft. She might develop any one of a number of undesirable faults, including an inability to get out of her own way." None of these undesirable practices came about. Instead, Mitchell wound up with his perfect yacht, probably the greatest cruiser-racer ever made. *Finisterre* won three straight Bermuda Races (1956, 1958, 1960), beating a total of 332 competitors for an unprecedented feat beyond Mitchell's wildest dreams. She had been the smallest yacht ever to win a Bermuda Race and, for her size, probably the most expensive yacht to do so. She cost in excess of $75,000.

Finisterre was immediately copied and the distance races on the East Coast were soon infested with fat little centerboard yawls. It just so happened that the Cruising Club's rating rule favored hulls of this type, although Mitchell long maintained that he had ordered his design with no intention of exploiting a loophole in the rule. But was there a loophole?

The C.C.A.'s committee on the measurement rule seemed to think so and modifications were made so that boats with extreme beam measurements were no longer favored. *Finisterre* won her third Bermuda Race with less of a handicap advantage than the first time, and after that she was more or less retired from competition.

Finisterre made obsolete big yachts like *Bolero,* the 73-foot yawl that John Nicholas Brown built for himself and his family in 1949 at a cost of about $300,000. Brown had no particular racing pretensions at first. *Bolero's* initial competitive effort was a dud because the windward mark of a race off Marblehead was missing and the event had to be called off. As Mrs. Brown wrote years later, "It seemed only fair to let *Bolero* try her luck again. Thus it occurred that she raced her way to Maine at such a pace that when a friend in Pulpit Harbor announced to her small son that the Browns were coming to supper he exclaimed, 'Gee, not the *Bolero* Browns!' The fat was in the fire. It was just as if one's pet pony had turned out to be Man o' War. John was pleased if somewhat apprehensive. I was appalled, for we had suddenly to change our whole way of life on the water. From that moment on, the public owned *Bolero* and *Bolero* owned the Browns."

Brown, a commodore of the New York Yacht Club, raced his famed black beauty for six seasons and then the pressures became too oppressive. He sold her and returned to anonymity in a 40-foot yawl. *Bolero* wound up in San Francisco Bay, sailing against her old rivals—*Baruna, Good News,* and *Doris.*

A *Bolero* was within the reach of only a very few wealthy yachtsmen like Brown, an investment banker from Newport. But a *Finisterre* reproduction in fiberglass for $40,000, or less, was within the reach of a lot of enthusiasts. So out poured the cruising yachts—sloops, and yawls in the 35- to 42-foot range—and up went the entries in the Bermuda Race, from eighty-nine in 1956 to 111 in 1958 and 135 in 1960. The Royal Bermuda Yacht Club, whose very small bar was taxed beyond its limit when faced with serving 1,000 thirsty ocean-racing heroes, then asked its co-sponsor, the C.C.A., to place a ceiling on entries. This was done in 1962.

The Bermuda Race is quite something. Alfred Loomis, a navigator and writer who has sailed in more of these events than any other man, is startled by the casual approach to the 635-mile passage now taken by so many competitors. They set sail from Newport, having kissed their wives good-bye and having said: "See you Thursday in Bermuda." When Loomis set sail for Spain in the ocean race of 1928, he was not at all sure he would ever arrive.

The voyage to Bermuda is not always a lark. Ask Jack Weston who fell overboard from *Scylla* during the night gale in the 1960 race. He was saved only because his life

*Opposite: Youngsters
in Blue Jay sloops find
it hard to avoid
fouling one another.
Fending off helps. Bottom:
The man on the flying
trapeze—which is
suspended from mast.
Weight outboard helps keep
boat flat. It is a
Flying Dutchman, a swift,
Olympic class sloop.
Above: Dismasting of a
Star just below
the spreaders. Star on
left is spilling
wind to ease strain
on rigging. Left: Hiking
is hard, wet work.*

jacket was equipped with a new kind of powerful light which illuminated the rescue.

The morning following that blow the sea was still in a turmoil and there was water over the flooring around the galley aboard *Reindeer.* The cook was a Philadelphia lawyer named Ned Madeira and he was trying to get out a breakfast of fried eggs. He passed an egg to the boat's skipper, Newbold Smith, but the serving fell into the bilge water. Madeira took a look at his old pal Newbold and saw that he was concentrating on another matter taking place in the cockpit. The cook scooped up the egg and served it to the unknowing skipper, who gulped it down, saying, "Yum, yum." Another member of the crew observed all this and promptly became sick.

Mal de mer is no hazard in America's Cup races, which are postponed if the sea is heavy or threatening. But nervous tension has everyone aboard the contending boats keyed to a high pitch, for the old mug is still yachting's greatest prize.

Cup racing was dormant for some twenty years after Harold Vanderbilt's final victory in the J boat, *Ranger,* in 1937. The revival did not come about until a commodore of the New York Yacht Club, Henry Sears, asked the New York State Supreme Court in 1956 to permit two changes in the original deed of gift. He wanted to reduce the permissible minimum water-line length of yachts competing for the cup from 65 feet to 44 feet and eliminate the provision that demanded all challengers to "proceed under sail or on their

own bottoms to the port where the contest will take place." The court approved.

The first change opened up cup racing to the Twelves (water-line length 45 to 46 feet), a class consistent with the traditions of the trophy. The cup is and always has been for closed-course match racing in yachts of the largest class currently active in the challenging and defending countries. The twelve-meter class was not exactly active in England or America, but boats did exist and competition could be revived. It obviously was impractical to ask a challenging nation to sail or tow a Twelve across the ocean, so the elimination of the second provision permitted transport on the decks of freighters.

Sears obtained assurances within the New York Yacht Club that one or two new Twelves would be built (*Vim*, the newest at the time, had come out in 1938), and then he went to England seeking a challenge. He found interest in the Royal Yacht Squadron and a syndicate resulted. The Royal Yacht Squadron challenged the New York Yacht Club in 1957, and a match was arranged for 1958 off Newport.

Three new Twelves were built in the United States: *Columbia, Weatherly,* and *Easterner.* And *Vim* was refurbished. The four competed in a long series of trial races in the summer of 1958, *Columbia* finally being selected over *Vim* after the closest kind of match racing. The challenger was *Sceptre,* a heavy and—it developed—slow vessel that *Columbia* defeated easily in four straight races. The winning skipper was Briggs S. Cunningham, a wealthy, fifty-two-year-old amateur sportsman with a long and distin-

Top: MANU KAI, *a 40-foot cruising catamaran with immense, 14-foot beam. She was built in Hawaii for Lance Reventlow's use in Southern California waters. Left: Frostbite dinghy racing at Cedar Point Y. C., Westport, Conn.*

guished record in smaller racing craft of the six-meter and Atlantic classes.

One of the members of the British syndicate which paid for *Sceptre* was Captain Loel Guinness. He was a guest of Harold S. Vanderbilt aboard the latter's motor sailer, *Versatile,* for the first race. Five minutes after the start, *Columbia* had sailed right through *Sceptre* in very light air. Vanderbilt turned to Guinness and said, "I'm sorry, Loel, but I'm afraid that's it." Guinness had come 3,000 miles to see his investment perform and after five minutes of action the greatest living authority on America's Cup racing told him the boat had no chance. Guinness was shocked, but Vanderbilt proved to be right.

The 1958 revival was an artistic, if not a competitive success. An Australian press tycoon, Sir Frank Packer, took notice and decided upon a challenge, although his country had never before tried for the cup and no Twelve had ever been built on that continent. Sir Frank commissioned a brilliant young Australian designer named Alan Payne, who conducted an exhaustive study in America of twelve-meter design and tank testing.

Payne produced an excellent Twelve, *Gretel,* for a 1962 challenge. Following trial races again, the New York Yacht Club selected *Weatherly* as the defender. This yacht had had her keel and sail plan modified and "Bus" Mosbacher, who had raced *Vim* with distinction in 1958, took command as skipper. The series was a close one, *Weatherly* winning four races to one. Packer's yacht was just as fast as *Weatherly,* and credit for the victory went to the Mosbacher crew. It simply outsailed the less experienced Australians.

The 1958 and 1962 contests once again established the America's Cup as a great international sporting event and produced new enthusiasm for yachting. The great white fleet sails on.

POWERBOATS
BY
THE
MILLION
—
12

POWERBOATS
BY
THE
MILLION

*A vast, fast,
and venturesome
array of
runabouts and
cruisers
maintain America's
reputation
for being a nation
of sailors.*

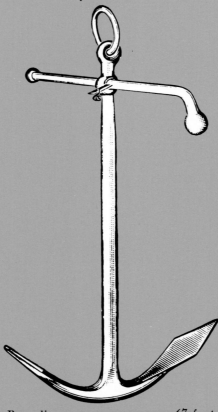

Preceding pages: MAIMELEE, *a 67-foot
power cruiser, had world's largest fiberglass
hull when built in 1961.*

In 1925 two men and a dog crossed America from the Pacific Ocean to the Atlantic in an 18-foot open boat powered by two outboard motors. Their names were Frank Wilton, John Hogg, and Spy. Their route covered 5,286 miles and the voyage required 137 days. They had a fairly rugged time.

Thirty-four years later the lone survivor, Hogg, went over the route again from east to west. Hogg, now sixty-seven, had a thirty-year-old companion, John Dahl, and his boat was a modern, 19-foot Glasspar outboard cruiser, laden with a ton of equipment. The trip had certain promotional aspects to it and took a leisurely 102 days. Hogg said it was a pleasure. The voyage began in New York City and went north to the St. Lawrence River at Montreal, then west through the Great Lakes and into the river system of mid-America. The adventurers ran out of water at Fort Benton, Montana, and the boat was portaged by truck 400 miles over the continental divide to the Snake River at Lewiston, Idaho. The terminal point was Astoria, Oregon, where Lewis and Clark spent the winter of 1805 and where the Columbia River empties into the Pacific Ocean.

Since the 1925 passage from west to east had been nearly the same, no one was about to dispute John Hogg's claim to being the first and only person to make a round trip across the country by boat.

A major difference between Hogg's first trip and his second was in communication. In 1959, Hogg and Dahl had a radiotelephone. They could listen to or request weather reports from commercial radio stations or the Coast Guard at almost any time. In this way they were seldom caught in open water when wind and waves made progress uncomfortable or downright dangerous, as well might be the case in the perilous Great Lakes.

The first boat, a wooden one called *Transcontinental*, or *Transco* for short, had a mini-mum amount of navigational equipment: a compass, a chronometer, and a sextant. (A deviation error in the compass caused the boat to miss its landfall on a crossing of Lake Michigan by thirty miles.) Charts were sufficient for the Great Lakes, but almost nonexistent for rivers. Automobile road maps, which showed the course of a river in only the vaguest way, often were the best references available. Time and again the boat ran aground in uncharted, unmarked waters.

Transco II, the 1959 fiberglass cruiser, was equipped with a direction finder, a sonic depth finder, invaluable in twisting river channels, a correctly adjusted compass, a barometer, hundreds of charts covering every mile traveled, and guidebooks listing the facilities of yacht clubs and marinas.

Marinas! The word had not even been coined in 1925 and the concept of a public boating facility providing a host of nautical services was still to be imagined. It was even difficult to find fuel for the outboards. In 1959, except for bleak parts of the upper Missouri River, Hogg found recreational boating everywhere. In the western states, for example, flood-control and hydroelectric projects had created vast lakes for pleasure boating where none had existed before. And when *Transco II* struck a submerged object at the south end of Lake Champlain and broke the drive shaft on one motor, a replacement shaft was obtained and installed in hours. Thirty-nine years before it would have taken a week or more.

Two engines were carried on both trips, the first time twin two-cylinder Evinrudes of five horsepower that weighed 100 pounds each. *Transco II* had twin two-cylinder, electric-starting Evinrudes of thirty-five horsepower, weighing 150 pounds each. Both times the motors did yeoman service, but *Transco II* could go thirty miles an hour, three times the speed of *Transco I*.

Top: KRAFT V *is a stock Huckins cruiser built in 1962. It is 64 feet long and powered by twin diesels. Above: Intracoastal Waterway offers protected, 1,000-mile passage along East Coast to Florida waters. Top right: First modern marina, Bahia-Mar, at Fort Lauderdale, Fla., can berth nearly 1,000 boats. Right:* ALISA V, *at 96 feet, is a very large contemporary yacht. Broward Marine of Fort Lauderdale was custom builder in 1956.*

TRANSCONTINENTAL OUTBOARD CRUISE
5,286 MILES – NEW YORK to OREGON

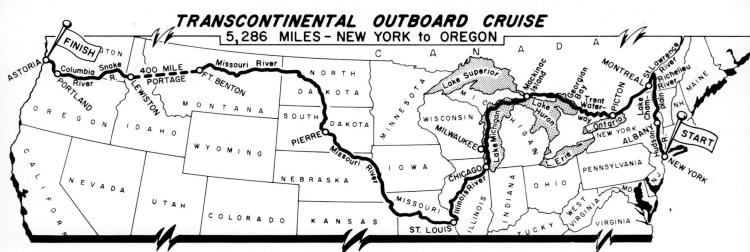

Top: TRANSCO I *in New York at end of 5,286-mile, transcontinental voyage from Astoria, Ore., in 1925. John Hogg waves, Frank Wilton steers, and Spy mans the foredeck. Right:* TRANSCO II, *which duplicated the voyage in 1959, but from East to West. Hogg again waves, as does his shipmate, John Dahl. Above: Map shows route of second trip.*

The contrast between these trips illustrates how and where boating made an impact on the American society. In the Roaring Twenties, the Hogg-Wilton trip was just another stunt. The boat carried a banner that read, "Heaven, Hell or Hoboken." The modern voyage, on the other hand, was underwritten by various boating firms to prove that a transcontinental jaunt by outboard was entirely feasible for anyone.

The change in attitude was largely due to the boating boom the United States experienced during the decade of the 1950's. For ten years sales of boats, motors, and other marine products went up and up and up, as Americans discovered that the fun of boat ownership was within reach of those who were neither wealthy, mechanically inclined, nor located near water. For instance, the combination of an outboard motor, a de-luxe 14- or 16-foot outboard boat, and a trailer to haul the rig cost $2,200—about the same as a low-priced car—so there were more than enough customers.

As the newcomers poured into boating, the trade organizations spouted impressive statistics on the amount of money being spent on marine products. According to the National Association of Engine and Boat Manufacturers the total retail dollars collected by the entire recreational marine industry were $645,000,000 in 1951, $1,000,000,000 in 1954, $2,085,000,000 in 1958, and $2,525,000,000 in the peak year 1960. By 1961, the peak figure had leveled off, but barely negligibly at $2,340,000,000.

Powerboats, most of them outboards, were largely responsible for the expanding figures. Outboard Marine Corporation, which annually markets some two thirds of the outboard motors sold in this country under the Evinrude, Johnson, and Gale brand names, claims that its sales in the 50's rose 470 per cent.

Growth was nice, but with it came problems. Many a neophyte was under the delusion that a boat operated just like a car. Dealers reported dozens of cases in which a novice bought a boat, found where the starter button was located, and drove away at high speed—some to eventual disaster. Accident reports began to increase alarmingly and in some places there was horror—as, for example, around Lake Texoma, a large, new reservoir lake on the Texas-Oklahoma border, where, as a result of boating mishaps, twelve people drowned during the 1956 season.

The means of educating newcomers to the fundamentals of boating were few. The United States Power Squadrons, a nationwide private organization of powerboat owners founded in 1914, had for years given public classes in basic seamanship and piloting, but they were unprepared to deal with the mass ignorance let loose on the water in the 1950's. The U.S.P.S. tried its best, as did a similar organization, the United States Coast Guard Auxiliary. Membership in these outfits grew steadily (by 1964 the U.S.P.S. had some 60,000 knowledgeable members, the U.S.C.G.A. 22,000), but the total was just a scoop from the big bucket compared to the total number of boatowners.

Boating's problems were soon brought to the attention of Federal and state authorities. The industry's two major trade organizations—the National Association of Engine and Boat Manufacturers and the so-called Outboard Boating Club of America—fortunately assumed leadership in directing a sensible approach to legislation. The Federal Boating Act of 1958 presented the states with a model boating law which almost all of them adopted. State codes provided for the registration of powerboats by state authorities (rather than the Coast Guard) and made mandatory the reporting of boating

*The modern powerboat fleet seeks to satisfy
all tastes. Below: Model designed for offshore fishing, with
hull by Lone Star and Mercruiser power unit with
outboard drive. Bottom: Houseboats provide lazy living
afloat in protected waters. Price range is
$2,500 to $8,000. Right: Speedy runabout with fanciful lines
can exceed 50 mph. This one is Century
Coronado, a 21-footer costing about $6,500.
Bottom right: A 15-foot water-ski boat by Sport Craft
Boat Company, of Perry, Fla. With four-cylinder
Mercury motor it can go 35 mph. Cost in 1960: about $1,700.*

*Gregarious outboard enthusiasts like
to travel in company. This is part of the
Kissimmee Boat-a-cade fleet which
cruises central Florida each October.*

accidents and the use of certain safety equipment. In some cases, the states also established water-skiing safety rules, minimum age limits for operating powerboats, and maximum speed limits in areas where they seemed necessary. Fees collected from registrations often supported local enforcement programs.

Intelligent legislation helped. The alarming climb of boating accidents leveled off after 1961 and declined somewhat in 1962.

There was one area where state legislatures and leaders of industry could not protect the public from itself. This was in the matter of quality standards. A number of shoestring manufacturers capitalized on the boating boom, seeking to share in the tremendous financial gains it made possible. A common remark made by boat dealers in the mid-1950's was, "I can sell anything that floats." And some of their wares just barely did that.

Most abused were the buyers of outboard boat hulls. Scores of small companies popped up to manufacture these, partially because of the ease with which fiberglass could be molded. The get-rich-quick technique was to buy a popular boat from an established, first-line company and use it as a plug for making a mold. Copies could then be turned out at "popular low, low prices." Often, however, they were inferior. Transoms tore out, fittings corroded, and the fiberglass hulls showed checks and cracks. An isolated few even disintegrated.

Other manufacturers made small cruisers of a poor grade of plywood and designed them without skegs or keels. Piloting them required more skill than most of boating's enthusiastic but misguided new sportsmen could muster.

Two factors eventually drove the irresponsible producers out of boating. One was the economic setback the industry suffered during the 1961 season, when the spectacular growth pattern faltered. Inventories began to pile up in warehouses and a number of firms went out of business. The other was the entry of several large corporations into the leisure-sports business. Seeking to diversify their interests, these corporations bought up small established boat companies, thereby giving the industry a greater degree of big-league financial stability. The Brunswick Corporation, for example, long famous for billiard and bowling equipment, paid some $15,960,000 in 1960 for the Owens Yacht Company of Baltimore, and $37,000,000 in 1961 for the Kiekhaefer Corporation, makers of Mercury outboard motors and the leading competitor of Outboard Marine Company. The well-known trade names of Owens and Kiekhaefer were continued, however. So was "Chris-Craft" when the NAFI Corporation, a manufacturer of automobile seat covers, bought the Chris-Craft Corporation in 1960 from Chris Smith's descendents for $40,000,000. NAFI modified the name only slightly to Chris-Craft Industries two years after the purchase.

There also was a chain of mergers within the industry. The resulting combines made competitive life very hard for the small, independent boatbuilder, and now many old brand names began to disappear as they had throughout the history of the automobile business: Baltzer, Bristol, Colonial, Cruis-Along, Grebe, Higgins, Hubert Johnson, Stephens, Wheeler.

In the outboard-motor field, Martin and Flambeau were discontinued. Sole survivors remaining to share the market were Outboard Marine, Kiekhaefer, West Bend, and Scott Atwater, which eventually changed its name to McCulloch.

During the boom years these manufacturers engaged in a horsepower race which raised the ratings of their largest models over and over again. In ten years the largest

Evinrude-Johnson went from two cylinders and twenty-five horsepower to four cylinders and ninety horse. Mercury jumped from four cylinders and twenty-five horsepower to six and one hundred. The average horsepower rating of newly sold motors climbed from five to almost thirty. The new outboards also gained gear shifts, remote controls, separate gas tanks, quieter operation, and electric starters and generators.

As a result of these advances, a multitude of outboard runabouts had become capable of going a jarring thirty to forty miles per hour with great ease—but with a great deal of discomfort to the passengers. Many boats were overpowered, and to take these muscular motors, the hull makers had to beef up their products.

At first there had been little change in hulls, and when in 1957, instead of improving the fundamental design, the manufacturers built nonutilitarian fins on the aft gunnels of their runabouts, they did them-

selves no service. They were, of course, copying the automobile makers, then in their fin period, and they seemed to think that whatever Detroit did in pursuit of the American dollar, they should do too. Fins happily did not last very long on boats—"If it has no purpose, it's no good," Nat Herreshoff used to say—and it took good New England common sense to advance powerboat design.

C. Raymond Hunt, the same Ray Hunt who could sail rings around most competitors in sloops and yawls, had long been an advocate of an advanced V-shaped hull for small powerboats. The Hunt design had deep V sections forward, tapering to a shallower V bottom aft, and it produced a much softer ride, particularly in rough water. Another feature was longitudinal strakes along the hull, which gave improved control and reduced skidding.

Hunt had designed a handful of large powerboats along these lines and an outboard runabout of his went into production

in 1957, but in general his ideas had not yet taken hold. The time was ripe for progress, however, because the new power in outboards and inboards had to be harnessed. A softer ride was needed, as well as a hull design that could take it in rough water. Many first-time boatowners were dismayed to find that their enjoyable hours afloat were limited by weather and that less than perfect conditions could make boating not only uncomfortable but dangerous.

The break-through came with a boat called *Moppie* and a competitive event billed as the world's toughest boat race. Richard Bertram, a Miami yacht broker and a fine sailor, was a member of the *Vim* crew during the 1958 America's Cup trials. He noticed a fast outboard runabout with a V-hull that often drove through the fleet at high speeds in the hands of Ray Hunt's son, Jim. Bertram asked Hunt if he would design a larger inboard model for the 180-mile Miami-Nassau powerboat race, a new event that sent small boats into the Gulf Stream and across to the Bahama Islands.

Hunt produced the lines for *Moppie*, a 30-footer built of plywood in Miami for Bertram and Sam Griffith, a race driver and a superb boatman. Griffith proceeded to smash every record in winning the 1960 Miami-Nassau run with *Moppie*. And Bertram, the navigator of the team, was quick to realize that he had something—a powerboat that could plane at high speeds and still provide reasonable comfort over rough seas. He and Griffith went back to Miami and started producing 31-foot fiberglass versions of *Moppie* for general sale. With their twin Chrysler engines, they were hideously expensive ($19,000 for the express cruiser), but there was a market that grew as Griffith and Bertram continued to win marathon races in Florida, on Long Island Sound, and in England. The V hull, which like most yacht designs could not be patented, was soon adopted by other boatbuilders.

Boston Whaler (left) introduced
new kind of outboard hull. Immense,
5½-foot beam gave unusual stability for
such a small boat. Fiberglass
hull is 13¼ feet. Hull was made in
sandwich form with flotation
material in middle. Below: Result?
An unsinkable craft even
when sawed in half. Boat also
has superior riding qualities among
outboard types. Instrument panel
(top right) looks complex
for twin-engine powerboat, but is
simply operated, thanks
in part to new hydraulic controls.
V-shaped hull (bottom right)
has been big advance for powerboats
in 1960's. This Bertram 31 has
V bottom with longitudinal strakes.
Such hulls make operation in heavy seas
practical, even comfortable.

So was the Boston Whaler — another Hunt innovation. Fisher-Pierce, a small company in South Braintree, Massachusetts, began producing this beamy, open outboard boat in the late 1950's, anticipating a limited market. The rectangular hull with its blunt, squared-off bow was radical in appearance, and boat buyers are historically conservative. The boat was 13 feet, 3 inches long, with a 5-foot, 3-inch beam. It weighed some 250 pounds, cost $600, and could take motors up to forty horsepower. The hull was made of two layers of fiberglass with buoyant foam in the center of the sandwich. It could float even when sawed in half, as publicity pictures proved. It also provided good speed, loads of room, and a comfortable ride. It was, in general, an outstanding small boat and a good seller. Not only did Fisher-Pierce have to expand production facilities, the company, furthermore, was paid a supreme compliment by the giant Outboard Marine Corporation, which decided to go into boat manufacturing in 1959. After its research staff had surveyed the entire small-boat field for the best possible design, Outboard Marine settled on a 16-foot fiberglass runabout with a squared-off bow and enough flotation to make it unsinkable. Advertising copy glowingly described the boat in this way: "It's a new design concept. Basically a deep V hull, traditionally soft riding. Two outer keels at the chines [they were sponsons] gives her wide-track stability. What happens between the stabilizing keels is more important. Water thrown up into spray channels creates hydraulic lift. The shock of pounding waves is absorbed. The bigger the waves the greater the lift. You ride on a cushion of spray. And not a drop comes aboard. If you expect to get wet, you'll have to wait for a rainy day."

Outboard Marine's boat had a lot of the Boston Whaler in it, and something of the old Hickman sea sled that caused a flurry in

the 1920's. The power plant of the O.M.C. boat was advanced too, being an outboard-inboard type. The horsepower race had made motors so large and heavy that outboards lost one of their best features—portability. Once on the transom, the big outboard could not be moved by anything less than a crane. It made better sense in the eighty- to one-hundred-horsepower bracket to put the motor inboard and run the shaft through the transom to a propeller on an outboard-type lower unit.

A four-cycle outboard-inboard, furthermore, was far thriftier with fuel than the two-cycle outboard. Instead of a separate rudder, the lower unit did the steering and preserved the good outboard feature of protecting the propeller. The unit lifted so that the boat could be beached, and when the propeller struck something, the unit kicked up, preventing damage to the prop. Gone

was the old expensive complex of shaft, strut, rudder, and fixed propeller. Outboard-inboards (also called stern-drive engines) found their way into many new small and medium-sized boats and delivered from eighty to 310 horsepower.

Models like the Boston Whaler and the O.M.C. boat were healthy because they were safe (stepping on the gunnel was like stepping on a rock) and comfortably spacious. They reversed the trend of squeezing the boatman into smaller and smaller spaces, and their funny looks attempted to alter the taste trend. That wasn't easy. It has been slow going for Outboard Marine's sales.

O.M.C.'s experience is illustrative of the current powerboating scene. Producers naturally attempt to give the public what it wants. But sampling the public taste is difficult. The powerboaters are largely a shapeless, formless mass. Unlike sailboat sailors,

SANTA MARIA, *106-foot steel yacht, was built in Netherlands for Henry Ford II in 1963 for $700,000.*

Chuck Mersereau went 91 mph in 17-foot catamaran hull powered by twin one-hundred-horsepower motors.

they do not generally belong to organized fleets and clubs. The activities of powerboat owners and enthusiasts vary. Fishing is the excuse for the majority of powerboats, from the $100 flat-bottomed skiff of the Middle West to the $100,000 sport fisherman of Florida's Gulf Stream. Then there is water skiing, which has fast become popular since its beginnings in 1939-40. Racing in stock outboards and inboard hydroplanes attracts its share of sportsmen, and predicted-log competition, which amounts to a piloting contest, appeals to a small, mathematically inclined group. And, of course, there is just plain cruising.

Surveys indicate that one of the power-boat owner's main problems is finding enough to do with his toy. Just plain riding for hour after hour exposed to droning, vibrating engine noise can be a bore. Marinas are full of yachts that seldom leave the dock; the owning family can be seen at night sitting in the saloon watching television on a portable set. What would Joshua Slocum think of that? Sailboat fleets are getting a few converts from the stinkpots (the sailorman's traditional label for the powerboat). One reason for the conversion is children. There is plenty for them to do around a sailboat, but not much on a powerboat.

One area of powerboating that thrives

as never before is expense-account yachting. The hefty tax increases of the 1930's doomed conspicuous yacht consumption. The 200- and 300-foot yachts are gone, but there are many 60- to 100-foot powerboats around, especially in Florida in the wintertime. Looking them up in Lloyd's Register of American Yachts, one finds that the owners do not have names like Mrs. Cadwalader or J. P. Morgan, but rather the Randolph Shoe Company, Forbes Publishing Company, Ingalls Shipbuilding Corporation, and so on. These yachts are used by executives who need a place to relax and to entertain their customers. Bahia-Mar, the enormous city-owned marina in Fort Lauderdale, Florida, is a haven for the corporate yacht. Two thirds of the craft berthed there belong to companies rather than individuals.

An expert in this field is Miami's Richard Bertram, whose brokerage firm operates a world-wide business of selling and chartering used yachts. In an average year, the firm will collect commissions ranging from five to ten per cent on $5,000,000 worth of sales. Ninety per cent are powerboats, the average length of which is 45 feet. Bertram, who grew up in sailboats, says, "I used to think people with motorboats just didn't have sense enough to take up sailing, but I was cured of that idea in a hurry. Sailing can take a lifetime to learn, but thousands of people can quickly become good skippers in a power-boat." One fourth of Bertram's customers have never before owned a boat.

An example of big yachting 1963 style can be found in the vessel built in Holland that year for Henry Ford II, chairman of the Ford Motor Company. Mr. Ford launched his yacht in secrecy, but the following facts came to light. Name: *Santa Maria*. Length: 109 feet. Cost: $700,000. Home port: Cannes, France. Crew: five plus the captain, forty-year-old Glenn Hargrave of Miami. Features: passenger accommodations for only six, air conditioning, five bathrooms, two bars, television, dishwasher, two speedboats in davits on deck, three refrigerators, a main saloon (24 by 14 feet), the inevitable gold-plated bathroom taps, radar, automatic pilot, a salt-water converter delivering 2,000 gallons of fresh water each day, stabilizers, and three generators and two diesel engines made by General Motors.

The grandeur of the Ford yacht makes it a contemporary equivalent of George Crown-inshield's *Cleopatra's Barge* and is evidence that pride of boat ownership has not waned between 1817 and the present day. Gilding a yacht has pleased the Detroit auto maker as it did the Salem merchant prince. Crownin-shield, however, was the only yachtsman of his day. Ford is one among millions. A look at a recent issue of *Yachting* magazine shows just how vast the sport has become:

A man sailed a 20-foot sloop singlehanded from California to Hawaii in twenty-eight days and steered the boat himself for only twenty hours. An elaborate self-steering system performed the trick the rest of the time, and the skipper had ten hours' sleep every night. . . . The members of a yacht club on Cape Cod were in furious debate about what kind of a new class boat to buy. . . . Two yachtsmen attempted to take their new boat through the New York state canal system in late fall. En route to their home port at Rochester on Lake Erie, the ice caught the boat and it had to be laid up for the winter at Cohoes, New York, not a noted seaport. . . . The Cruising Club of America awarded its coveted Blue Water Medal to a couple from the Canal Zone who can claim to have cruised in most parts of the world aboard their 30-foot ketch. . . . A young man in California drove his boat a record 137 miles per hour in a drag race at the Long Beach marine stadium. . . . Then a fearless youth on water skis hitched a ride behind the boat and skied a recorded 117 miles per hour before he took a head-over-heels flip, fracturing his pelvis and sacrum. . . . A sand bar formed in the mouth of the Rocky River at Cleveland harbor, blocking yachts from the channel, and the army engineers had to come and dredge it out. . . . A California yachtsman reported that his yacht had been machine-gunned and sunk off the coast of Venezuela, and that he and his wife had been taken off and thrown into prison . . . Fifty-six-year-old Ray Hunt was awarded a medal in Massachusetts for his "distinguished services to yachting.". . . A charter fishing captain, Bill Norton, and his mother took his boat south from Newport to Nassau for the winter, towing mother's houseboat all the way. . . . Fishermen and water skiers, avowed enemies, were bickering over the territorial rights in the crowded waters of Lake Hopatcong, New Jersey. . . . A club commodore spoke out against the proposed idea of requiring automobile-type licenses for operators of boats. "After all," he said, "this is still a sport."

The commodore is right. The present being the product of the past, it is the same sport that Crowninshield pursued and one that has given America a grand heritage since the time of *Cleopatra's Barge*. Ours has been and is a nation of sailors.

PICTURE CREDITS

AD-Arie de Zanger, photographed at Mystic Seaport, Connecticut, with co-operation of Marine Historical Association.
CI-Currier & Ives prints, Library of Congress.
CP-Culver Pictures, New York.
EM-Evinrude Motors.
HM-Henry A. Mott, **The Yachts & Yachtsmen of America,** New York, 1894.
KC-Kiekhaefer Corporation.

LH-Winfield Thompson and T. W. Lawson, **The Lawson History of the America's Cup,** Boston, 1902.
MR-Morris Rosenfeld and Sons, New York.
PC-Picture Collection, New York Public Library.
PM-Peabody Museum, Salem, Massachusetts.
RM-Richard Meek, photographed for **Sports Illustrated** magazine.
YC-New York Yacht Club.

CHAPTER ONE
10-11-AD. 12-PC. 14-15, 16-17, 18, and 20-21 (all)-PM.

CHAPTER TWO
22-23-YC. 24-LH. 26(top, left)-CP; (top, right)-PC. 27(both)-PC. 28-AD. 30-LH. 31(bottom, left)-LH; (bottom, right)-CP. 32-Frederic S. Cozzens, **American Yachts, A Series of Watercolor Sketches,** New York, 1884. 33(all)-YC. 34-LH. 37(top)-CP; (bottom)-LH. 39-Henry G. Peabody, **Representative American Yachts,** Boston, 1891. 40-41(both)-AD.

CHAPTER THREE
42-43-CI. 44-PC. 46(left)-Brown Brothers, New York. 47-CI. 49-CI. 50(top)-HM; (bottom)-YC. 51-HM. 52-Brown Brothers, New York. 53-Cozzens, opp. cit.

CHAPTER FOUR
54-55-AD. 56(both)-PC. 58(both)-PC. 59-Maurice Prendergast, "The Yacht Race," Courtesy of the Art Institute of Chicago. 60-61(all)-CP. 63(top)-CI; (bottom)-HM. 64(top)-T. G. Dutton, **Yachting,** London, 1877. 64-65(bottom)-YC. 65(top)-CI. 66-67-PC. 68-69(top)-CI. 69(bottom)-Cozzens, opp. cit. 70-71-CP. 72(top)-YC; (bottom)-Cozzens, opp. cit. 73-L. A. Shafer, **The Cup Races,** New York, 1899. 74-CP. 76-Peabody, opp. cit. 77-CP. 78-79(both)-CI. 81-**Leslie's Illustrated Newspaper,** August 5, 1876.

CHAPTER FIVE
82-83-Marine Historical Association, Mystic, Connecticut. 84-G. Foster Howell, **Howell's Steam Vessels,** New York, 1896. 87-PC. 88-N. L. Stebbins, **The Yachtsman's Souvenir,** Gardner, Massachusetts, 1888. 89-Dutton, opp. cit. 90(top, left)-HM. 91(top, left)-Marine Historical Association, Mystic, Connecticut. 92-93(both)-AD. 94-Edward Burgess, **American & English Yachts,** New York, 1887. 95-CP. 96(all)-AD. 97-HM. 98-99-CI. 100-Howell, opp. cit. 101-Marine Historical Association, Mystic, Connecticut. 102-103-Cozzens, opp. cit. 104-PC. 105-CP.

CHAPTER SIX
106-107-AD. 108-Joshua Slocum, **Sailing Alone Around the World,** New York, 1901. 110-MR. 113(top, left and bottom)-MR; (top, right)-PC 114-John Macgregor, **A Thousand Miles in the Rob Roy Canoe,** London, 1886. 115-PC. 116-118 and 120(all)-MR. 121(top)-PC; (bottom)-MR. 122 and 124-127(all)-Slocum, opp cit.

CHAPTER SEVEN
128-129-MR. 130-PC. 132-133 and 134-135(all photos)-MR. 136-CP. 137, 138-139, 140-141, 143, and 144(all photos)-MR.

CHAPTER EIGHT
146-147-MR. 148-EM. 150-151 and 152-153(all photos)-MR. 154(all but middle, left)-MR; (middle, left)-PC. 157(all but top, right)-MR; (top, right)-Cape Cod Shipbuilding Company, Wareham, Massachusetts. 159-KC. 160(top, left)-EM; (top, right)-MR. 161(top, right)-Chris-Craft Corporation. 162(both)-MR.

CHAPTER NINE
164-165-Smith Schuneman. 166-Great Lakes Historical Society, Cleveland, Ohio. 168-169(both)-San Francisco Maritime Museum. 171-PC. 173-San Francisco Maritime Museum. 174-175(both)-Burt Glinn, Magnum Photos. 176(left)-State of Illinois Department of Conservation; (center)-State of Washington Department of Commerce. 176-177-State of Ohio Department of Natural Resources. 177(center and right)-Michigan Tourist Council.

CHAPTER TEN
178-179-RM. 180-PC. 183, 184-185, and 186-187(all photos)-MR. 188-RM. 189-MR. 190-United Press International. 192-RM. 193-United Press International. 194(top, left)-MR; (bottom)-RM. 195(top; bottom, right)-MR; (middle, left)-RM. 197, 198-199, and 200(all photos)-MR.

CHAPTER ELEVEN
202-203-RM. 204-PC. 207(both)-MR. 208-RM. 209(top, right)-RM. 210-211 and 214-MR. 215-R. G. Aulik. 218, 220-221, and

223(all photos)-MR. 224(top)-MR; (bottom)-RM. 225(bottom)-MR. 226-227-AD. 228(top)-Barry Feinstein.

CHAPTER TWELVE
230-231-MR. 232-PC. 234-235(all)-MR. 236(top)-MR; (middle and bottom)-EM. 238(top)-KC; (bottom)-MR. 239(top)-MR; (bottom)-KC. 241-KC. 242-State of Washington Department of Commerce. 242-243 and 243-Johnson Motors. 244(both)-Fisher-Pierce Company. 245(both)-MR. 246-Wide World Photos. 247-KC.

BIBLIOGRAPHY

ANDREWS, WAYNE, **The Vanderbilt Legend.** Harcourt, Brace and Company, New York.

BELL, HELEN G., **Winning the King's Cup.** G. P. Putnam's Sons, New York, 1928.

BLANCHARD, FESSENDEN S., **The Sailboat Classes of North America,** Doubleday and Company, Inc., New York, 1963.

BOWMAN, HANK W., **Encyclopedia of Outboard Motorboating.** A. S. Barnes and Company, New York, 1955.

CHAPELLE, HOWARD I., **American Small Sailing Craft.** W. W. Norton Company, Inc., New York, 1951.

CHAPELLE, HOWARD I., **The National Watercraft Collection.** The Smithsonian Institution, Washington, D. C., 1960.

CRANE, CLINTON, **Clinton Crane's Yachting Memories.** D. Van Nostrand Company, Inc., Princeton, New Jersey, 1951.

CROWNINSHIELD, FRANCIS B., **The Story of George Crowninshield's Yacht.** Merrymount Press, Boston, 1913.

DEVINE, ERIC, ed., **Blow the Man Down.** Doubleday, Doran Company, New York, 1937.

FOSTER, CHARLES H. W., **The Eastern Yacht Club Ditty Box, 1870-1900.** Plimpton Press, Norwood, Massachusetts, 1932.

HERRESHOFF, L. FRANCIS, **An Introduction to Yachting.** Sheridan House, New York, 1963.

HOYT, C. SHERMAN, **Sherman Hoyt's Memoirs.** D. Van Nostrand Company, Inc., Princeton, New Jersey, 1950.

JULYAN, HERBERT E., **Sixty Years of Yachting.** Hutchinson, London, 1946.

KELLEY, J. D. JEROLD, **American Yachts.** Charles Scribner's Sons, New York, 1884.

KUNHARDT, CHARLES P., **Small Yachts.** Forest and Stream Publishing Company, New York, 1885.

LOOMIS, ALFRED, **Ocean Racing.** William Morrow and Company, New York, 1935.

MAXWELL, HARRY L. & STONE, HERBERT L., **The New York Yacht Club Centennial, 1844-1944.** New York Yacht Club, New York, 1944.

MORRIS, EVERETT B. & COULSON, ROBERT, **Racing at Sea.** D. Van Nostrand Company, Inc., Princeton, New Jersey, 1959.

O'CONNOR, RICHARD, **Gould's Millions.** Doubleday and Company, Inc., New York, 1962.

PARKINSON, JOHN, JR., **Nowhere Is Too Far.** Cruising Club of America, Springfield, Massachusetts, 1960.

RIMINGTON, CRITCHELL, ed., **The Sea Chest.** W. W. Norton Company, Inc., New York, 1948.

ROSENFELD, MORRIS, **Under Full Sail.** Prentice-Hall, Inc., Englewood Cliffs, New Jersey, 1957.

STACKPOLE, EDOUARD A. & KLEINSCHMIDT, JAMES, **Small Craft at Mystic Seaport.** The Marine Historical Association, Mystic, Connecticut, 1959.

STEPHENS, WILLIAM PICARD, **American Yachting.** The Macmillan Company, New York, 1904.

STEPHENS, WILLIAM PICARD, **Traditions and Memories of American Yachting.** Hearst Magazines (Motor Boating), New York, 1942.

TAYLOR, WILLIAM H. & ROSENFELD, STANLEY, **The Story of American Yachting.** Appleton-Century-Crofts, New York, 1958.

TAYLOR, WILLIAM H. & STONE, HERBERT L., **The America's Cup Races.** D. Van Nostrand, Princeton, New Jersey, 1958.

TELLER, WALTER M., **The Voyages of Joshua Slocum.** Rutgers University Press, New Brunswick, New Jersey, 1958.

THOMPSON, WINFIELD M.; STEPHENS, WILLIAM PICARD, & SWAN, WILLIAM U., **The Yacht "America."** Charles E. Lauriat Company, Boston, 1925.

INDEX *Italic numbers refer to illustrations.*